Full Employment and High Growth in Europe

Full Employment and High Growth in Europe

A New Cycle of Reforms to Play a Leading Role in the New World Economy

Mario Baldassarri
University of Rome, 'La Sapienza'

Francesco Busato
Columbia University, New York

First published 2003 by
PALGRAVE MACMILLAN
Houndmills, Basingstoke, Hampshire RG21 6XS and
175 Fifth Avenue, New York, N. Y. 10010
Companies and representatives throughout the world

PALGRAVE MACMILLAN is the global academic imprint of the Palgrave Macmillan division of St. Martin's Press, LLC and of Palgrave Macmillan Ltd. Macmillan® is a registered trademark in the United States, United Kingdom and other countries. Palgrave is a registered trademark in the European Union and other countries.

ISBN 1–4039–2070–2

This book is printed on paper suitable for recycling and made from fully managed and sustained forest sources.

A catalogue record for this book is available from the British Library.

Library of Congress Cataloging-in-Publication Data

Baldassarri, M. (Mario)
    Full employment and high growth in Europe : a new cycle of reforms to play a leading role in the new world economy / Mario Baldassarri, Francesco Busato.
        p. cm.
    Includes bibliographical references and index.
    ISBN 1–4039–2070–2
    1. Full employment policies--European Union countries. 2. Unemployment--Effect of monetary policy on--European Union countries. 3. Labor supply--Effect of taxation on--European Union countries. 4. Budget deficits--European Union countries. 5. Monetary policy--European Union countries. 6. Fiscal policy--European Union countries. 7. Government spending policy--European Union countries. 8. European Union countries--Economic policy. I.Busato, Francesco II. Title.

    HD5764.A6B27 2003
    338.94--dc21

                                                            2003054913
10   9   8   7   6   5   4   3   2   1
12   11   10   09   08   07   06   05   04   03
Printed and bound in Great Britain by
Antony Rowe Ltd, Chippenham and Eastbourne

Contents

List of Figures

List of Figures

List of Tables

Acknowledgments

The number of people who have made helpful contributions is very great indeed. In particular, we are indebted to Bruno Chiarini, Paolo de Santis, John Donaldson, Franco Modigliani, Edmund Phelps, Gustavo Piga, John Thomas and the participants of seminars and conferences at Johns Hopkins University, Harvard Business School, MIT Sloan School of Management, International Bankers Club of Luxemburg. A special thanks to Francesca Caponi, Andrea De Leonardis, Teresita Foggia, Marzia Lavinia Frezza, Amedeo Panci, and Angelica Vaccarini, for their research, data and table management assistance.

PART ONE

INTRODUCTION AND CONCLUSIONS

1. A Discussion and a Proposal on How to Revive Europe... without Waiting for *Godot the Prince*

1.1 A Theoretical Error and an Empirical Misconception.

A theoretical error and an empirical misconception have in large part stalled European economic policy since the birth of Monetary Union.

The theoretical error lies in defining the re-establishment of financial equilibrium in the budget solely as the reduction and eventual elimination of national deficits. The imposed limits on budget deficits and national debt, as well as the transfer of monetary sovereignty to the European Central Bank and the European system of central banks, have led some to talk of the "death" of national economic policy. Indeed, monetary policy decisions are made in Frankfurt, and budget policy is blocked by the zero deficit rule.

In reality, the government budget has an effect on the entire economic system, yet not just through its actual financial balance, meaning the difference between revenues and expenditures. The system is especially affected by the amount and make-up of those same revenues and expenditures.

For over a quarter century, within the context of economic growth theory, it has been shown[1] that given an equal deficit, the level and composition of revenues and expenditures affect how economic systems expand. For one, it is easily understood (and maybe just common sense) that a country that has a zero deficit from having balanced revenues and expenditures in the government sector that are equal, for example, to 90% of gross domestic product, will develop quite differently in the medium to long term from a country that has a balanced budget that is equal to just 30% of GDP. In addition, the

---

[1] See, among the many contributions, Solow (1956), Swan (1956), Baldassarri (1978).

different composition of expenditures (for immediate needs or for investment) and revenues (direct and indirect taxes and contributions on labor or production, etc.) can have additional and different effects on the way that an economic system develops. It is therefore evident that an economic system's dynamic condition in the medium to long term does not react only to the size of the deficit and the ways in which funds are raised to cover that deficit, but as much and more so to the overall weight of the budget on the economy and to the individual items that make up government revenues and expenditures.

For these reasons, the constraints set by the Maastricht Treaty and the current zero deficit requirement of the Stability Pact do not kill national budget policy at all. On the contrary, they lead to an interpretation and an implementation of budget policy in its truer sense: deciding what to spend on and how much, and what to tax and how much, instead of resorting to the budget deficit and national debt scam that temporarily allows limitless spending, but leaves to the future and later generations the burden of covering that expense. Therefore, this means that when an increase in spending is needed, it is necessary at the same time to decide how and where new taxes will come from. The converse also holds true: when there's a need to reduce taxes, it must be decided how and where new spending reductions will be made.

That a one-time easing of fiscal policy can give a boost to the economy, creating a larger tax base and therefore bringing in higher overall tax revenues, is not an issue. Nor is issue taken with the possibility that higher spending financed by a deficit can give a boost to the economy in the short term. In these circumstances, however, it is also necessary to evaluate the impact in the medium to long term of that same budget deficit and the accumulation of debt.

It is thus a question of assuring "ex-ante" that conditions of a balanced budget are being met, and of assessing "ex-post" what greater resources might eventually be generated by higher growth, which could then be used to further reduce taxes or increase investment spending.

The **empirical misconception** over the three years since the introduction of the Euro lies in the idea that a recovery in the international economy and a simultaneous devaluation of the Euro would alone spur a strong export-led economic rebound in Europe as well as Italy. That in turn would create full employment without having ever having initiated the process of structural reforms in government spending, the social welfare state, the labor market in terms of more flexibility or the goods market in terms of privatization and liberalization to produce greater efficiency and competitiveness. The idea is resources would even be generated automatically, allowing for a reduction in fiscal pressure without containing spending in the meantime. The deficit would be covered later with the greater tax proceeds that accompany an economic upturn, which comes like a godsend from the heavens activated "externally" by the positive developments from the rest of the global economy.

This was shown to be an illusion by the slowdown in the American economy that began in 2000, and as economic activity was almost definitively snuffed out by the radical changes in the international cycle in the aftermath of the September 11th terrorist attacks.

Even now, however, Europe does not seem capable of launching its own autonomous cycle of economic recovery, showing that it is still directly dependent on the performance of the American economy and the economy of the rest of the world.

1.2 Previous Researches on the Italian Economy: is there any Meaningful Message for Europe?

Following the shocks of the 1970s oil crisis, Europe attempted to steer a convergence process that would lead toward a European Monetary System (EMS). In the beginning, the strong discrepancies between various countries gave rise to the introduction of limits with differentiated width on the exchange rate fluctuations between different currencies, especially for Italy and similar countries, which presented more divergent aspects. Only in 1987 an attempt was made to put in place more rigid monetary constraints, pushing the EMS just a step away from a system of fixed exchange rates. Italy did not take advantage of this cyclical period of expansion, a favorable time to adjust its own internal economy, most importantly in terms of inflation and national debt. Therefore Italy continuously lost ground in terms of competitiveness, leading to expectations of a devaluation of the lira. In September 1992, these imbalances led to a serious monetary and financial crisis, resulting in the lira's being pulled from the EMS, the first sign of the end of that very same monetary system, as it had been conceived in the late 1970s. This is the point at which plans for Economic and Monetary Union began to take shape, with the aim of creating a single currency. Under the conditions then, it appeared that it would be all but impossible for Italy to stabilize its economic and financial indicators in a short time to participate from the very beginning in the new challenge of the single currency.

At that time, Mario Baldassarri, Franco Modigliani and Fabio Castiglionesi proposed a challenge-provocation to the Italian economy, giving priority to the goal of bringing inflation to zero[2]. It was called the "possible miracle," which was none other than a serious application of income policy in such a way as to drastically cut inflation, while breaking the vicious cycle of salaries-prices-currency depreciation. This logical argument and its concrete proposal were put into motion with the July 1993 agreement between the government and the unions on the cost of labor.

In this essay it was assumed that bringing inflation to zero would have had a direct result in terms of a reducing the nominal interest rate differentials between Italy and the rest of Europe, in particular Germany. Consequently, there would be a reduction in the nominal expenditures on interest, in effect streamlining the "additional" amount of the budget deficit that comes from the impact of inflation on nominal interest rates. In this way, a more realistic representation of the deficit would emerge, which could be used to devise a policy of structural containment on current spending that would in turn make balancing the budget a serious and feasible goal. It would then be possible for Italy to participate in European Monetary Union.

Entry to the Euro was gained by a swift reduction of the budget deficit, thanks in large part to the lowering of interest rates and the quasi elimination of interest rate differentials with the rest of Europe. The rest of the reduction in the deficit came from an increase in fiscal pressure, rather than through controls on current government spending. For Italy as well as other European countries, once a financial equilibrium was established, it was then a matter of judging just what sort of weighting of the national budget to put on the economy, in terms of expenditures and revenues, would encourage more solid possibilities for economic growth and for reducing unemployment. And maintaining and reinforcing financial equilibrium would have to be done in the context of having already assigned the European Central Bank with the task of controlling inflation and maintaining monetary stability.

Three years later, in the beginning of 1999, Mario Baldassarri, Marco Malgarini and Giorgio Valente produced a study which demonstrated that a positive trend in the world economy could certainly push the Italian economy toward a recovery in production

---

[2] Baldassarri M., Modigliani F., Castiglionesi F., *Il miracolo possibile: un programma per l'economia italiana (The Possibile Miracle: a Program for the Italian Economy)*, Bari, Laterza, 1996.

activity.[3] Without deeper domestic structural reforms, the future of that rebound remained fragile and precarious. In fact, the decreases in interest rates on European and international markets and the narrowing of the exchange rate differential between Italy and the rest of Europe had accounted for more than two-thirds of the rebalancing of the Italian budget and the ensuing entry of Italy into the Euro. On the other hand, Baldassarri et al. show that a jolt in the international interest rate cycle with an increase of just 2 percentage points would have carried Italy, hindered by its national debt, above the budget deficit threshold equal to 3% of GDP, pushing the debt-to-GDP ratio toward the high end. In the space of two years, therefore, Italy would have found itself in violation of the Maastricht criteria. Moreover, even given that a strong rebound in the world economy were to spark a recovery within the Italian economy that would make it possible to maintain its European obligations regarding budget deficits and national debt, only an unsatisfactory performance would be derived, with a slow reduction in the unemployment rate that would not have reached the minimum levels desired in the medium to long term of approximately 4-5%.

The proposal for the Italian Economy detailed in this second contribution, entailed instituting a measure of combining a cut in current levels of spending and taxation with an increase in government investment, to be initiated in a period of financial stability, which would pave a way toward more sustained growth capable of achieving the goal of full employment within 4 to 5 years. Under conditions of monetary and financial stability, it meant restructuring the national budget with the aim of lessening the budget's burden on the economy, as well as better qualifying the composition of expenditures and revenues. The results showed it is possible to build a solid framework for expansion of the Italian economy, through structural reforms of current government spending, the fiscal system, and the labor market, so as to reinvigorate investments and lower unemployment.

---

[3] Baldassarri M., Malgarini M., Valente G., *"Il secondo miracolo possibile: la sconfitta dell'inflazione, un progetto per la piena occupazione" (The Second Possibile Miracle: the Defeat of Inflation, a Project toward Full Employment)"*, Milano, Editrice Il Sole 24 Ore, 1999

1.3 A Confused European Debate: Never-ending Coordination or Coordination with an End.

Adding to the theoretical error and the empirical misconception, the three biggest countries of continental Europe (Germany, France and Italy) are involved in a tricky conceptual dilemma. In fact, the theme of so-called **fiscal coordination** circulated around Europe for a long time. The idea was that along with a single monetary policy and a single currency, there should also be a coordinated fiscal policy or, in other words, a "common" policy, so-called not because it would be decided by a single, nonexistent European Government, but would be agreed upon together by individual national governments. In reality, the trouble arises from the fact that behind the term fiscal coordination is hidden a will to not reduce fiscal pressures in Europe, practically creating a *"cartel of governments"* aiming to avoid fiscal competition. In opposition to this are those European countries, such as UK, Ireland and Spain, that had already lessened fiscal pressures and achieved improved performances from their economies as well as more solidly balanced national budgets.[4]

Certainly fierce fiscal competition among the different European states could have effects that in some ways would be disruptive.

Certainly coordination among national governments can be useful.

But only so long as the plans are clear: that is, bringing revenue levels closer to approximately 40% of GDP, instead of current levels in all the continental European countries of closer to 50%. It is therefore evident that this implies structural reforms focusing on government spending in all of these countries, in order to guarantee financial equilibrium.

It's a fact that this interpretation of European coordination has long represented an excuse for national decision-making, as if nothing should and could be done on the reform front within every single country unless it were agreed upon and/or imposed at a European level.

---

[4] Notice, however, that the European Commission too seems not to have a clear picture, as appears from Ireland's being reprimanded in April 2001 for lowering fiscal pressure, while enhancing demand and by this end inflation. That was motivated by the possibility that the Irish inflation, due to the strong domestic demand, might raise the area-wide inflation rate.

1.4 Full Employment in Europe: Mission Possible!

Based on Oxford Economic Forecasting's highly regarded econometric model, we have attempted to measure the *inertial trend* from 2002 over the next four years for all the member countries of the European Monetary Union.[5] The econometric exercises presented herein regarding the impact of alternative economic policies refer to the 2002-2006 period. Considering structural information about the sensitivity of economic systems, it can be presumed that largely the same effects would be reproduced if the simulation were to be deferred to a later time period.

Keeping the weight of national budgets on the economies at current levels, in other words without structural reforms, the results show European growth rates would remain modest, even taking into account the possibility of an international economic recovery after the sudden halt caused by the September 11th terrorist attacks. Unemployment rates would remain high and none of the countries would be in a position to eliminate their budget deficits within the deadlines set under the Stability Pact. An additional worsening in the international economic cycle would obviously mean an even more negative outlook.

Therefore, using the same econometric model, we then set out to check the impacts produced by three different economic policies on the European economy and on its individual economies.

The first (**Easy Monetary Policy: Effectiveness and Limits**) is the traditionally use of an easy monetary policy for its expansive effects on the economy, either through a shock reduction in interest rates or through a gradual lowering of rates. Without making parallel and coordinated adjustments to budget policy and the labor and the good market policy, the effect is to give a boost to the economy in the short term, while leading to a rebound in inflation in the medium term. This policy, however, does not seem capable of structurally improving growth prospects in the medium to long term.

---

[5] OEF provides a suite of user-friendly programs which allow clients to develop their own forecast scenarios or conduct 'what if' simulation analysis. The software can also be used to build satellite models within models. Data from resultant forecasts can be tabulated, graphed or exported to other packages. The model is built for every individual country with links connecting all of the economies of the Euro zone to one another, and this, in turn, to the rest of the world. For more details, see the website www.oef.com.

The second (**Higher Spending, Higher Taxes and No Reforms**) considers an additional increase in government spending, which necessitates, however, a parallel increase in fiscal pressure to maintain the conditions of financial equilibrium. This assumption is required to respect the Stability and Growth Pact (SGP).[6] This strategy of adding even more to the weight of the budget on the economy can even have the effect of producing a brake effect on the conditions for development in the different European economic systems. Growth is lessened, and unemployment increases and in the short and in the medium run. This policy, thus, not only does not seem capable of improving the current economic scenario, but also appears to have a negative impact also on the long-run perspectives.

Consequently, we have defined a third economic policy strategy (**Lower Taxes, Lower Spending, Higher Employment**). For this we refer to the theoretical assumptions summarized in Chapter 2, as well as some significant correlations that have emerged in all of the European countries regarding the existence of links between growth and unemployment, and between the size of government budget and growth rates. Also the prior positive performances of a similar economic policy over the Italian economy suggested to consider it as a candidate strategy for reaching *full employment and high growth in Europe*. In particular, we analyze the impact and the effectiveness of a budget policy spread over four or five years aimed at simultaneously reducing fiscal pressure and current account government spending by about 1% of GDP per annum against a background of increased flexibility within the labor and increasing competition in the goods and the services markets. With this third economic policy strategy we thus sought to verify if the Italian economy's possible miracle via a strategy of reforms could also be made for a Europe that supposedly is capable of and wants to take on the role she is requested to play in the new world economy. Anticipating results, presented in more details in the sequel, the answer is yes.

The goal of this analysis is to measure four different aspects.

The **first** consists of understanding the macroeconomic consequences of a policy that simultaneously reduces revenues and expenditures, based upon two precise agreements (*do ut des*) with families and with businesses. Families are promised a reduction in personal income tax, a highly progressive move favorable to low incomes and large families, while raising the retirement age by about

----

[6] More details on the SGP are presented in the Appendix and the end of the manuscript.

three years compared with the retirement age as stated by the rules in force. Businesses are proposed a fiscal reduction in corporate income tax and social contributions, while eliminating the thousand streams of subsidies, supports, and various transfers from the national budget. Therefore, this would mean measuring each individual country's potential for improvement by taking steps internally, without relying on eventual positive effects from moves made in other countries.

The **second** scenario presumes, instead, that this step be enacted simultaneously in all the countries. Consequently, in contrast to the first, this would result in a measurement of the eventual synergetic impact of policies "coordinated" at a European level.

The **third** policy simulation combines the same fiscal interventions with an expansionary monetary policy. In other words it puts together a reduction in fiscal pressure with an easier access to the credit market, while enhancing, by this end, private investments and consumption.

The **fourth** aspect, then, addresses the possibility that a country could consider so-called "free-riding," or in other words, not taking any domestic steps in the hope high growth obtained in all other countries through the structural reforms, could produce positive effects and solve the problem by having growth spurred from the outside. This argument is based upon the possibility that full employment and high growth would be achieved without having to deal with the eventual political costs of making reforms internally.

Briefly, these are the results we obtained:

1. without structural changes in government expenditures and government revenues, unemployment in all of the countries remains high and they have difficulty in maintaining financial equilibrium;

2. with lower taxes and lower current spending, there is more growth, full employment and zero deficit. However, inflationary risks begin to appear owing to the restrictions and to the existing rigidity in the labor market and therefore on the supply side;

3. adding flexibility to the labor market appears to bring inflation under control, even with a high growth rate and a strong increase in employment;

4. coordination does not seem to improve significantly the results obtainable for each single country independently. A very large part of the impact on growth and the reduction in unemployment appears to be due to the domestic effects of structural reforms decided by each single country, and only one-fifth of the synergetic effects inspired by the measures effected in all of the other countries;

5. combining this fiscal intervention with an easier monetary policy improves economic growth, reduces further unemployment, and improves government finance scenarios, without negative feedback on the inflation side;

6. *there's no room for sneaks*: whoever attempts to not make structural reforms in hopes for positive effects induced by others' reforms would be left behind in competitiveness, would expand little, and would maintain high unemployment and run risks on the budget deficit front.

These results were obtained based on an outline of a world economy that after the strong two year halt in 2001-2002, tends to regain a consistent pace of growth starting in 2003. But even in this scenario, doubts and uncertainties can emerge. So we sought to verify the impact of an international economic cycle that is less optimistic, characterized by a slowing of the world economy that extends into 2003, as it seemed to happen in mid-2002, on account of uncertainties over the American recovery.

So, in these conditions, the results obtained indicate that the impact of structural reforms is still important and their realization still necessary. Greater possible difficulties in the world economy should consequently inspire Europe to realize its own internal structural reforms "better and before" without falling back into the illusory wait for an "external" recovery in the world economy to make more resources available, and thus make the realization of those same structural reforms easier, less painful or maybe even possible to postpone.

1.5 The Basic Message to Reach a High and Stable Growth: Reform, Reform, Reform.

Even keeping in mind the obvious precautions that always accompany every econometric simulation, it then seems possible to draw a clear conclusion from these data: each country "must" take its domestic economic policy seriously.

It is here important to translate into economic and social terms the policy strategy implemented in our simulations.

The recovery in growth and employment, above all in the biggest countries (Germany, France and Italy), comes through reestablishing the relationships between the State, on one hand, and citizens, families and businesses, on the other hand. A social-political pact that would see a reduction in the budget's burden in terms of the levels of spending and revenues and broadens the scope of decisions of citizens, families and businesses, yet without destroying the State or the Welfare State. Instead, they have both to be given their essential and determinant role within a clear, not invasive, economic resource allocation.

All these elements can be imagined as a *new social, political and institutional pact*. As already indicated, it can take the form of a policy of reducing government revenues and government expenditures ex ante by about 1% of GDP per annum for four or five years. Stronger growth and higher employment ex post makes for a reduction in fiscal pressure and government spending equal to, and in some cases higher than, 1.5% per year. This relationship between ex-ante interventions and their ex-post effects seems to be confirmed in the case of Italy, as already seen in the preceding works, and seems extendable to other countries in the Euro area.

In reality, it's a matter of streamlining the economic burden of the State and reforming the Welfare State to render the first more efficient and more effective, and the second more just and inspired to a real solidarity. Both are prevented from weighing excessively on the economic system, producing privileges and social inequities within and between generations, and holding back the present and future potential for growth, employment and the welfare of the entire continent. It's therefore a matter of reducing quantitatively the redistributing effect the government budget has on the economy, making it qualitatively more efficient by allowing a larger share of income for families and businesses in order to accelerate accruals, development, and growth in employment.

1.6 How to Respect the Stability Pact and Live Happily in Europe.

The accentuated slowdown in the American economy caused by the events of September 11 greatly worsened the outlook for the international economic cycle. The poor performances of the stock markets, caused also by serious doubts over governance and transparency of American corporations, have emphasized the risks and the uncertainties regarding the world economy over the next few years.

Moreover, Europe as a whole does not seem capable of giving an internal and autonomous push to grow its own economy and remains strongly and directly connected to the performance of the American economy, both in terms of the real business cycle as well as the financial markets.

Increasingly emerging within this context is the problem for many countries of respecting, in punctual terms, the parameters assigned to each one under the Stability Pact, with the aim of redirecting all European countries toward zero deficit.

In reality, the zero deficit criterion was from the beginning based on medium term projections and a normal evolution in the economic cycle. Just for this reason, the idea of automatic stabilizers was introduced which, while guaranteeing a balanced budget under normal conditions, could allow for margins of fluctuation in the budget deficit above and below zero, specifically to account for positive and negative phases in the economic cycle.[7]

In this way it was expected all of the European countries could achieve a balanced budget and, once the zero deficit condition was met, could confront the alternative ups and downs of the cycle.

Instead a strong, anomalous and unexpected negative cycle hit the world economy (and consequently the European one) before the individual countries were able to complete the adjustments to achieve a balanced budget. It's as if the referee had blown the whistle to start the game before the teams had finished lining up on the field. At this point, there is need to reevaluate those same parameters of the Stability Pact with pragmatism and good sense, without abandoning

---

[7] In the recent years, however, several studies analyzed the possibility/necessity of revising, in some sense, the Stability and Growth Pact. Among the many, see Blanchard and Giavazzi (2002), Fiorito (2002), Wyplotz (2002).

the medium to long term goal of eliminating the deficit, which, on the contrary, has to be maintained.

During the course of 2002, these themes emerged with increasing frequency at different European summits, during which the concept of an automatic stabilizer began to be defined and the concept introduced of financial equilibrium being "close to balance," instead of referring in a timely and numerical way to a fateful "zero." The rationale behind this choice it that for budgets that amount to about or just less than half of GDP, a couple decimals higher or lower doesn't seem to take on any significant economic relevance.

Moreover, other fields of thinking are also beginning to discuss that same definition of budget deficit that under the Stability Pact is linked to the overall budget balance. Some proposals (Fitoussi, 2002) tend to distinguish between various items of government spending, for example, by not including investments in the Stability Pact's parameters, or measuring interest payments in a different way from other government spending items. Still others (Fitoussi and Creel, 2003) propose a different assessment of assigned economic policy goals, implying a different role for the European Central Bank (ECB) than that which it was assigned at the time it was instituted. The final aim is a redefined mix of fiscal and monetary policies. Others have criticized and are criticizing (Modigliani and Fitoussi, 2002) the ECB's interest rate policy over the past few years. Certainly a less phobic interest rate policy in the way it detects faint or even nonexistent inflationary risks and more attentiveness to the actual economic conditions could render a more pragmatic and effective use of the instruments of economic policy. It should also be remembered that the objective of monetary stability can certainly be pursued via the lever of using interest rates to contain inflation, but without forgetting that the strength of a currency depends also, and maybe above all, on the growth outlook of an economic system.

However, as has emerged from our work, without structural reforms within budget policy, an easing of monetary policy wouldn't have great effectiveness in itself. There would even be a risk of feeding the illusion that the strategy of restructuring the budget could be less necessary and more deferrable in time. In this sense, here we want to reaffirm the centrality of a triangle of structural reforms that is capable of giving self-propelling autonomy to the Old Continent. Only on this basis can a more pragmatic monetary policy prove itself useful without giving rise to a "wait and see" attitude or risks of monetary instability.

At present, without abandoning the necessary line of monetary and fiscal rigor, the objective conditions of the world economy in general and Europe's in particular make these contributions and debates useful (and maybe also necessary) to assure a pragmatic and more sensible use of the instruments of economic policy, instead of an ideological and excessively rigid one.

In our work, however, we do not intend to enter into the matter of how to modify or interpret the Stability Pact. Given the conditions posed by the pact, however, we do intend to propose a strategy of economic policy (or rather structural reforms) capable of building, presuming there's monetary and financial stability, a pathway toward economic expansion that is more coherent with the system's potentials. In addition, the growth path would be more in line with the goals of seeing a full use of resources, an increase in potential growth and a better social distribution of incomes, also in cross-generational terms. Our "proposal" does not require barring eventual changes or more or less elastic interpretations of the dictates of the Stability Pact. These could render the strategy proposed here even more effective and, either way, more – not less – necessary and urgent.

It is not about changing the Stability Pact in order to not make structural reforms. On the contrary, it's about realizing the necessary reforms in all of Europe, or better yet in all the countries that are far behind on this front. In this case, these countries will be able to respect and obtain a solid and durable financial equilibrium and not a fragile and precarious one with respect to the mutable conditions of the international cycle. In this context, a reexamination of the shifting outline of the deficit trend in parallel with an implementation of structural reforms would simply be a reasonable interpretation of the Pact and not a radical alteration of it. Rather it would be an intelligent and farsighted confirmation of the true objectives of financial stability posed in that very Pact.

We therefore believe it is fundamental that the debate not be limited to a quasi ideological struggle between those who are "pro" and those who are "con". It is really not a matter of deciding simplistically to change the parameters of the Pact. It is a matter of putting on the same table the job of making reforms and of respecting a flexible interpretation of the Pact, one that is the most intelligent and farsighted.

The econometric exercises presented in our work are therefore meant as a thoughtful contribution to show that Europe can set itself higher goals with regard to what simple inertial trend lead to believe.

Certainly it means assuming responsibility for one's self, for single countries and for the Continent as a whole, but also toward the rest of the world. What that means is steering one's own necessary reform processes. In this way European growth would increasingly assume self-propelling characteristics and would be less dependent on the old export-led model that in past decades has guided the experiences of single national entities.

We maintain that this is the deepest meaning of the process of European integration, which until now, has seen its culmination in the creation of the single currency.

The Euro, on one hand, and the single market, on the other, make it so that summing up 12, 15 or more countries is not a simple arithmetical operation. The single national states were all more or less small economies characterized with a high degree of openness toward external trade. Today, however, the Europe of the Euro (and in the near future an enlarged Europe) is a large closed economy with a notable reduction in openness toward international extra-European trade.

In these conditions we can no longer allow ourselves to wait for an external positive economic cycle to improve our outlook for growth. We have to take on the responsibility of building these favorable conditions domestically, in this way helping to determine, in synergy and in alternation with the world's great economic areas, a solid pathway toward expansion for the international economy. For Europe the world economic cycle can no longer be taken as a datum that is "exogenous." The dimensions that an integrated European economy is now assuming within the world economy must make it understood that the performance of the world economy is also based on what is taking place in the Old Continent. Europe, that is, must begin to acknowledge not only that the rest of the world cannot resolve European problems, but also and most importantly that same evolution of the rest of the world is dependent on the European economy's ability to create self-propelled development.

1.7 There is a Problem in the World Economy, and There is a Problem in Europe.

The European social conquests in the past were able to find adequate resources based on a favorable trend in the terms of trade between the prices of industrial products on one side, and agricultural and mineral commodities on the other side. Indeed, a considerable part of the

European welfare state was effectively made possible by taking advantage of the real income derived from the Third World countries caused by falling relative prices for agricultural products and commodities in general. In addition, a reduced commitment to defense and security spending left even wider resources available for building welfare state and social protection.

Indeed there is a problem in the world economy, and there is a problem in Europe. These growth-related issues (that are the relations among the industrialized, the developing and the transition economies, and the new role that Europe wants and deserves in the modified international scenario) call for more attention.

Concerning the former, it represents a problem for the world economy that can be defined as *serious* nowadays, but that may become *dramatic* within the next ten/twenty years. To better appreciate it, it is interesting to analyze the World Map where continents' sizes are weighted by corresponding population's size (Figure 1.1), by corresponding mineral resources (Figure 1.2) and corresponding agricultural resources (Figure 1.3). In the following figures, the larger a continent is, the larger is the size of population or the amount of resources available.

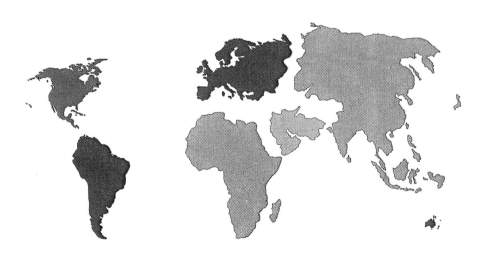

Source: Cova (1996)

Figure 1.1 World Map: Continents Weighted by Population's Size

Source: Cova (1996)

Figure 1.2 World Map: Continents Weighted by Mineral Resources

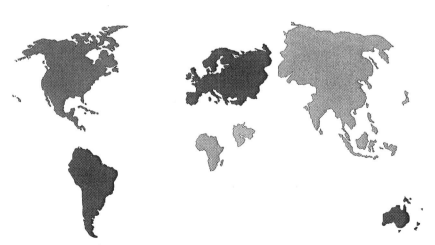

Source: Cova (1996)

Figure 1.3 World Map: Continents Weighted by Agricultural Resources

Nature or God, as somebody could say, has been, indeed, quite generous in terms of geographical distribution of resources, as we can see from previous figures. Indeed, their distribution appears, more or less, proportional to the population's needs. The only exception may be raised when looking at the African Continent, which is quite large in term of population's size and of mineral (non-oil) resources, but it shrinks significantly when weighting its size by agricultural resources.

Weighting, finally, each continent with its corresponding GDP, the picture presents a very different scenario (Figure 1.4). There are three giants accounting for a very large part of the World's GDP: north America (US and Canada), Europe, and Japan. The Latin American and the Asian countries become relatively small, while Africa almost disappears. This depicts what is commonly defined as *the tragedy of Africa* (see Easterly and Levine, 1997 or Sala-I-Martin and Subramanian, 2003, Collier and Gunning, 1999 for a survey of these issues within development economics).

Source: Cova (1996)

Figure 1.4 World Map: Continents weighted by GDP

This is not the result of God's will, but of the organization and the market power built by men. Notice indeed, that this economic scenario is not the consequence of the scarcity of resources, but of market structure. In particular, developed economies produce technologically advanced products and services, which are produced and traded within oligopolistic markets. On the contrary, natural (mineral and agricultural) resources are located in developing and transition economies,[8] but traded in more or less perfectly competitive markets. It is clear that when there exist heterogeneous market structure within the same production chain, the results in terms of World income distributions heavily depend on the different power of the agents operating in different markets.[9]

To verify that income reallocation is clearly a market structure related problem, it is convenient to compare the evolution over time of the term of trade between industrial countries and oil producing countries with the term of trade between industrial countries and non-oil-producing countries. In fact oil-consumer countries are organized as an almost oligopolistic system, as well as oil-supplier countries, which are organized within the OPEC cartel. On the contrary, agricultural and mineral resources are allocated within a competitive market, which demand side, however, is organized as an oligopoly.[10]

The term of trade between industrial countries and oil producing countries increased by near 350% since 1973, thirteen years after the creation of OPEC cartel (created at the Baghdad Conference, September 1960) (Figure 1.5).[11] Most importantly, after more than 30 years, oil price per barrel still fluctuates around that level. The OPEC cartel has been able, up to now, to optimally dynamically manage its power by controlling oil extraction.[12]

---

[8] Precisely, they are traded at the Chicago Exchange Market.

[9] With heterogeneous market structures, we refer to the possibility of having a sector behaving competitively, while relying, however, on an intermediate sector that is dominated by a monopolist, or vice versa. These scenarios turns out to be troublesome in terms of resource allocations and rent extractions. More technically, in such a context, an equilibrium is not anymore Pareto optimal.

[10] In other words, we want to verify whether a case where two oligopolistic markets confront each others (OPEC Vs Technology Markets) is more or less desirable than a case where an oligopolistic market face a competitive one (Natural Resources Market Vs Technology Market). The comparison is made on the basis of the term of trade, which measures the relative power of the market structures.

[11] During the war between Arabs and Israelis, Arab financial needs occasioned by war increased desire for an higher income. Hence OPEC reduced output causing oil price to more that triplicate between 1973 and 1975.

[12] Notice that this cannot be necessarily interpreted as the product of an ideological and/or religious confront, but it can be seen as the application of a neoclassical scheme of analysis, that is commonly quotes as the oil extraction problem, and it is a straightforward application of dynamic programming

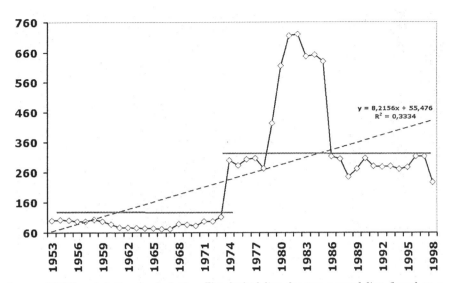

Source: OECD and Authors' calculation. The dashed line denotes a trend line (based on a linear regression, which coefficients are presented in the Figure). The lighter lines denote the average level of term of trade before and after 1973.

Figure 1.5 Term Of Trade Between Oil-Producer Countries And Industrialized Countries

On the contrary, the term of trade between industrial products and raw (non-oil) materials is steadily falling since 1953. Among the possible interpretations, we argue that this is due to the rent extraction operated by oligopolistic markets that demand agricultural and mineral (non-oil) resources. What is more critical, in our opinion, is that a part (more or less large) of this rent has been used to finance European growth, and, for a smaller share, the US growth. In the US, indeed, the relative prices change effect was mitigated by the relatively higher share of domestic production of oil, with respect to European Countries. In both countries, however, the agricultural production has been subsidized with government intervention, in order to save domestic producers from the fall of agricultural good prices. Two consequences have been produced: on one side the fall of agricultural relative prices have compressed growth of the third world countries, and on the other side, consumers of the industrialized countries had to pay higher prices on agricultural protected products, or higher taxes to subsidize them.

techniques (see Stockey, Lucas, and Prescott, 1989 for more details).

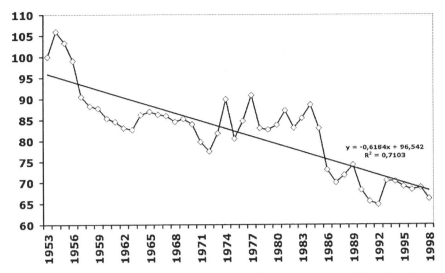

Source: OECD and Authors' calculation. The dashed line denotes a trend line (based on a linear regression, which coefficients are presented in the Figure).

Figure 1.6 Term Of Trade Between No-Oil-Producer Countries and Industrialized Countries

It can be suggested that there exist an *easy solution* of this problem, which is to transform agriculture-based economies into industrialized economic systems. In our opinion this is not an easy job, or a proposal consistent with actual economic and political scenario. To analyze it, suppose that this program could be realized in some way.[13] Even in this case, however, there exist a problem due to the transition between the two regimes, since it may take a lot of time, and it is difficult to imagine how it would happen (it could involve, for example, a civil war). Moreover, there might exist a scarcity problem of agricultural products once the transition is completed. Indeed, once all developing economies, which in current economic context are responsible for supplying agricultural products, become industrialized countries, the world economy will still need a supply of corn, rice, bananas and mangos.

---

[13] In early months of the year of 1789, when the French population was starving without even a piece of bread, it has been suggested to give them croissants, instead of bread. This sounds much similar to suggesting to developing economies to stop producing corn, or mangos and to start producing high tech mobile phone. It may be worth to recall that few months after that famous line, the French Revolution begun.

Hence, it follows that this scenario is not consistent with a sustainable development scheme. It can be easily imagined that in few years the developed economies will observe large migrations from the poor to the wealthy regions, starting with the case of Europe, which geographically faces north African countries.

We need to look and make every possible effort to find a way out to world-wide sustainable growth. Global problems requires Global Institution. IMF, Worldbank, and WTO should be reformed in order to accomplish to this new mission. In particular, the WTO should become the true World-wide Antitrust, while preventing the raise of monopoly power within chain value, and preventing, by this end, the extraction of rents from underdeveloped economies.

Notice that there exist already evidences of organized oligopolistic markets, like for example the case of ICO (International Coffee Organization), which has been set up in 1963, even earlier than the OPEC. ICO is the main intergovernmental organization for coffee, bringing together producing and consuming countries to tackle the challenges facing the world coffee sector through international cooperation.

It would be useful for developed economies first, and for the world economy too, having more and more of organization like this. The true *liberal thought* is indeed having competition among oligopoly powers, and not competition between a monopoly (oligopoly) and thousands of small competitors. In fact, it is not consistent to imagine a world where only a fifth of the population is rich, while everybody else is starving in developing and transition countries. The growth and the development of western countries depend on the development and the growth of Latin America, of Africa, and of Asia. And the new engine for the future growth of developed economies has to be found in the development of the above mentioned areas of the World. This means that rich countries can be selfish, but they cannot be any longer myopic, or worse, economically and politically foolish.

The second problem refers directly to Europe. It is represented by the composition of government expenditure of European countries and to the US one. A casual inspection of Figure 1.7 shows that during the decades before the fall of Berlin Wall, defense expenditure, as a percentage of GDP, ranged between the 6% of the US and the 2.5% of Italy. UK, France, and Germany were in between.[14] After the fall of

---

[14] Notice, however, that the UK defense expenditure share of GDP is much more closer to the US one, while France and Germany are closer to Italy.

Berlin Wall, however, defense expenditure steadily decreased since 1989, while generating the so called *peace dividend*.

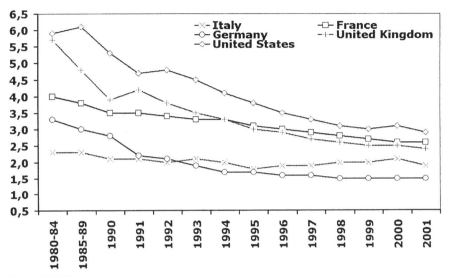

Source: NATO

Figure 1.7 Defense Expenditure (% GDP)

In particular, at the end of 2001, the US defense expenditure is close to 3.5% of GDP, France and UK are close to 3%, while Germany and Italy devote to Defense expenditure between 2 and 2.5 points of GDP. Also the composition of defense expenditure in each of the above mentioned countries deserves more attention, as well as the structure of the army. There are countries (like Italy, for example) where a large part of this government budget chapter is represented by current expenditure (e.g. wages, salaries), while a relative smaller share is allocated to capital expenditure (e.g. machineries, infrastructures, research). In other countries (like the US and UK) this proportion is reversed. There exist, moreover, a difference concerning the kind of army. In particular some countries have a small-size but professional Army, while others a draft-based, large and obsolete Army.[15]

---

[15] The obsolescence here refers to the fact that the mutated international scenario does not requires anymore large Armies, but small and highly efficient army, able to move and to be operative in a short time.

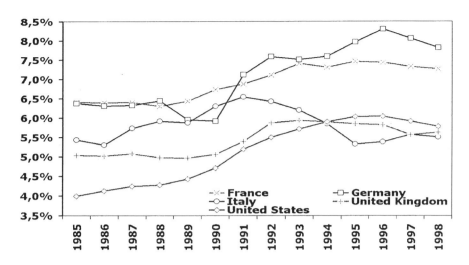

Source: OECD

Figure 1.8 Health Expenditure (% GDP)

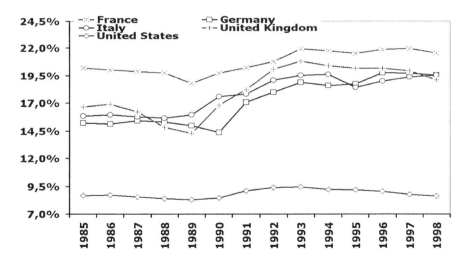

Source: OECD

Figure 1.9 Social Expenditure (% GDP)

When looking at the Social and the Health expenditure, the orderamong the same countries is almost reversed over the sample 1985-2001. In particular, The US are the country with the lowest Social Expenditure share of GDP, and one of the bottom end with regard Health Expenditure's share of GDP. On the contrary, European countries presented since 1985 a large and increasing social and health expenditure.

It can be imagined that, after the Second World War, European countries chose an implicit (or explicit?) coordination equilibrium with the US. In particular, European countries chose to allocate the smallest possible share of their GDP to defenses, while relying on the US defense shelter (for example European countries were and are able to benefit from consistent American resources as part of NATO).[16] Many resources, then, become freely available for being allocated to other uses, like social security and health.

Now, the processes of economic and financial integration also entail parallel processes of institutional integration and reform. On the other hand, however, economic phases also often require assuming responsibility even when political and institutional phases seem necessarily longer and more extended.

In addition, after September 11th, the World is changed, and it is possible that previous equilibria are not efficient anymore. European integration is becoming tighter and tighter, and Europe wants and deserves a leading role in this modified worldwide scenario. Needless to say, significant resources are necessary to play this role.

By a long-lasting low growth profile, totally dependent and lagging behind North American cycle, Europe faces a very difficult choice: either to accepts its secondary role in defense and global security, or to drastically cut its social expenditure and welfare state.

Only shifting upward the current depressed growth path, the European countries will have the opportunity to generate new resource making possible to invest into these new activities, without disinvesting them from current budget chapters, like the social and the

---

[16] Alternatively, this equilibrium could be interpreted in the light of the classical theory of comparative advantages (Ricardo, 1837), where Europe specializes in the production of social goods (welfare and health services), while the US specializes in the production of defense related and military goods. There exist a subtle but critical difference with Ricardo's contribution. In Ricardo's comparative advantage theory countries involved in production specialization trade produced commodities. In the context of the military and the social expenditure, there exist an important asymmetry, in the sense that defense expenditure is tradable in some sense, while social expenditure is a social public good that is country specific! Even US tourist could not take the benefits of European Welfare state, since they would pay if using European health services, for example.

health expenditures. Once the new resources becomes available, that choice could be better affordable. Both *social standards* can be maintained, while security and defense can be faced. There exist, however, many other possible uses, which analysis does not belong to our goals. For what concerns our perspective, it is important to create more resources, by reaching full employment and sustainable high growth, which use belongs to each government decision set.

In summary, it is important to underline how this new equilibrium would give Europe the opportunity of having a new and a leading role in the World Economy. Indeed, an improvement of economic performances has a clear impact in strategic positioning over the political and international scenario.

The recent events on the world political and economic scene impel Europe to grow on the front of both economic and political responsibility. In other words, Europe should avoid the temptation that has presented itself here and there over the last years to seem too indulgent with the economic conquests obtained over the past decades through its model of social and civil development.

Sometimes Europe appears on the world scene like a sleeping beauty waiting for a foreign prince capable of rousing her from her long sleep.

Unfortunately it is also necessary to remember that the foreign prince capable of leading a reawakening today doesn't always assume the characteristics of a chivalrous prince, but rather the more ominous features of international terrorism. Also for this reason, structural reforms should be introduced in the short term, because waiting the long term required for the coming of the European prince is a luxury that can't be afforded.

PART TWO

THEORETICAL BACKGROUND,
EUROPEAN UNION GUIDELINES,
AND EMPIRICAL EVIDENCES

2. Three Theoretical Achievements

2.1 Basic Themes on Macro and Microeconomics.

One of the main issues of economic theory has always been the role and the impact of the government budget and fiscal policies on both individual decisions of families and businesses (microeconomic effects) and on the overall state of the economic system (macroeconomic effects).

The first topic we'll address concerns the results obtained through economic theory regarding the relations between size, composition of the government budget, and development of an economic system. To be complete, we'll analyze the problem first from the standpoint of neoclassical theory, and then in the context of endogenous growth models.[1]

The synergy between efficiency and distributive equity represents the second of the economic theory assumptions which we intend to refer to for the empirical themes dealt with in this work. Going over the most recent literature on the subject[2] we'll demonstrate how distributive equity and efficiency represent a binominal synergy, rather than two variables in opposition to each other, as according to the most traditional trade-off suggested by the most significant writings produced in the 1950s and 1960s.[3]

Finally, on the microeconomic front, with important macroeconomic implications, there is a whole series of studies connected to game theory and the theory of industrial organization. In

---

[1] For further detail, see Baldassarri (1978), Barro and Sala-I-Martin (1994), Aghion (1999), Aghion and Howitt (1998), or Masson (2000).
[2] In this context, we include contributions of Alesina and Rodrik (1994), Persson e Tabellini (1994), Perotti (1993), Baldassarri e Piga (1997) and Murphy Schleifer and Vishny (1997),
[3] See also Kutnez's example.

particular, reusing Curnot's model, an aspect that's often not considered in the current debate emerged. In other words, in the case of fiscal coordination, without a clear final objective of stability or a lessening of total fiscal pressure, there could in reality be a paradoxical result, that is an increase in that same fiscal pressure.

2.2 Economic Growth and Government Budget.

The literature that analyzes the relationships between economic growth and fiscal policy is particularly vast and rich, and a complete review of it would go beyond the scope of the present essay. As such, in the following pages we present only some aspects that we think are the most important for the purpose of our "argument," reviewing the most notable contributions concerning economic growth models, both exogenous and endogenous.

We begin with **neoclassical growth theory**, otherwise known as the theory of exogenous growth.[4] In this area, government intervention in the productive structure of market economies has been analyzed since the dawn of modern economic theory, with reference in particular to two specific situations: the presence of private monopolies in crucial sectors of the productive system and the necessity of taking care of so-called government goods. Starting in the 1950s, however, and maybe unexpectedly, a form of "mixed" market gained growing weight in different European countries, in which government-owned businesses operative in various private markets were acting in competition with private businesses. The situation of so-called "businesses with a public interest" also fall into this category. It took on considerable dimensions in the case of Italy and was adopted by many other European countries. It must be emphasized that this form of market presents a double aspect: on one hand it can reduce competition in the market, on the other the presence of public enterprises operating under conditions of competition in various markets seemed to be able give additional vigor as an instrument of economic policy aimed at stabilizing the economy and promoting development.

In this type of "mixed" government-private economy, the limits of an analysis of fiscal policy interventions that are based exclusively on the levels of revenues and expenditures, or even more simply, on only the balances of the government administration's budget,[5] seem clear.

---

[4] The writings on growth theory are particularly numerous: among them we note the roots by Solow (1956) and Swan (1956).
[5] Major criticism of the selected criteria of the growth and stability pact:

In this context it appears necessary, if not indispensable, to include evaluations and comments with respect to the structure and composition of spending and revenue items (see Baldassarri, 1978). The message of this essay must be very clear. In fact, it is not possible to evaluate economic policy on the sole basis of size or the number of interventions, but the quality of those also has an important role, especially for economies characterized by a large burden of the State. The concept of "quality of government spending" actually refers to a measure of quantity relative to its composition, with particular regard to the amount destined to productive spending and/or for investments, as well as to current spending destined for collective consumption.[6] Significant doubts have to be raised toward those analyses that refer only to the aggregate values of the budget and overlook the available possibilities, and the imposed constraints, of maneuvers to reorganize the budget through changes in its very structure.

To *extrapolate* the economic policy message from this part of theoretical literature, the key variables as regards government spending are represented by the amount destined for consumption and the amount destined for investments, or rather the propensity for consumption and for investment of the government sector. By comparing these with the behaviors expressed by the private sector, the optimal choice for the level and the composition of government spending in order to maximize economic growth and/or the collective welfare, is derived. The literature does not exclude the possibility that government businesses and/or the government budget as a whole show greater efficiency and/or effectiveness. The entire efficiency frontier of production would undergo a shift toward the outside with growth in the share of the market of the government sector, and if the opposite were true, the relation mentioned above would be seen going in the opposite direction. In these two extreme cases, the decision of policymakers is altogether easy: in the first case, it's convenient to reallocate the resources of the private sector to the government one, which guarantees better performance, while in the second case, the reallocation should be directed toward the private sector.

From this, a precise message is derived: either the State and the government sector prove themselves more efficient in stimulating growth over the long term (and in this case they can have the right to absorb and manage an increasing share of the economy), or the State has to perform its proper function as collective decision-maker, using a

---

comment or refer to a later point.
[6] In fact it's clear that the impact of interventions in government spending targeting only consumer goods is quite different from the impact following interventions in government investments, including in private sectors.

minimum of necessary resources and leaving a maximum of possible resources to families and businesses, whose decisions in turn will determine a much more consistent and satisfactory pathway toward economic growth.

A second class of models with which it is useful to evaluate the interventions of economic policy is **the theory of endogenous growth**.[7] We are taking as a given that neoclassical growth theory (see above all Solow, 1956) considers that technical progress is exogenous and that growth in GDP in the long term depends solely on growth in the population. In this context, economic policy, in the kinds of interventions applied to stimulate savings, influences only the level of per capita income, but does not change the rate of growth of the economy. On the other hand, in more recent growth models, technical progress is endogenous and that offers, at least in principle, larger spaces for fiscal policy since it permanently changes the rate of growth of GDP.

As emphasized by Baldassarri (1978) and Barro and Sala-i-Martin (1998), fiscal policy interventions encourage investments, guaranteeing a higher rate of growth, as long as the social yield on investments exceeds the private yield. In this case, the interaction between fiscal policy and the market economy generates positive external effects that we see as higher productivity of government investments. Fiscal policy interventions applied to stimulate investments are welcome in this context, as long as businesses do not internalize the positive externalities, generating a flow of investment inferior to the optimal profile.[8]

The literature about endogenous growth also allows the possibility of elaborating interesting considerations about the role of fiscal policy in respect to the debate on efficiency-equity. In this class of models, the

---

[7] In conclusion, similarly to as was seen with the neoclassical models, given the richness of the endogenous growth models, the present review doesn't seek to summarize every general conclusion on the subject of fiscal policy, except for the desirability of productive spending or investments in areas where social productivity is greater than private productivity. For example, see Aghion and Howitt (1998), Aghion (1999), or Tanzi and Zee (1997), for a description of the relationships between fiscal policy and growth in a fuller context.

[8] It is superfluous to underline that all of the considerations here quoted are valid in a decentralized economy. A Benevolent Planner confronts and resolves the problem of the optimum allocation of resources by assigning quantities. Based on the first theorem of the economy of welfare we are sure of the Pareto-optimality of this allocation.

social redistribution of income doesn't necessarily produce a reduction of economic growth, differently from what was originally suggested by Kuznetz. Re-distributive policies can in fact reduce social conflicts (as pointed out by Benabou, 1996), or otherwise increase the productivity of the less privileged classes (Aghion, 1999).[9] Both of these interventions result in higher demand, and consequently in a higher rate of growth.

An additional aspect of endogenous growth theory is the joint analysis of the economic cycle and growth in the long term. The so-called Shumpeter approach (Shumpeter, 1939) dominant in the arena of modern theory of endogenous growth emphasizes the purgative role of recessions. In these phases, indeed, the less efficient businesses and those that are too financially exposed come to be eliminated, in this way boosting the average productivity of the economy and creating the basis for future growth.

We see it as an obligation to refer to the so-called conjecture of Harberger, according to whom, on the other hand, fiscal policy, on a par with monetary policy, proves to be substantially neutral with respect to growth over the long term. We cannot say we're able to share this hypothesis, both because few studies seem to be able to validate it (Mendoza, 1997), and because results of this type appear fragile and uncertain.

Other channels through which fiscal policy can stimulate economic growth relate to the hypothesis of supporting scientific research and technology with interventions directed in a way as to create positive externalities, and make it so that businesses incorporate those effects into their decision-making process. It is clear that the success of the targeted interventions depends much on the quantity and the quality of the information available to policymakers. A valid alternative, in the case that information is of low quality, consists of creating a scheme of compatible incentives, and afterward to let the market act independently.

A second aspect regards the way in which technological developments have an impact on the economic system. These can come from the research itself, or from learning and experience (so-called learning by doing). The phenomenon of learning by doing, however strongly endorsed by macroeconomic and industrial literature, presents a notable risk represented in the marginality of its effects for individual businesses that don't incorporate the benefits meant to fall

---

[9] For more detailed analysis, see Aghion (1999).

back on the economy in its entirety (including those same businesses). This fact gives reason to think that subsidies meant for businesses, lacking precise content, can be transformed into a dispersion of resources.

One last comment is based on the so-called "multi-good" or "multi-sector" models, in which goods are produced in different sectors with different technologies. These models suggest that growth could be stimulated through policies addressed at increasing the mobility and the flexibility of the work force (see, for example, Lucas, 1993; Aghion and Howitt, 1998). In this case, an optimal reallocation of resources across sectors according to factor demand and final goods demand is guaranteed.

2.3 Economic Growth and Social Equity.

The link between distributive equity (understood as a redistribution geared toward reducing income inequalities) and efficiency (understood as the greatest possible productivity attainable with given resources) has taken on great importance in the context of economic theory and represents one of the supporting pillars of the economic policy strategy we propose in this essay.[10] Before presenting the two schools of thought that characterize this literature, a distinction must be made, as according to Baldassarri and Piga (1997), between an "internal evaluation" of the welfare state and an "external evaluation." The former regards consequences and conditions (advantages, inefficiencies, and damages), on the base of which the welfare state is managed, while the second answers the question of whether it is convenient and/or useful to have a welfare state, which we assume to be efficient.[11]

We believe that the welfare state is indispensable in an economic system, but we are also convinced that quantity and quality of the social state influence the path of growth of the economy. For this reason, in the following pages we revert to the literature that has analyzed the "internal evaluation," although somewhat briefly.

---

[10] It must be emphasized that the analysis we present herewith takes into examination a concept of equity that is decidedly economic, in the sense that ethical and sociological considerations are not taken into account.
[11] In fact, if we weren't to assume within "external evaluation" the efficiency of the welfare state, quite probably the answer would tend toward a pure market economy.

The traditional approach considers the objectives of distributive equity and efficiency in opposition, or, in current English usage, a trade-off. This type of result leaves little space for purely economic speculation, as the debate is framed in the fundamental question about the relationships between ethics and economics.

Beginning in the early 1990s, economic literature reconsidered the relationship between equity and efficiency in a different light: it is in fact possible to identify historical, institutional and technological conditions which determine a synergetic interaction that, owing to a clearer interaction between equity and development, generates a stronger growth of the entire economy. It's possible to organize different levels of equity with respect to the corresponding level of efficiency. In this context, it can be demonstrated how the relation between social equity and economic growth is positive, for lower levels of equity, and then later shrinks. Economically speaking, the expansion part of the relation can be traced to the greater demand created by the redistribution of resources toward the less privileged classes. The shrinking part depends on the redistribution of income from investments and from the consequent drop in net income on capital, which therefore reduces the incentive to invest. Given the continuity of the relation, one or more equity values exist for which the relation with efficiency is maximized. We denote this combination as the "golden rule." In this context, Baldassarri and Piga (1997) propose using a function of social welfare defined with respect both to equity and to efficiency, in a way to settle most optimally the trade-off that comes to be created.[12] The most recent writings point out how the mechanisms based on which distribution influences the production frontier are three: the existence of heterogeneity among agents, the existence of fixed costs in technology and finally, the presence of imperfections in the markets.

As far as the first aspect is concerned, the two most significant essays are those by Alesina and Rodrik (1994) and Persson and Tabellini (1994).[13] The first two authors connect heterogeneity to the different availability of physical capital and the work factor, while in the second contribution heterogeneity owes to the initial availability of wealth. In both these essays, the existence of non-lump-sum taxation and the redistribution of income through a system of transfers are assumed. Alesina and Rodrik obtain an equity-efficiency frontier that

---

[12] The authors refer to this as the modified golden rule, or rather the platinum rule.

[13] Both seek to explain the link between distributive equity and growth rates, omitting phenomenologies described by Kutznez's curve and by the relations between equity and income levels.

is first increasing and then decreasing, as the positive effects of the redistribution through government spending prevail, above a certain threshold, against the negative effects derived from the ability to appropriate the yields on investments. On the other hand, Persson and Tabellini show that greater equity can generate more rapid expansion. It should be emphasized, however, that an increase in the wealth of the average voter, as described by Persson and Tabellini, prompts that person to internalize the yield on investments before taxation, and to therefore invoke a reduction in taxes.[14]

In a second class of models it is emphasized that redistribution can render investments that require an initial fixed cost impracticable, because of taxes. Among the various authors, it is interesting to consider Perotti's contribution (1993), which lies between this class and those models that are based on imperfect markets. He proposes a model with fixed costs for investments and imperfect credit markets. In detail, in this model there are two classes of agents, the "poor" class, subject to liquidity constraints, and the "rich" class, free from financial constraints. Investments are financed by the affluent class and require an initial fixed cost. In this context, it is easy to see that the redistribution takes away from the "rich" classes resources otherwise destined for investment, transferring them to the social classes that don't have access to the financial markets. If the rich class is "sufficiently rich" to be able to continue to invest, the "greater equality" widens the demand for goods and services, boosting the growth rate of the entire economy. If, however, this condition is not met, the redistribution of resources has a depressive effect on the economic system. The model therefore allows for an increasing equity-efficiency frontier at first, and decreasing afterward, similarly to what was seen before. Note that the problem is serious: heightened inequality doesn't supply the poor classes sufficient resources to invest, and, almost paradoxically, strong equality takes resources destined for investment away from the affluent classes. The conclusion is that maximizing the size of the middle class has to be the crux of redistributive policies. In addition, it is interesting to note that this aspect can be seen as an additional source of cyclical fluctuation of the economy.

The third class of models assumes the existence of imperfect markets. Two important contributions are those of Galor and Zeira (1993) and of Murphy, Schleifer and Vishny (1989). The first gives prominence to the imperfections in the credit market, showing how the results depend on the initial distribution of resources, similarly to

---

[14] It is also necessary to emphasize that an increase in the wealth of the average voter does not necessarily imply greater equality within the society.

what was seen in Alesina and Rodrik. The model of Murphy, Schleifer and Vishny is particularly articulated in describing two sectors, one characterized by the existence of increasing yields and the other by decreasing yields. While considering imperfections in capital markets that do not allow all individuals to invest in technologies of growing scale, in the model inequality weighs on the demand side, in the sense that only some classes (for example, individuals not possessing stock or land) consume goods of only primary necessity and invest only in products with decreasing yields, while the other classes (for example, entrepreneurs and specialized investors) put part of their income into goods of high technological content. In this case an extremely egalitarian distribution of income discourages covering fixed costs, and too unequal a distribution does not allow the majority of individuals to enjoy capital yields and to consume produced goods. All of the models considered (except for Persson and Tabellini (1994)) show a relation between efficiency and equity that is initially increasing (in which instance greater equity feeds greater economic development) and afterward decreasing (in which instance greater equity slows economic growth) often indicated as the equity-efficiency frontier (Figure 2.1).

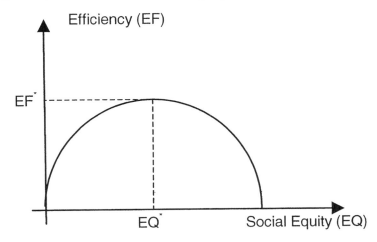

Figure 2.1 Social Equity -Efficiency Frontier
Source: Baldassarri and Piga (1996)

Baldassarri and Piga (1996) point out how in contributions to theory that analyzes the link between growth and redistribution, a representative parameter of equity is not explicitly incorporated in the function of social utility. This represents a weak point of the analysis, as the equity-efficiency combination cannot be chosen directly by the policymaker. In other words, we cannot depict a map of indifference curves in the equity-efficiency plane. To obviate this problem, the authors introduce a map of the functions with an aversion to inequality.[15] Technically speaking, Baldassari and Piga show how it is possible to define a function of social utility with regard to equity and efficiency, and how it is therefore possible to trace a map of the indifference curve along with the equity-efficiency frontier. The tangent between the two curves indicates the optimal point, which corresponds with the best combination of equity and efficiency (an example is represented by the EQ** and EF** pair in Figure 2.2. For further details and possible cases, refer to the original essay).

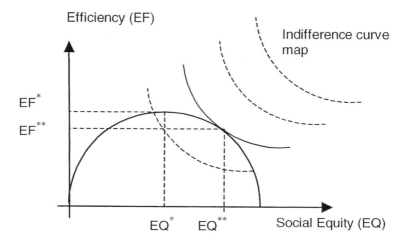

Figure 2.2 A Social Utility Function over Efficiency and Social Equity
Source: Baldassarri and Piga (1996)

Finally, Baldassarri and Piga emphasize how the true challenge doesn't consist of the optimal choice between equity and efficiency, as much as the maximization of efficiency (or rather of economic growth) for every distribution of income or wealth. In graphic terms, this means that policymakers should not think only of how "to move along the equity-efficiency frontier," but also about how "to move the same curve higher". (Figure 2.3)

----

[15] Thanks to the Atkinson theory, we can affirm that if in an economic system the so-called principle of transfers is valid, given two companies with the same average income, if the Lorenz curve of one company is always superior to that of the other one, then the health of the first will be superior to that of the second.

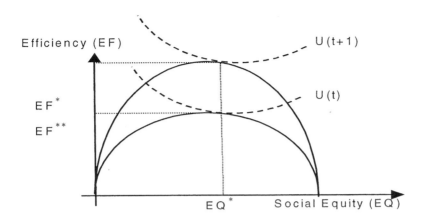

Figure 2.3 Moving Social Equity- Efficiency Frontier Upward
Source: Baldassarri and Piga (1996)

More precisely, it is a matter of understanding how the parameter of distributive equity enters into the function of social utility and in what way that same function of social equity changes in respect to different stages of development of the economic system. There's a need to judge whether in a growing economy society tends to value more or less the level of distributive equity, and conversely, to measure the greater or lesser impact that distributive equity determines on economic growth. Here, two evident polar conditions are being discussed: on one hand, an absolutely egalitarian society, but where everyone is poor and there is no growth, and, on the other hand, an absolutely egalitarian society that is only obtained after a strong process of development where everyone is rich and, given the increasingly marginal yields between equity and efficiency, where the parameter of equity prevails in the social utility function, leading to an egalitarianism of wealthy people. On the contrary, in the case of decreasing yields between equity and efficiency, a optimal solution will exist that maximizes welfare without arriving at the extreme situation of pure egalitarianism.

2.4 A Microeconomic Caveat.

From the theory of industrial organization (IO), we derive a simple model that permits us to frame within a theoretical scheme the problem of coordination and/or fiscal competition. The model we will use is the one proposed by Cournot (1838), and we will compare two solutions: the cooperative solution (which represents the case of fiscal coordination), with the non-cooperative one (as an approximation of the case of fiscal competition).

We suppose that two States, indicated as 1 and 2, have to decide the corporate income tax rate, which we indicate as $0 < t^i < 1$ with $i = 1,2$. We assume that investors will look to invest capital in the country that has the lower fiscal pressure. We indicate as k^1 the capital stock of country 1 and as k^2 that of country 2.

Tax revenues are equal, for country 1, to:

$$R^1 = t^1 k^1 \tag{2.1}$$

and for country 2

$$R^2 = t^2 k^2 \tag{2.2}$$

Now we hypothesize that the flow of capital is represented by the following equations:

$$k^1 = 1 - t^1 + \frac{1}{2} t^2 \tag{2.3}$$

and

$$k^1 = 1 - t^1 + \frac{1}{2} t^2 \tag{2.4}$$

The economic assumption on which equations (2.3) and (2.4) are built implies that, in considering number (2.3), as the tax rate in country 1, t^1, increases, capital stock transfers from country 1 toward country 2, while an increase in the tax rate in country 2, t^2, involves a flow of capital toward country 1.

We analyze first the case of **fiscal competition**, in which each country chooses the tax rate, t, independently. For the first country, we'll have:[16]

---

[16] Technically speaking, we resolve an optimization problem, for which the control variable is t¹. Given the quasi-concavity (in fact it's linear) of the target function, the optimization problem is defined and the first order conditions are necessary and sufficient for a maximum.

$$\max_{t^1} R^1 = \max \ t^1 k^1 = t^1 \left(1 - t^1 + \frac{1}{2} t^2 \right)$$

From the necessary and sufficient first order conditions, we obtain a reaction function for t¹

$$t^1 = \frac{1}{2} + \frac{1}{4} t^2 \tag{2.5}$$

For country 2 we resolve a symmetrical problem,

$$\max_{t^2} R^2 = \max \ t^2 k^2 = t^2 \left(1 - t^2 + \frac{1}{2} t^1 \right)$$

From which we obtain the reaction curve of country 2

$$t^2 = \frac{1}{2} + \frac{1}{4} t^1 \tag{2.6}$$

In this context we use as a concept of a non-cooperative solution a definition of equilibrium borrowed from game theory, the Nash equilibrium. In slightly more technical terms, the Nash equilibrium is located at the intersection of two reaction functions, equations (2.5) and (2.6). Thus, resolving the system of two equations (2.5 and 2.6) in two unknowns (t^1 and t^2) we obtain the rate of equilibrium in the case of fiscal competition, that is $(t^1)^* = (t^2)^* = \frac{2}{3}$. Substituting, finally, these values in number (1) and (2) we are given the equilibrium values of tax revenues and capital stocks, $(k^1)^* = (k^2)^* = \frac{2}{3}$ and $(R^1)^* = (R^2)^* = \frac{4}{9}$.

Then we move on to analyze the case of **fiscal coordination**. We hypothesize that the two governments choose to maximize tax revenues together, which we define as equal to R¹ + R². Formally we will have:

$$\max_{t^1 \geq 0, t^2 \geq 0} \left(R^1 + R^2 \right) = \max_{t^1 \geq 0, t^2 \geq 0} \ t^1 \left(1 - t^1 + \tfrac{1}{2} t^2 \right) + t^2 \left(1 - t^2 + \tfrac{1}{2} t^1 \right)$$

Solving the first order conditions, regarding t¹ and t², we obtain: $(t^1)^{**} = (t^2)^{**} = 1$. And similarly to what was done previously, we recalculate the tax revenues and the capital stocks: $(k^1)^{**} = (k^2)^{**} = \dfrac{1}{2}$ and $(R^1)^{**} = (R^2)^{**} = \dfrac{1}{2}$.

In the following table, we compare the value of tax rates, of tax revenues and of capital stocks in the case of fiscal coordination and in that of fiscal competition. Technically speaking, the case of Fiscal Competition refers to solution of maximization problem of each government, separately; that of Fiscal Coordination refers to the maximization of joint revenues.

	Rate	Capital Stocks	Revenues
Fiscal Competition	$(t^1)^* = (t^2)^* = \dfrac{2}{3}$	$(k^1)^* = (k^2)^* = \dfrac{2}{3}$	$(R^1)^* = (R^2)^* = \dfrac{4}{9}$
Fiscal Coordination	$(t^1)^{**} = (t^2)^{**} = 1$	$(k^1)^{**} = (k^2)^{**} = \dfrac{1}{2}$	$(R^1)^{**} = (R^2)^{**} = \dfrac{1}{2}$

Table 2.1 Fiscal Coordination and Competition

Immediately it must be pointed out that in the fiscal competition system the equilibrium values of the tax rates are lower than those in the coordination system. In addition, in the system of fiscal competition each country obtains greater capital than the amount produced in the case of coordination, while tax revenues are greater in the case of coordination. This result is particularly important, in that it shows how the natural consequence of fiscal coordination, in absence previously agreed constraints concerning the final level of fiscal pressure, is an increase in tax rates.

This simple formal model brings to light the risks of coordination, which are particularly accentuated in the case where governments aim to maximize the fiscal yield, without taking into account the effects on unemployment and growth. Obviously, the model presented here represents stylized behaviors and is formulated in a context of partial economic equilibrium, which does not allow for an appraisal of the boost in demand generated by the reduction in fiscal pressure. If, however, the goal of the policymaker were that of reducing unemployment, as in our case, from the analysis of this model exactly the opposite message emerges. The reduction in unemployment happens through a reduction in fiscal pressure and growth in production activity, and thus through a system of fiscal competition, or in any case of a system of coordination in which the common goal of reducing fiscal pressure is agreed upon ex-ante.

3. Economic Policies in the European Union

3.1 Economic Policy after the Euro.

With the birth of European Monetary Union, management of monetary policy was transferred to the European Central Bank and the European System of Central Banks, and for member countries of the Union, fiscal policy remains the only instrument of economic policy directly controllable by national governments. Over the last few years, given an unemployment rate of about and higher than 10 percent of the work force and a monetary policy that is certainly not accommodating, the debate on management of fiscal policy didn't take long to materialize, and the points of the dispute have concerned choosing the best combination of fiscal policies.

In a certain sense, however, the relationship between the budget and fiscal policy, on one hand, and economic development, on the other, as well as the consequent existing relationship between economic development and social equity, have not appeared clearly defined in the European institutional debate. This debate has often seemed disconnected from the underlying economic reality and from the different potential outlooks of European economic systems. In many cases, it's been limited to comparing the assignment of roles and powers between European institutions and national governments, rarely assessing the effects that exercising these same powers has on both the prospects for development and the conditions of distributive equity. The debate has in fact long been concentrated on three different scenarios: competition, coordination and fiscal harmonization.

Since 1997, the European Commission has urged member countries of the Monetary Union to take steps toward fiscal harmonization with the precise goal of reducing existing distortions within the Single Market, also with the good intention of reducing in that same way European unemployment (See the Report "Measures to fight against tax competition in the European Union" European Commission, Bulletin 6-1997). But not having clarified ex ante if such a harmonization process should lead to maintaining, increasing or reducing the taxation level, even that good intention has remained rather vague and indefinite.

At the summit in Feira, Portugal, in June 2001, an important agreement was reached among member countries of the Union as to a first form of coordination of taxation on capital income. In principle, the countries of the Union are committed to systematically exchanging a set of information in order to correctly tax capital income generated on foreign investments but received by residents. The economic ministers also adopted a code of conduct to prevent a rise in harmful fiscal competition on capital income (word for word, it talks of harmful tax competition).[1]

Even more recently, during the Barcelona European Council in March of 2002, various themes were tackled and as for the fiscal aspects, it was repeated that the coordination of fiscal policies hinges on the commitment to ensuring healthy government finances as well as on the rules set by the Stability and Growth Pact.

3.2 Four Crucial Aspects.

We hold that the economic policy of individual countries of the European Monetary Union has not been, since 1996, equal to its full potentials. We have attended a number of conferences and meetings, from Santa Maria of Feira in 1997 to Barcelona 2002, we've seen the European Monetary Union press for forms of fiscal coordination to combat fiscal competition, but not yet has a clear and concrete strategy of economic policy been proposed to push growth and reduce unemployment. There's been on more occasions the distinct feeling that Europe has been lulled into the illusion of solving its economic problems through a recovery in international demand.[2]

It seems useful to us to emphasize here four critical aspects that have emerged in the context of the debate about the choices in economic policy.

---

[1] A brief inset presented in the appendix offers greater detail on the accords of Feira, Portugal. Briefly, the idea of the accords consists of creating an efficient system of taxation based on residency and on the related exchange of information about the origins of capital income so as to avoid double taxation. In this case, every country could choose the optimal level of income taxation without fear of an outflow of capital, assuming implicitly that the beneficiaries of the aforementioned income were not "overly mobile."

[2] It's superfluous to point out that we're not taking into consideration the last 18 months, for which performance has been much worse.

The first point regards the "**what**."

In other words, we believe that the economic policy objectives have not been specified with clarity and firmness: reducing unemployment? Increasing the rate of growth? Financial equilibrium of all the member countries? Zero inflation? While being firmly convinced of the necessity of the Stability and Growth Pact, we also believe that it only provides limits to be respected, which different economic structures can conform to. In this context, we believe it's correct to propose as a central goal of economic policy a full use of resources (which also means reducing unemployment) and maximizing the potentials for development in terms of innovations and technical progress, as well as training and growth of human capital. The Lisbon summit finally moved in this direction, recommending a precise path toward increasing the growth rate for all the European countries, evidently reachable with structural reforms that raise the real and potential growth.

The second, much more debated aspect regards the "**how**."

Assuming the main objective is increasing the rate of activity and reducing unemployment, within the European institutions it hasn't yet seemed clear what could be a coherent economic policy strategy, even within the conditions of monetary stability assigned as the ECB's objective and the conditions of financial stability stated in the Stability Pact. On the other hand, proposals and suggestions have come from various sources aiming for the clearly expressed goal of lowering unemployment in Europe. Among these contributions, the clearest seems to be the one proposed by Modigliani et al (1998), in which, however, the use of monetary policy is supported without directly entering into the merit of interventions in budget policy or fiscal policy, even though it raises the possibility that the Stability Pact might need to be redefined to exclude government investments from the parameters of financial equilibrium.

The third aspect is the "**when**".

To disclose one result of our analysis, we'll see how a strategy of economic policy based on structural reforms of tax revenue, the welfare state and the labor market seems necessary, also in light of the tragic events of September 11, 2001. And the sooner it's adopted the better, also based on the positive experiences of those European countries that for the most part have already implemented reforms in the course of the 1990s. In this way, the causal link connecting the wait for a possible rebound in the world economy to the availability of the necessary resources to realize reforms in Europe is broken. The opposite seems true, which is that the more the international economic cycle seems uncertain and stalled, the more those structural reforms are urgent, to actually create better conditions for the economic cycle, and above all, for the structural growth trend in the medium to long term.

The fourth and last aspect concerns the aim of possible **fiscal coordination and/or harmonization**. In the sphere of the economic policy strategy that we intend to propose here, it in fact appears necessary to state with clarity that the final end has to be reducing fiscal pressure in all of Europe.

These crucial aspects have made us think and have led us to verify the efficiency of an economic policy strategy, based on solid theoretical foundations, that aims to reduce unemployment and raise the growth potential of European economies in a context of greater and more genuine levels of social equity.

3.3 In Summary.

Raising potential growth and bringing continental Europe to full employment seems a reachable goal.

However, this objective cannot be obtained simply through a messianic wait for a strong and prolonged rebound, from abroad, of the world economy.

Instead, a determined and conscious structural reform strategy is necessary, the responsibility for which lies with national governments. A coordinated action on a European level can little improve the results of each country. These possible results instead remain dependent on the internal decisions of each economic system.

This work is meant to show the necessity of a deep revision of government budget policy, aimed at realizing in the space of four or five years a reduction in fiscal pressure, a reduction in current government spending, and an increase in government investments, both in terms of physical and non physical infrastructure, as well as innovation research and training aiming for an improvement in technology and human capital. Such a strategy must have two solid support bases in the labor market, introducing more flexibility and more access opportunities, and on the market for goods and services, bringing about more liberalization, more privatization and more competition.

It's therefore not a matter of counterweighing the objectives of financial equilibrium and the objective of economic growth. It's not by chance that European authorities came up with the name Stability and Growth Pact.

It is thus a matter of interpreting with wisdom and flexibility the parameters that point the way toward a balanced budget, so as to achieve acceptable conditions of development in the medium to long term of at least 3% per year. It is therefore necessary to assess the status of the budget deficit, both in relation to the economic cycle and to the quantity and quality of structural reforms that gradually come to be implemented.

It's pretty reasonable to understand that it's better to have a 1% deficit that however incorporates important parts of structural reforms rather than no deficit that excludes undertaking reforms. Real growth and financial balance in fact are not in opposition. It is to give medium to long term solidity to the conditions of financial equilibrium of the government budget, that it is necessary to build a solid path of development so as to raise the rate of activity and achieve full employment.

Without reforms and without investments, a zero deficit would remain a fragile and precarious result, however. It would also leave the European economy almost totally dependent on the international economic cycle all the same.

With reforms and with more investments, even in light of the difficult and uncertain international cycle, eliminating the deficit could be achieved in a longer time, but, if in the meantime the season of reforms is launched with decisiveness, budget equilibrium would appear more solid and less subject to the vicissitudes of the rest of the world economy.

4. Empirical Evidences

Throughout the course of the 1990s, the performances of some European economies were on average modest: low growth, high unemployment, high fiscal pressure, high government spending, financial imbalances in terms of the government deficit, and, in some countries, a worrying accumulation of national debt. Compared with a large part of the European continent that limped along for the entire decade, the American economy, as well as several European economies, recorded the longest and most sustained period of growth ever.

4.1 Europe and the United States: Economies Face to Face.

We have therefore made a comparison of economic aspects that allow us to identify some characteristics of European and American economies.[1] The following sections, then, mainly focus on European countries.

As can be seen in Figure 4.1 and Figure 4.2, the 1970s and 1980s saw the European economies and the American economy grow at rates that were quite similar, one overtaking the other in turns throughout the two decades. Around the middle of the 1980s, a change in the power relationships occurred. The United States undertook a course of expansion of production and a reduction in unemployment that was due to be broken only at the end of 2001, for sadly notorious reasons. Figure 4.2 compares then the growth rate index (year base in 1961) for the European and the American economies. It offers an alternative, and may be clearer, perspective growth speed of the two systems.

---

[1] It might be superfluous to specify that the analysis described in these pages doesn't claim to be a rigorous comparison between two economic systems, but a snapshot of the principle macroeconomic aspects. One should refer to the economic literature for analyses that are more detailed and technically more rigorous.

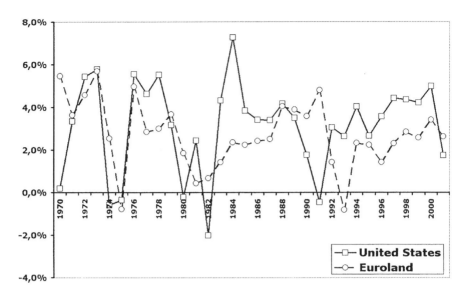

Source OECD Economic Outlook

Figure 4.1 Annual Growth Rate in Euroland and in the US.

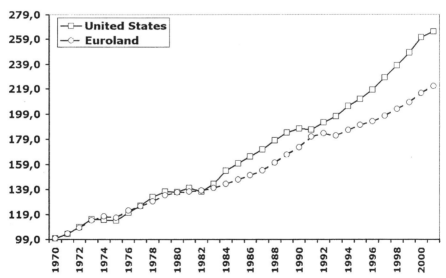

Source OECD Economic Outlook, and Authors' Calculations.

Figure 4.2 Annual Growth Rate *Index* in Euroland and in the US.

The brilliant growth performances of European countries of the 1980s are replaced by growth results well below the potentials of the system. What is even more surprising in this situation is how the

European economies of the 1980s didn't benefit from or didn't succeed in taking advantage of the resulting externalities of the economic integration process that culminated with the introduction of the single currency in 2001.

At the same time, up until about the middle of the 1980s, the European labor market proved itself more efficient in managing the workforce, as can be seen from an unemployment rate of less than 6%. In those same years, the American economy experienced higher unemployment with a rate of around and higher than 6% per year. In Europe, on the other hand, unemployment begins to spread through the labor market, transforming itself, year after year, into a structural problem (Figure 4.3).

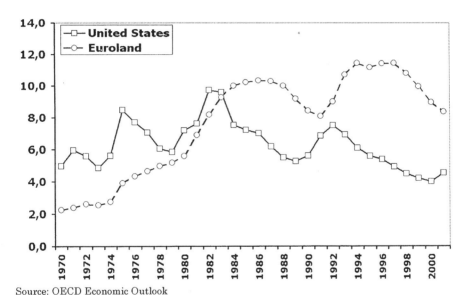

Source: OECD Economic Outlook

Figure 4.3 Unemployment in Europe and in the US.

Moreover, European countries had the lead regarding the participation of the population in the labor market until the middle of the 1980s, after which the situation was reversed up until the last years of the 1990s. Regarding the results, it is rather interesting how it's shown that the aggregate performances of an economic system do not depend only on the average differentials of growth, but also on the cyclical component. In other words, it's not only important that a country achieve higher levels in the rate of growth during the positive phases of the cycle, but it's maybe even more important that these phases last a long time.

As far as government finance is concerned, we have taken into consideration national debt, net borrowing, total government revenues and total government spending.

In regard to the first two items Figure 4.4 and Figure 4.5 clearly show how the United States overtakes Europe in the second half of the 1990s. American debt and underlying net indebtedness, expressed as a percentage of GDP, fall below the corresponding European items. This result is in good part attributable to the different pattern of development and growth of the two macro-areas in the previous five years. As already shown in the preceding pages, the European Union, having grown at a average rate of about 3%, has always been "pulled along" by the economy of the United States, which developed at rates of between 4% and 5%, and, even more importantly, with more firmness.

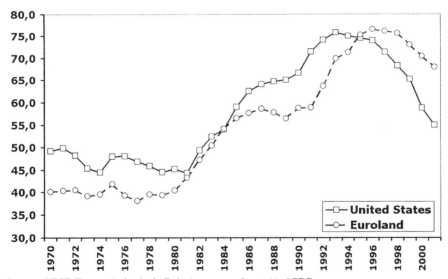

Source: OECD Economic Outlook. Debt is expressed as a % of GDP.

Figure 4.4 High and Sustained Growth Reduces Government Debt: the US Experience of the 90s.

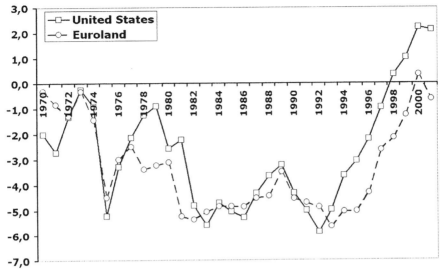

Source OECD Economic Outlook. Deficit is expressed as a % of GDP.

Figure 4.5 High and Sustained Growth Reduces Government Deficit: the US Experience of the 90s.

The last aspects we take into consideration in the context of the government finance picture are the levels of total government revenues and expenditures, expressed as a percentage of GDP.

As shown in Figure 4.6 and Figure 4.7, the levels of fiscal pressure and government spending of the two macroeconomic areas are structurally different. The American economy shows values of around 30% of GDP, while the European countries register about 40%.

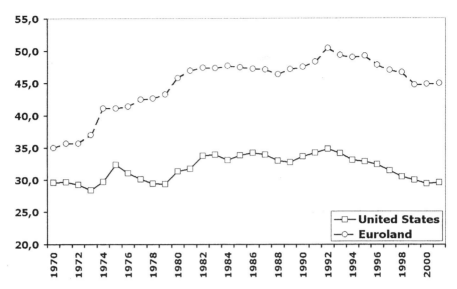

Source OECD Economic Outlook. Aggregate Government Expenditure are expressed as % of GDP

Figure 4.6 Aggregate Government Expenditure in the US and Euroland.

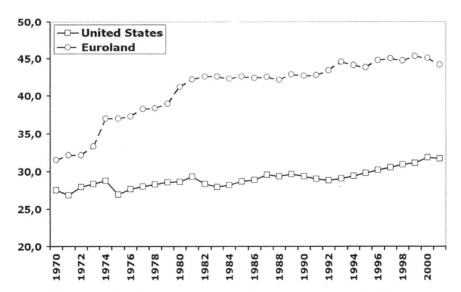

Source OECD Economic Outlook. Aggregate Government Revenues are expressed as % of GDP

Figure 4.7 Aggregate Government Revenues in the US and Euroland.

In summary, the two economic systems show structural differences, some of which were pointed out in these pages. Some of them concerns the structure itself, while some other refers to countries economic performances. At the same time, it's important to note that there are substantial historical-institutional and social differences among the member countries of the European Union, which need further explanation.

The following section addresses these issues investigating whether there exist any correlation and of which sign among growth, unemployment, and government size.

4.2 A Brief Journey into Europe of the 1990s: Two Europes in Europe ... or even Three?

On the subject of average European data, which were deeply unsatisfactory for all of the 1990s, a closer observation of the economic performances in different European areas and within individual countries allows us to see that "not all birds of a feather flock together".

Let's first look at the data from the period (1991-2001) regarding the rate of growth and the rate of unemployment. As can be seen in Table 4.1 and Table 4.2, the differences in the empirical evidence of individual economies are significant. In addition, it would seem possible to divide the different countries into groups that include economies that appear to have experienced similar trends amongst themselves.

Country	Average Growth Rate	Country	Average Unemployment Rate
Ireland	7.2%	Austria	4.1
Finland	3.2%	Netherlands	5.1
Portugal	3.1%	Ireland	5.3
Spain	2.8%	Portugal	5.5
Netherlands	2.7%	Sweden	6.3
Greece	2.6%	UK	7.8
UK	2.5%	Belgium	8.5
Sweden	2.4%	Germany	8.7
Denmark	2.2%	Denmark	8.8
Austria	2.2%	Greece	10.0
Belgium	2.1%	Italy	10.8
France	1.9%	France	11.0
Italy	1.7%	Finland	12.2
Germany	1.6%	Spain	15.5

Source: OECD Economic Outlook and Authors' calculations. The Average Growth and the Average Unemployment Rates are computed over the sample 1991-2001.

Table 4.1 Growth and Unemployment Rates of European Countries

Country	Unemployment Rate in 2001		Country	Government Revenues
Netherlands	2.4		Greece	28.1%
Ireland	3.8		Ireland	28.2%
Austria	3.8		UK	37.8%
Sweden	4.2		Spain	38.5%
Portugal	4.3		Portugal	40.9%
UK	5.1		Netherlands	44.2%
Denmark	5.3		Belgium	46.0%
Belgium	6.9		Italy	46.3%
Germany	8.2		Germany	46.9%
France	8.7		Austria	47.7%
Finland	9.3		Finland	50.6%
Italy	9.5		France	54.1%
Greece	10.4		Denmark	54.1%
Spain	13.1		Sweden	56.6%

Source: OECD Economic Outlook and Authors' calculations. The Average
Growth and the Average Unemployment Rates are computed over the sample
1991-2001.

Table 4.2 Unemployment Rate in 2001 and Government Revenues of European Countries

Say we assume a rate of growth equal to 2.5% per year, at random.
The exceptional Irish performance dominates over all the European
countries, with average growth above 7%, some distance behind that
come Finland, Portugal and Spain with growth of about 3% per year,
and Holland, Greece and the United Kingdom have growth of higher
than 2.5%. Sweden, Denmark, Austria and Belgium register average
development rates of higher than 2% per year. What is significant and
worrying for the whole of Europe is that the three biggest continental
countries (France, Italy and Germany) show more modest rates of
growth below 2%, with the biggest European country, Germany,
registering the lowest growth rate, a very modest 1.6% over the sample
1991:2001.

Let's assume just as arbitrarily an average rate of unemployment
of 8%. From this point of view, Austria, Holland, Ireland and Portugal
are the best, showing unemployment of about or below 5%. Just behind
them comes Sweden with just above 6%, and the United Kingdom joins
the winners' circle of those below 8%. Far above that, and in increasing
order, come Belgium, Germany and Denmark, falling a bit below 9%,
Greece, Italy and France, registering between 10% and 11%, and
finishing with even higher rates, Finland, above 12%, and Spain, above
15%.

However, it's interesting to more closely analyze these average unemployment rates compared with the data relative to the last year of the period, which is 2001 (Table 4.2). The phase of economic recovery, experienced in all of the countries in the years 1999 and 2000, allowed a reduction in unemployment to be seen somewhat in all of the countries. But in fact the overall situation didn't appear to change much, with the sole exception of Denmark, which from an average unemployment rate of barely below 9%, brought itself to a rate of a little above 5% in 2001, thus, from this viewpoint, entering the group of the best performing countries.

Still referring to average data of the last ten years, we turn now to analyzing the weight of the government budget on the economy, expressed in terms of percentage of total spending and revenues to GDP, and to the conditions of financial equilibrium indicated by the government deficit/GDP ratio (Table 4.2 and Table 4.3).

Country	Government Expenditure		Country	Average Government Deficit
Ireland	30.4%		Ireland	-0.1%
Greece	37.6%		Denmark	-0.6%
UK	40.7%		Finland	-1.4%
Spain	41.5%		Netherlands	-1.6%
Portugal	44.8%		Germany	-2.2%
Netherlands	46.7%		Austria	-2.8%
Germany	49.3%		UK	-2.9%
Belgium	49.9%		Sweden	-3.0%
Austria	50.6%		France	-3.3%
Finland	51.8%		Belgium	-3.3%
Italy	52.6%		Spain	-3.5%
Denmark	54.8%		Portugal	-3.8%
France	57.4%		Italy	-5.6%
Sweden	60.2%		Greece	-7.9%

Source: OECD Economic Outlook and Authors' calculations. The Average Government Deficit is computed over the sample 1991-2001.

Table 4.3 Government Expenditure and Government Deficit of European Countries

Here we also randomly assume a level of the weight of total government revenues on gross domestic product of above and below 40%. The countries whose budgets absorb a lower level of the economy's resources are Portugal, Spain, the United Kingdom (which come in between 37% and 40%), Ireland and Greece (which are below the threshold). Most of the other countries place between Holland's 44% and the 50% of Finland, while France, Denmark and Sweden fall far above 50%.

If we then consider the weight of total government spending on GDP, we see that Ireland sets itself far ahead of the rest with a value of about 30%, then Greece, Great Britain and Spain, ranging between 37% and 41%. Portugal already begins to show a higher value below 45% (as we'll see, tied to more contained fiscal pressure, placing this country among those that show more significant financial imbalances). In all the other countries, the weight of government spending on GDP is much higher, with Holland approaching 47%, Germany, Belgium, Austria, Finland and Italy about and above 50%, and finally, Denmark, France and Sweden ranging between 55% and 60%.

Concerning the government deficit level, we refer to the 3% limit stipulated by the Treaty of Maastricht. The conditions of financial equilibrium obviously imply that countries with low fiscal pressure must also have a more contained weight of government spending, and those with high government spending must have a higher level of fiscal pressure. So, from the point of view of the government deficit, we find Ireland and the United Kingdom fitting into the first front, while Denmark, Finland, Holland, Germany, Austria and Sweden fall into the second front.

As regards the deficit/GDP ratio of countries, on average over the ten years, France, Belgium and Italy appear to fit in with countries that show a heavy burden of the government budget on GDP, a situation in which revenues lag behind an even higher level of spending. On the other hand, Spain and Portugal, which generally have a more contained weight of the government budget, also consistently had excessive spending in relation to revenues for the decade. Finally, there's the case of Greece, which shows the lowest level of European fiscal pressure, but where there's an excess of government spending compared with revenues that brought the average deficit/GDP ratio to about 8%. It's not coincidence that Greece could only join the Monetary Union two years after the launch of the single currency.

The overall picture of these empirical experiments can lead us re-divide the European countries into two, or even three different groups.

The first group could be composed of Ireland, the United Kingdom, Spain, Portugal, Greece and also maybe Holland, where the weight of the government budget appears to be much less in relation to the other countries. In this first group, economic growth is stronger and unemployment more contained, keeping in mind that in Spain the level is still high, but progress in its reduction has been consistent, while on the other hand Greece continues to show high levels of unemployment.

The second group of countries, where the overall weight of the government budget on the economy is much higher with respect to the first group, could include Germany, France, Italy, Belgium, on one hand, and Sweden, Austria, and Denmark on the other, with Finland setting itself far above the others.

In fact, in this second group, the first four countries have experienced low expansion conditions and high unemployment, while the second three, although having a heavy burden of the State on the economy, have had better growth and a much more satisfying unemployment situation. Section 4.3.2 offers a more detailed discussion, while motivating the choice of further dividing the second group of countries.

Moreover, one separate case seems to stand out in Finland, which showed a heavy weight of the government budget on the economy, maintained however in the conditions of relative financial equilibrium associated with a steady rate of growth. That didn't, however, result in satisfactory progress in unemployment, neither on average for the period nor for 2001, which places it among the poorest performing countries of Europe.

This overall consolidated picture of average data from the decade 1991-2001 can be integrated with some additional considerations obtainable from the economic profiles of the individual national economies.

As can be seen from Figure 4.8, the most impressive growth is observed in Ireland, with rates so high that in the same graph they apparently produce the effect of squeezing the growth rates of all the other European countries into a more restricted range.

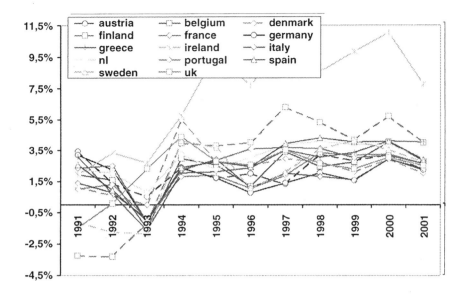

Source: OECD Economic Outlook

Figure 4.8 Growth Rates in Euroland from Ireland to ... Germany

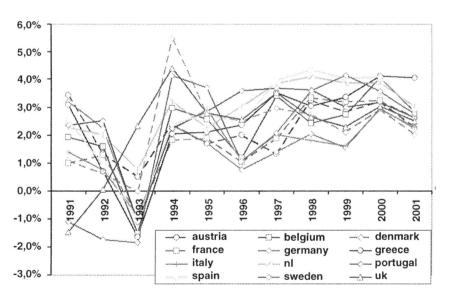

Source: OECD Economic Outlook

Figure 4.9 Growth Rates in Euroland ... but Ireland

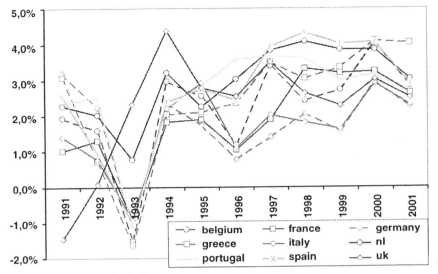

Source: OECD Economic Outlook

Figure 4.10 Growth Rates in "Good" and in the "Ugly" Countries in Euroland

In reality, if we exclude the data of the Irish economy, the great diversity of growth rates among the different European countries becomes totally evident (Figure 4.9). It can also be noted how the economic cycle of the rest of the world certainly influences the European economies, but the diversifications seem almost wholly due to the reality of and the endogenous capacity of development of the separate economies. It could be said, as has already been suggested elsewhere, that a true and proper "European" economic cycle doesn't exist, and moreover, that national economic cycles react to the international economic cycle in a way that is extremely diversified amongst themselves (Correja, Neves and Rebelo, 1995). Finally, Figure 4.10 excludes from the graph four countries: Ireland (for the already quoted reasons), and Austria, Denmark, Finland to have a clearer picture of growth performances. Provocatively, we refer to Belgium, France, Germany and Italy as to "The Uglies" and to Portugal, Spain, UK, Netherlands and Greece as to "The Goods".

Setting each country's GDP in 1990 equal to 100, it is very interesting to look at the accumulation of growth throughout the course of the 1990s until 2001, as presented in Figures 4.11-4.13.

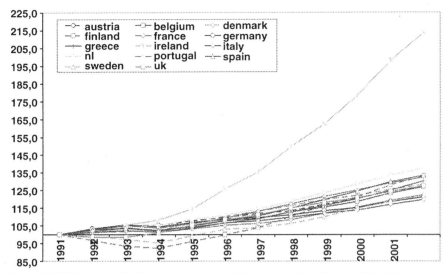

Source: OECD Economic Outlook, , and Authors' Calculations, Base Year is 1991=100

Figure 4.11 Growth Rate *Index* from Ireland to ... Germany.

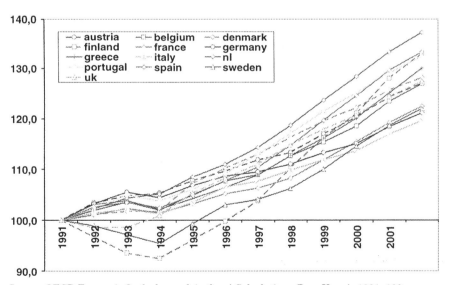

Source: OECD Economic Outlook, , and Authors' Calculations, Base Year is 1991=100

Figure 4.12 Growth Rate *Index* in Euroland... but Ireland.

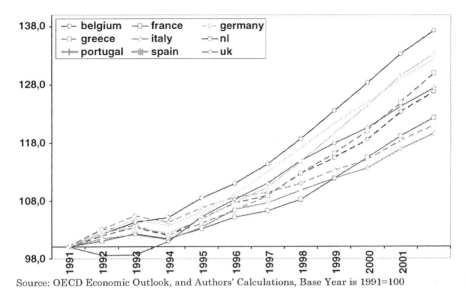

Source: OECD Economic Outlook, and Authors' Calculations, Base Year is 1991=100

Figure 4.13 Growth Rate *Index* in the "Good" and in the "Ugly" Countries in Euroland....

The enormous jump in growth achieved in Ireland looks even more remarkable, having increased its GDP by 215%, more than doubling it in the space of twelve years. Also in the case of this graph, the *Ireland effect* makes the performance of all the other European countries appear modest and compressed together. In reality, excluding Ireland and readjusting the scale of values, the diversification of the individual countries' growth profiles is clearly marked. In the same twelve years, in fact, Finland and Portugal increased their own income by approximately 40%, Spain and Holland by about 35%, Greece, the United Kingdom and Sweden by more than 30%, Denmark and Austria by some 28%, followed by Belgium at 25%, and, the very last, the three largest continental economies, with France and Italy just a bit above 20%, and last, Germany, even below 20%.

Also in terms of unemployment rates, the diversification of the experiences of single countries is strongly accentuated, even if the trend in nearly all of the countries is of a gradual increase in unemployment in the first half of the period followed by a slow reduction in more recent years (Figure 4.14).

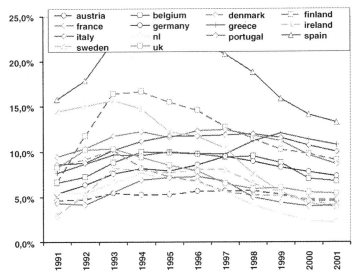

Source: OECD Economic Outlook

Figure 4.14 Unemployment in Europe across the 90s.

However, the country that presents an anomalously high rate of unemployment for the entire period is Spain, even if it must be recognized that from 1994 until 2002 it succeeded in drastically reducing unemployment from 23% to 13%. From this point of view, the most successful country is Austria, which constantly maintained its unemployment around 4%. Ireland's reduction in unemployment is huge, from 15% in 1993 to values smaller than 4% in 2001. The performances of the United Kingdom and Netherlands are also notable, from a peak of 10% in 1993 to 5% in 2001, and from more than 7% to less than 2.5%, respectively. Finally, the progress Portugal has shown is positive, which passed from more than 7% in the middle of the period to around 4% in 2001.

The diversity of performances appears even more striking if we refer to the following Figures, which show the reduction or the increase in the rate of unemployment for the successive years after 1993.

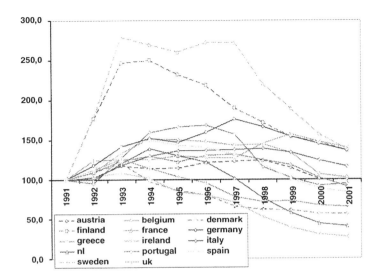

Source: OECD Economic Outlook and Author's calculation. Base Year is 1991=100.

Figure 4.15 Unemployment Rate *Index* in Euroland from Sweden to Ireland.

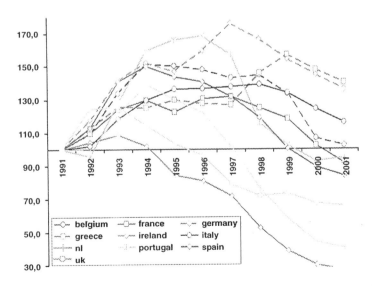

Source: OECD Economic Outlook and Author's calculation, Base Year is 1991=100

Figure 4.16 Unemployment Rate *Index* in the Goods and in the Ugly countries of Euroland.

Two countries, Greece and Germany, turn out to have actually seen their rates of unemployment increased. Italy also saw its unemployment rate soar above the already high 1993 level, and only in 2001 was able to bring itself back below that figure. France, Belgium and Portugal, however, reduced their unemployment rate by about 20%, Spain and Finland by about 40%, Sweden and the United Kingdom by 50%, Holland and Denmark by just more and just less than 60% respectively. Once more Ireland sets itself far ahead, having reduced its unemployment rate by nearly 80%.

Let's analyze more closely the structural and dynamic weight of total revenues, total spending and the deficit in the experiences of the different countries over time.

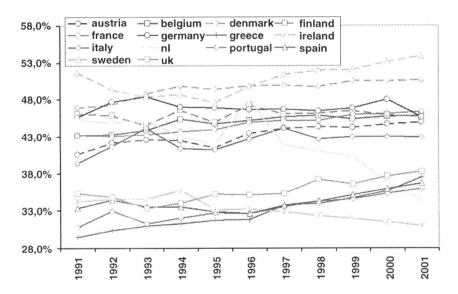

Source: OECD Economic Outlook

Figure 4.17 Government Revenues, from Sweden to ... Ireland

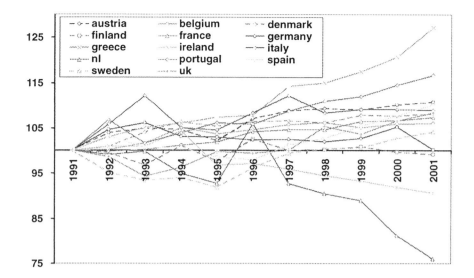

Source: OECD Economic Outlook, and Authors' Calculations, Base Year is 1991=100

Figure 4.18 Government Revenues *Index* from Sweden to ... Ireland

Consider first Government Revenues. Figure 4.17 and Figure 4.18 confirm what was already indicated based on the average data for the period cited in the previous table. It is worth noting how the fiscal pressure of the different countries moves compared with the average data in the same stretch of time. Four countries are shown to have reduced it: Sweden and Finland by about 4%, Holland by more than 7%, and Ireland by more than 15%. Great Britain shows to have reduced its fiscal pressure at first, up to a peak of 6%, then to have increased it by about 4% in more recent years, still using the reference year. In all of the other countries, fiscal pressure increased or at best remained equal to the level reached in 1991. Greece seems to be a separate phenomenon, having increased the total percentage of government revenues on GDP by more than 25%, but which as already seen and as we'll recall in the future, experienced even greater increases in government spending.

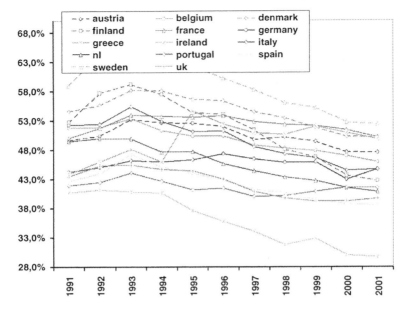

Source: OECD Economic Outlook.

Figure 4.19 Government Expenditure, from Sweden to ... Ireland

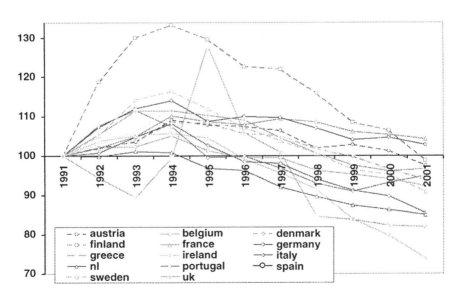

Source: OECD Economic Outlook, and Authors' Calculations, Base Year is 1991=100.

Figure 4.20 Government Expenditure *Index*, from Sweden to ... Ireland

Also on the other aspect of the government budget, that is the total of government spending on GDP, the data regarding the performance of all the 1990s confirm the ideas expressed previously about the average data for the period. Interesting additional conclusions can however be derived from the analysis presented in Figure 4.20, which shows the dynamic over time of the weight of government spending on GDP in the individual countries. Still in respect to 1991, Ireland shows to have reduced the weight of government spending on GDP by more than 25%, followed by Greece, then Holland, then Italy, but also keeping in mind that Italy relied mostly on a reduction in interest rates that strongly reduced spending on interest connected to an enormous national debt. In Finland, there's an enormous leap in the weight of government spending for the first part of the period, then followed by a strong reduction that practically brings it back, in the last year of the period, to the levels of the first year. By contrast, Germany and France, which were already starting with high levels of government spending, further increased its weight on GDP, which in 2001 is even higher than the figures for 1991.

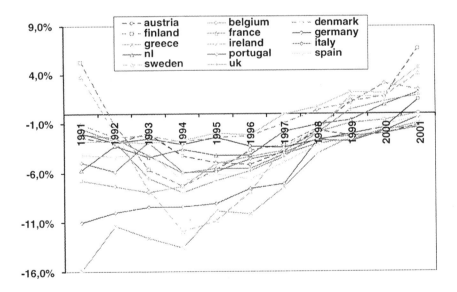

Source: OECD Economic Outlook.

Figure 4.21 Government Deficit in Euroland

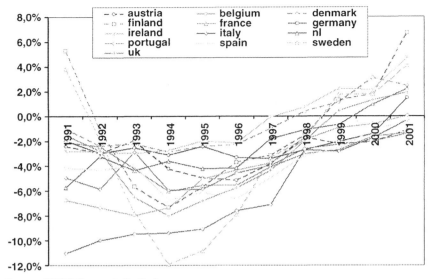

Source: OECD Economic Outlook.

Figure 4.22   Government Deficit in Euroland... without Greece

Lastly, the national diversification of the conditions of financial equilibrium that were presented over the space of the entire period remain to be analyzed. As Figure 4.21 shows, the process of rebalancing the government budgets and of convergence toward more sustainable financial conditions was very strong and generalized. If we exclude the anomalous and most disrupting case of Greece, however it can be seen (Figure 4.22) that there was a push toward rebalance and convergence, but it seems still very diversified from country to country, and above all, obtained in different ways and different time spans.

Some countries moved toward financial equilibrium by containing spending and also even reducing fiscal pressure (Ireland, Holland, Sweden, Finland, Portugal, Spain), others instead pursued progress in spending by increasing fiscal pressure (Austria, Greece, Belgium, Great Britain, France, Germany, Denmark, Italy).

As noted previously, from the perspective of the weight of the government budget on the economy, which partly seems to be reflected as an inverse relation to the state of growth and unemployment, the economic performances of the 1990s seem to point to the existence of two or three different Europes. It is still to be understood which kind of correlation/causality exist among macroeconomic quantities. This is the attempt of the next section.

4.3 Which correlations: Dr. Watson or Sherlock Holmes?

From this brief journey through the data of the European economies, some correlations seem to emerge for which a deeper and also more rigorous analysis is certainly necessary that is beyond the scope of this work.

Notwithstanding the institutional and socio-economic diversities of single countries, in fact strong indications emerge, however, regarding a significant connection that tends to tie the pace of development and the rate of unemployment in an inverse relation to each other, or as we'll see in more detail, the strength of economic growth and the variation of the unemployment rate.

Furthermore, in line with the theoretical references cited beforehand, strong indications seem to emerge with regard to an inverse correlation between the weight of the government budget, expressed in terms of total levels of revenues and spending in respect to GDP, and the progress of economic growth. There's a hint that there could be a phenomenon of crowding out between the size of the government budget and the activity of private citizens that could eventually lead to a slowing down of productive activity. This correlation seems to go far beyond what can be expressed from the existing relationship between the national deficit and economic growth. In this case, moreover, an inverse relation appears to emerge, according to which, in the medium term, an increase of the deficit tends to have a brake-effect on economic growth, in keeping with the most traditional definition of the financial crowding-out effect.

On these elements we sought to measure the signs and the intensity of the correlations that can emerge in some way from the empirical experiences of the 1990s. We proceed also in this analysis by first referring to overall European data, to then evaluate possible significant differences between the different subgroups of countries.

4.3.1 The Aggregate Data.

First of all, we tested the existing correlation between the growth rate and variations in the unemployment rate in reference (cross section — time series) to the 14 European countries for the demonstrated data for the 11 years from 1991 to 2001. Having used a logarithmic interpolation, the coefficient that results shows in itself the elasticity between the profile of the rate of unemployment and the rate of growth.

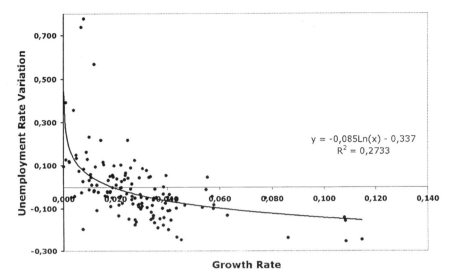

Source: OECD Economic Outlook and Authors' calculations. The solid line denotes a trend line (based on a logarithmic interpolation, which coefficients are presented in the Figure).

Figure 4.23 Growth Rate and Unemployment Rate Change in Euroland

As is shown in Figure 4.23, below a growth rate of 2%, unemployment tends to increase, while it tends to decrease with a growth rate greater than 2%. The correlation expresses a relation according to which for every additional 1% in permanent growth, the rate of unemployment (with a constant work force) falls by 8.5% per year. Thus, it could be concluded that unemployment would tend to be reduced by almost half within the space of five years.

On the other hand, let's test the correlation between the size of the government budget and the rate of growth, in reference to fiscal pressure, government spending and finally their financial balance, or in other words the government deficit.

The correlation between the weight of total government revenues and the rate of growth appears negative, as can be seen in Figure 4.14. This appears to indicate that in response to an increase of 10 points in fiscal pressure, GDP growth would see a decrease of 1 percentage point. In other words, each 10% increase in fiscal pressure results in a reduction in the growth rate of the economy equal to about 0.4%.

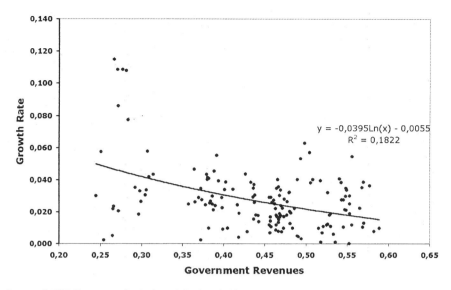

Source: OECD Economic Outlook and Authors' calculations. The solid line denotes a trend line (based on a logarithmic interpolation, which coefficients are presented in the Figure).

Figure 4.24 Growth Rate and Government Revenues in Euroland

Anticipating a results from next sections, this result is also confirmed by the estimate of correlations between government revenues and economic growth for the best performing countries and for those we've previously indicated as anomalous. It's interesting to note that the same correlation does not result as statistically significant in the countries of continental Europe (Italy, France, Germany, Belgium).

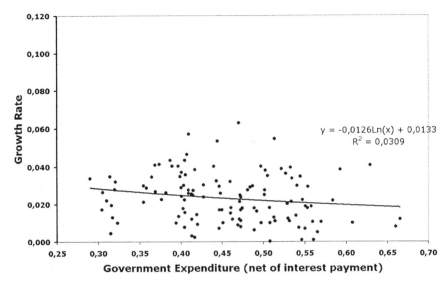

Source: OECD Economic Outlook and Authors' calculations. The solid line denotes a trend line (based on a logarithmic interpolation, which coefficients are presented in the Figure).

Figure 4.25 Growth Rate and Government Expenditure, net of interest payment in Euroland

The same correlation sign, that is negative, also exists between government spending net of interest and the growth rate of the economy. Clearly, it could seem surprising.[2] In reality, however, we have to consider that in the years 1991-2001 nearly all the European government budgets were in deficit, and the process of financial rebalancing initiated by the process of monetary unification involved a strong deficit reduction. Thus in these conditions it is not so surprising to happen to find that the economic actors (families and businesses) could have perceived increases in government spending as evident signals of even greater future increases in fiscal pressure. Therefore, the signal can give an explanation not only as regards the negative correlation that results, but also regarding the fact that the coefficient results higher than what appears in the correlation between fiscal pressure and growth. In fact, in this case, the pattern that develops is one in which every 10-point increase in government spending would cause about a 1.3-percentage point decrease in GDP growth. In other

---

[2] It should be pointed out that similar considerations are valid as far as aggregate spending (including the interest component) is concerned. However, it seemed more correct to present the item as spending net of interest to make countries with notably different amounts of national debt more comparable.

words, every 10% increase of the weight of government spending on GDP would incur a reduction of 0.52 percentage points of the rate of growth of GDP.

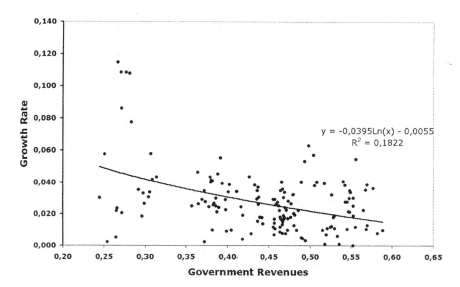

Source: OECD Economic Outlook and Authors' calculations. The solid line denotes a trend line (based on a logarithmic interpolation, which coefficients are presented in the Figure).

Figure 4.26 Growth Rate and Government Expenditure in Euroland

Consequently, a cut of five GDP percentage points in fiscal pressure would lead to an increase of 0.5 points in the rate of GDP growth. A parallel reduction of five percentage points of GDP in government spending would lead to an increase of 0.65 points in the growth rate of GDP. Thus it would be the case that an ex-ante balanced measure with a tax cut and spending cut of the same amount, would determine a 1.5 point increase in GDP growth. That greater growth rate would lead to a continuous reduction of the deficit ex-post. We will see, however, that the same is not true for all European countries. The analysis of disaggregated series shows that there exist "efficient countries" where government spending has a positive impact over economy development. In these cases its correlation with GDP growth turns out to be positive. In aggregation, the former effect seems to dominate, while generating a negative correlation between Europe-wide government spending and Europe-wide GDP growth.

Beyond the level of revenues and spending, the direct correlation between deficit and growth shows an inverse value, that is, a greater deficit corresponds to greater growth, and vice versa.

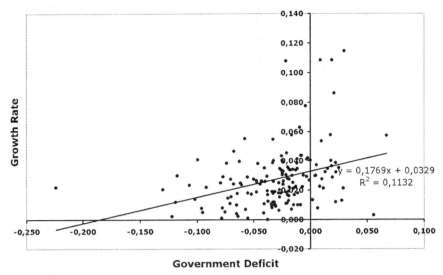

Source: OECD Economic Outlook and Authors' calculations. The solid line denotes a trend line
(based on a linear interpolation, which coefficients are presented in the Figure).

Figure 4.27 Growth Rate and Government Deficit in Euroland

This result is consistent with classic economic theory, and easy to explain with a simple intuition. A higher growth generates greater revenues, while reducing, *ceteris paribus*, government deficit. From the results obtained, it would seem that for every GDP point less of deficit, there would result about 0.18 points more of growth.

On the whole, therefore, based on the simple correlations obtained and with the proper caution in an analysis that needs further investigation and more accurate estimates, it could be affirmed that a reduction in fiscal pressure with a parallel reduction in government spending, and a streamlining of the deficit, would all three contribute to improving the growth conditions of the economic system.

4.3.2 Three Europes?

On the basis of these initial results, we wanted to test the strength of these correlations in regards to the different groups of countries and to the individual European economies, to check if the indicator of the correlation and the intensities undergo variations in relation to different structural levels of unemployment and to different weights of the government budget on the economy.

As far as regards the relationship between the rate of development and the status of the unemployment rate, let's begin with the group of countries that had modest growth and high unemployment in the context of a heavy weight of the government budget on the economy (Germany, France, Italy and Belgium).

As can be seen from Figure 4.28, the relation shows that the rate of unemployment tends to increase below a pace of growth of 1.8%, and vice versa, that the rate of unemployment tends to shrink for growth superior to that level. On the other hand, in the results obtained for all the countries of the European Union, that key rate of growth appears to fall a bit above or around 2%. This same key rate seems higher for the countries with a heavy weight of the government budget combined with good growth performance and low unemployment (Sweden, Finland, Denmark and Austria – Figure 4.29), while the group of countries with a low weight of the government budget combined with good growth performance and employment (Great Britain, Ireland, Holland, Spain, Portugal and Greece) fall in line with the overall average with a key rate of 2% (Figure 4.30).

These results seem to indicate, as can be reasonably expected, that in the countries with high unemployment, growth must be accelerated to above 1.8%. That acceleration has to be pegged at about 2% for the countries in which unemployment has been strongly contained, the weight of the government budget is lower and the labor market shows conditions of greater flexibility. On the other hand, in the countries where unemployment has been structurally maintained very low, a further reduction would require an ever greater acceleration in growth.

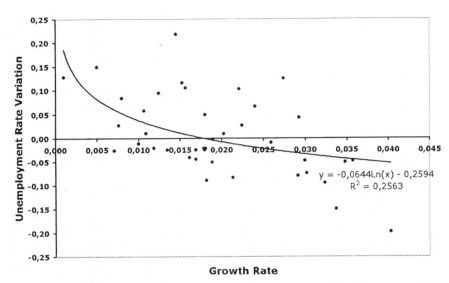

Source: OECD Economic Outlook and Authors' calculations. The solid line denotes a trend line (based on a logarithmic interpolation, which coefficients are presented in the Figure).

Figure 4.28 Growth Rate and Unemployment Rate Change within Italy, France, Belgium, Germany.

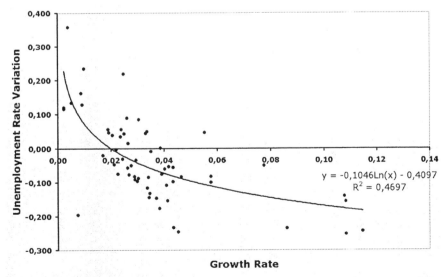

Source: OECD Economic Outlook and Authors' calculations. The solid line denotes a trend line (based on a logarithmic interpolation, which coefficients are presented in the Figure).

Figure 4.29 Growth Rate and Unemployment Rate Change within Netherlands, Ireland, Spain, Portugal, Greece, UK.

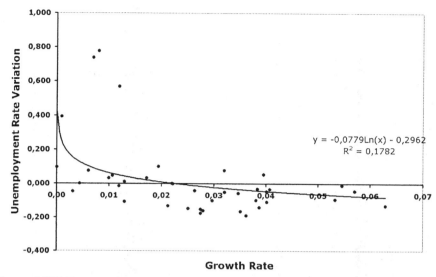

Source: OECD Economic Outlook and Authors' calculations. The solid line denotes a trend line (based on a logarithmic interpolation, which coefficients are presented in the Figure).

Figure 4.30 Growth Rate and Unemployment Rate Change within Austria, Denmark, Finland, Sweden.

What seems even more significant to us is the result regarding elasticity between growth and variations in unemployment (Figure 4.28-4.30). The coefficient obtained previously in regard to the whole of all of the countries in fact resulted equal to 0.085 and indicates that for every 1% of additional growth, a reduction of 8.5% in unemployment would be produced, therefore implying halving it in the space of five/six years.

So, compared with this result (the European average), a more contained elasticity emerges for the countries hat have a heavy weight of the government budget and strong rigidity in the labor market (Germany, France, Italy and Belgium), and an much higher elasticity for the countries that have a lower weight of the government budget and greater flexibility in the labor market (Great Britain, Ireland, Holland, Spain, Portugal and Greece).

Falling in the middle position are the countries with strong regulation of the labor market and a high weight of the government budget fall in a middle position, that have created a condition of efficiency within their economic system that lead them to experience positive conditions on both the growth and unemployment fronts. In the first group of countries, in fact, the coefficient equal to 0.064 would indicate that every additional 1% of growth could reduce the rate of unemployment by half only after seven/eight years. In the second group, this result could be had in the span of four/five years, while in the third group, between five and six years would be necessary.

Moving on to study the relationship between total revenues and the rate of growth of GDP in the three macro areas, this remains negative or null, even if the elasticity between the two variables differs in the three sectors (from Figure 4.31 to Figure 4.33). In fact, it comes in equal to –0.0243 for the group of "anomalous" countries, equal to – 0.0018 for the group made up of Italy, France, Germany and Belgium, and to –0.0055 for the remaining countries.

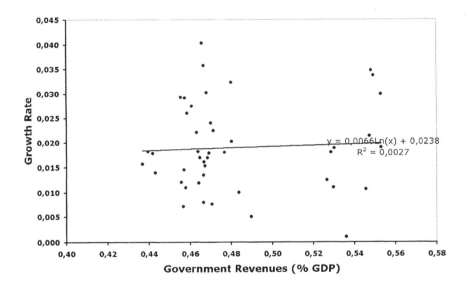

Source: OECD Economic Outlook and Authors' calculations. The solid line denotes a trend line (based on a logarithmic interpolation, which coefficients are presented in the Figure).

Figure 4.31 Growth Rate and Government Revenues within Italy, France, Belgium, Germany.

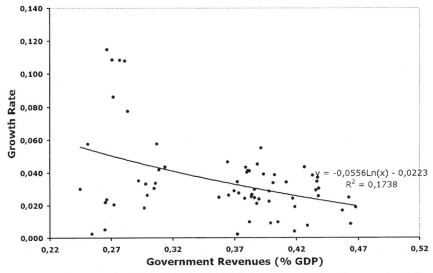

Source: OECD Economic Outlook and Authors' calculations. The solid line denotes a trend line (based on a logarithmic interpolation, which coefficients are presented in the Figure).

Figure 4.32 Growth Rate and Government Revenues within Netherlands, Ireland, Spain, Portugal, Greece, UK.

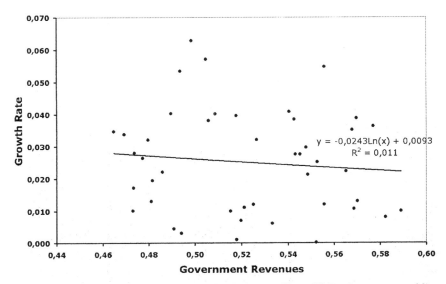

Source: OECD Economic Outlook and Authors' calculations. The solid line denotes a trend line (based on a logarithmic interpolation, which coefficients are presented in the Figure).

Figure 4.33 Growth Rate and Government Revenues within Austria, Denmark, Finland, Sweden.

It seems, therefore, that fiscal policy seems to have lost effectiveness in the countries of continental Europe (the correlation is in fact not statistically different from zero), while a reduction in fiscal pressure seems to have a greater effect in the countries that have already instituted structural reforms compared with the so-called anomalies. The message is clear: in order for interventions in fiscal policy have some impact (positive or negative) on the economic system, it's necessary that the system be put in a condition to respond to policy stimulations. In countries where the size of the government sector represents levels above 50% of GDP, but which prove capable of consuming and investing sufficiently (seen in Scandinavian countries), then variations in fiscal pressure have an impact, however modest, on the economic system in question. The effect of measures targeting revenues emerges as much more important for those countries that have reduced the weight of the government sector in the course of the 1990s (Great Britain, Spain, Ireland, the Netherlands). The same cannot be said for Italy, France, Germany and Belgium, whose economies seem practically blocked by a government sector that represents about 50% of GDP that has shown itself incapable of guaranteeing efficiency and effectiveness in its action. This leads to a quasi-neutrality of fiscal policies in absence of structural reforms, the impact of which cannot be analyzed on the same graph.

Differently from what was observed with government revenues, the correlation between total weight of government spending net of interest (% of GDP) and rate of GDP growth differs in the three macro regions.

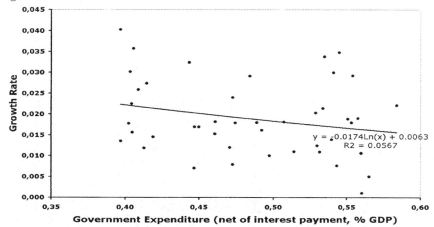

Source: OECD Economic Outlook and Authors' calculations. The solid line denotes a trend line (based on a logarithmic interpolation, which coefficients are presented in the Figure).

Figure 4.34 Growth Rate and Government Expenditure within Italy, France, Belgium, Germany.

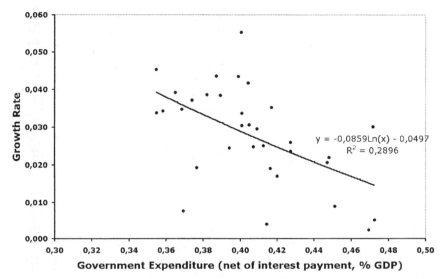

Source: OECD Economic Outlook and Authors' calculations. The solid line denotes a trend line (based on a logarithmic interpolation, which coefficients are presented in the Figure).

Figure 4.35 Growth Rate and Government Expenditure within Netherlands, Ireland, Spain, Portugal, Greece, UK.

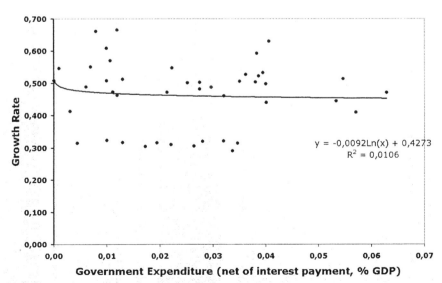

Source: OECD Economic Outlook and Authors' calculations. The solid line denotes a trend line (based on a logarithmic interpolation, which coefficients are presented in the Figure).

Figure 4.36 Growth Rate and Government Expenditure within Austria, Denmark, Finland, Sweden.

From Figures 4.34-4.36, a negative (or null, given the low value of the elasticity) relation between government spending and the rate of growth is seen in countries like Great Britain, Ireland, Spain, the Netherlands (the elasticity is equal to −0.0897) in respect to the estimate for Italy, France, Germany and Belgium (whose aggregate elasticity is equal to −-0.0041). Looking at countries like Denmark, Finland, Austria and Sweden the picture changes completely: government spending net of interest has a positive effect on the growth of the country.

This result confirms the hypothesis presented in the preceding pages, in as far as it emphasizes yet once more how the size itself of the government sector does not represent a hindrance for the economy when it is more efficient and effective than its private counterpart, indeed it guarantees better economic performances. The economic, and therefore political problem, lies in the case that the activity of the government administration does not guarantee standards at least equal to those of the private sector.

In so far as the relationship between overall net borrowing and the rate of growth is concerned, the analysis on a disaggregate level confirms what was determined for the aggregate data. A greater deficit is associated with lower economic growth, which confirms the financial crowding-out effect (Figure 4.37 to Figure 4.39).

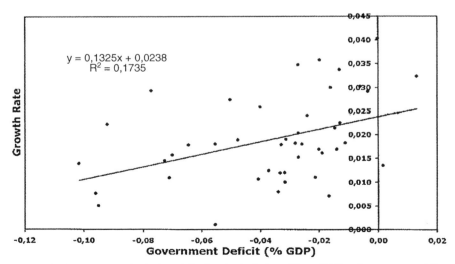

Source: OECD Economic Outlook and Authors' calculations. The solid line denotes a trend line (based on a linear interpolation, which coefficients are presented in the Figure).

Figure 4.37 Growth Rate and Government Deficit within Italy, France, Belgium, Germany.

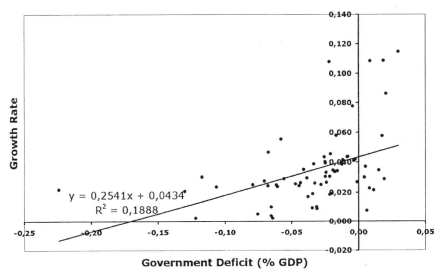

Source: OECD Economic Outlook and Authors' calculations. The solid line denotes a trend line (based on a linear interpolation, which coefficients are presented in the Figure).

Figure 4.38 Growth Rate and Government Deficit within Netherlands, Ireland, Spain, Portugal, Greece, UK.

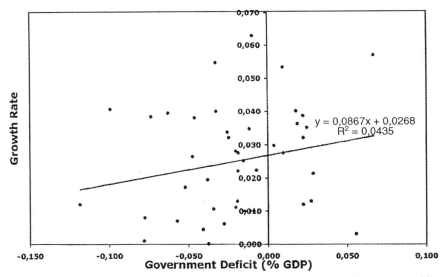

Source: OECD Economic Outlook and Authors' calculations. The solid line denotes a trend line (based on a linear interpolation, which coefficients are presented in the Figure).

Figure 4.39 Growth Rate and Government Deficit within Austria, Denmark, Finland, Sweden.

4.3.3 Details for Countries of the Union.

The data we've analyzed in these pages refer to the aggregate data, even though according to different criteria. These therefore represent the make-up of economic behaviors and historical-institutional aspects that are very different from one another, which it didn't seem right to us to neglect. For this reason, the study of the empirical evidence finishes by analyzing the same correlations within the individual European countries. To not weigh down the analysis, we've summarized the indicators for the four elasticities taken into consideration for the 14 (since Luxemburg is not included) countries in Table 4.3, while the graphs are summarized at the end of the chapter.

	Correlation between GDP growth rate and unemployment	Correlation between GDP growth rate and government revenues	Correlation between GDP growth rate and government expenditure*	Correlation between GDP growth rate and government expenditure**	Correlation between GDP growth rate and government deficit
Austria	−	−	−	−	−
Belgium	−	+	−	−	−
Denmark	−	+	+	+	−
Finland	−	−	+	+	−
France	−	−	+	+	−
Germany	−	+	+	−	−
UK	−	−	+	−	−
Greece	−	+	−	−	−
Ireland	−	−	−	−	−
Italy	−	−	+	−	−
Netherlands	−	−	−	−	−
Portugal	−	−	−	−	−
Spain	−	−	−	−	−
Sweden	−	−	+	−	−

Source: OECD Economic Outlook, Oxford Economic Forecasting (OEF), and Authors' calculations. (*) gross of interest expenditure, (**) net of interest expenditure.

Table 4.4 Correlations in Europe.

The negative correlation between growth and unemployment and the positive one between rate of growth and overall net borrowing turn out to be strong in the member countries of the European Union. The matter regarding the relationships between rate of growth and fiscal pressure and rate of growth and government spending (net and gross of interest) is different. For the first, Belgium, Denmark, Germany and Greece result positive, while it's negative for the rest of the countries. An increase in government spending net of interest has a positive impact on the rate of growth in Denmark, Finland and France, while it's negative in the remaining countries. The recurring theme of our analysis takes this form: Denmark, Finland and France are three countries that historically speaking are characterized by a government sector that, for historical, social or economic reasons, is particularly efficient. The same cannot be said for countries such as Germany, Italy, Spain or Portugal. Sweden's result leads one to think that maybe an upper limit exists for the size of the government sector, however efficient, in a market economy.

PART THREE

ECONOMIC POLICIES
FACE TO FACE

5. International Framework and Alternative Strategies

5.1 The International Economic Outlook.

The year 2001 was not particularly positive for the world economy: weaker growth in world demand associated with a marked decrease in securities values significantly reduced economic growth in both the United States and the Euro zone. At the same time, we witnessed an increase in unemployment in the majority of OECD countries. Consequently, the changing international conditions negatively influenced the government finance picture of various European and non-European countries. The situation was additionally worsened after the events of September 11th.

In this third part of the work, if we are to set ourselves the goal of measuring the effects of alternative economic policy strategies, then we must use an international framework, considered necessarily exogenous in the context of different econometric simulations. For this, we used the available information regarding the conditions of the world economy in the spring of 2002. The essential elements, summarized in **Table 5.1**, are characterized by a low rate of growth in world demand for 2001 and 2002, but which returns to high levels again for the remaining four years afterward. A revaluation in the Euro versus the dollar is also presumed, as well as an oil price that goes from about 21 dollars per barrel in 2002 to about 27 dollars in 2006, while international prices for raw materials are actually considered quasi-stable.

	2001	2002	2003	2004	2005	2006
Exchange rate US Dollar/Euro	0.89	0.94	0.98	1.04	1.09	1.1
International Commerce (% var.)	2.2	2.8	8	7.4	6.8	6.5
International Price of Raw Materials (% var.)	-13.7	-1.8	2.6	0.6	0.7	0.4
Oil Price ($ per barrel)	24.58	20.61	23.43	25.36	26.17	26.84

Sources: Oxford Economic Forecasting (release 2.0).

Table 5.1 International Framework

This international framework presented in Table 5.1 does not incorporate the Iraqi war, and the significant fluctuations of the oil price over the period October 2002-February 2003. Notice, however, that the robustness of our analysis has been tested with a sensitivity analysis discussed in the final chapter. It is there showed that the properties of the model and the conclusions of our simulations are preserved also in *a worst case scenario*. The Iraqi war of March 2003 can be considered as a case in point. We are therefore confident that the model properties and the economic message of our analysis are both preserved, and in some sense, strengthened.

Based on this exogenous international picture and by using the econometric model calculated by Oxford Economic Forecasting[1], we sought to measure the inertial trend over the next five years of all the member countries of the **European Monetary Union**.

Maintaining the weight of the government budget on the individual economies at current levels, that is without instituting structural reforms, what emerges is that European rates of growth would remain modest, the rates of unemployment would still remain high, and all of the countries would not be in a condition to eliminate the national deficit within the terms stipulated by the Stability Pact, even supposing a good possibility of international economic recovery after the sudden brake-effect due to the September 11 attack (see **Table 5.2**).

---

[1] This model is built for every individual country, and has links that connect all the economies belonging to the Euro zone one to another and, in turn, this area to the rest of the world.

		2001	2002	2003	2004	2005	2006
Austria	growth	1,0	0,9	3,5	3,2	2,7	2,5
	inflation	2,7	1,1	1,2	1,4	1,4	1,4
	unemployment	4,7	4,9	4,9	5,0	5,0	5,1
	gov. deficit	-0,9	-1,0	-0,4	0,1	0,4	0,4
	gov. debt	61,6	61,0	58,4	55,7	53,0	50,4
Belgium	growth	1,3	1,7	2,4	2,4	2,6	2,5
	inflation	2,5	1,2	1,9	1,9	1,9	2,0
	unemployment	10,8	11,0	10,8	10,6	10,4	10,1
	gov. deficit	0,2	0,0	0,5	0,5	0,5	0,5
	gov. debt	106,0	102,1	97,3	92,4	87,8	83,6
Finland	growth	0,3	1,3	3,6	3,5	3,2	3,1
	inflation	2,6	1,7	2,0	2,0	1,9	1,8
	unemployment	9,2	9,5	9,1	8,7	8,3	7,9
	gov. deficit	5,6	5,2	5,2	5,2	5,1	5,0
	gov. debt	41,3	38,7	35,2	31,6	28,2	24,8
France	growth	2,1	1,4	3,2	3,0	2,5	2,6
	inflation	1,7	1,5	1,9	1,8	1,7	1,7
	unemployment	8,9	9,3	8,5	7,9	7,5	7,4
	gov. deficit	-1,5	-1,9	-1,2	-0,8	-0,8	-0,7
	gov. debt	63,1	63,0	61,2	59,2	57,6	55,9
Germany	growth	0,7	0,7	2,5	2,4	2,3	2,3
	inflation	2,5	1,2	1,9	1,7	1,7	1,7
	unemployment	9,4	9,9	9,6	8,8	8,3	7,7
	gov. deficit	-1,7	-2,5	-2,1	-1,8	-1,4	-1,1
	gov. debt	59,4	60,0	59,7	59,2	58,6	57,6
Greece	growth	4,2	3,2	3,8	3,8	3,6	3,5
	inflation	3,4	2,5	2,6	2,4	2,7	2,6
	unemployment	12,0	12,3	12,3	12,3	12,3	12,2
	gov. deficit	-0,2	0,0	0,0	0,0	0,1	0,1
	gov. debt	98,4	93,3	87,7	82,5	77,6	73,0
Ireland	growth	5,8	3,0	5,1	5,2	4,7	4,7
	inflation	4,8	3,1	2,6	2,5	2,6	2,5
	unemployment	4,0	4,2	4,3	4,4	4,5	4,6
	gov. deficit	1,7	0,9	0,5	0,1	-0,2	-0,3
	gov. debt	34,1	31,5	28,4	25,9	24,1	22,6
Italy	growth	1,8	1,3	3,4	2,4	2,5	2,4
	inflation	2,8	1,8	1,8	1,8	1,8	1,8
	unemployment	9,8	9,7	9,5	9,1	8,7	8,5
	gov. deficit	-1,0	-0,9	-0,4	-0,3	-0,1	0,1
	gov. debt	105,0	102,3	96,8	92,5	88,4	84,4
Netherlands	growth	0,8	1,1	3,9	3,3	3,2	3,1
	inflation	4,5	2,4	2,0	1,9	1,9	1,9
	unemployment	2,0	2,3	2,6	3,1	3,5	3,9
	gov. deficit	0,6	0,6	0,6	0,5	0,5	0,4
	gov. debt	54,0	52,2	48,4	45,3	42,4	39,7
Portugal	growth	1,9	2,0	3,2	2,9	2,7	2,7
	inflation	4,3	2,5	2,1	2,1	2,0	2,0
	unemployment	4,1	4,2	3,9	3,8	3,8	3,8
	gov. deficit	-1,9	-2,0	-1,6	-1,4	-1,2	-1,1
	gov. debt	52,4	55,7	55,8	55,0	54,1	53,0
Spain	growth	2,7	2,0	3,3	3,1	3,0	3,0
	inflation	3,6	2,1	2,1	2,1	2,0	2,0
	unemployment	13,0	13,1	12,8	12,4	12,1	11,8
	gov. deficit	-0,1	-0,2	-0,3	-0,4	-0,6	-0,8
	gov. debt	65,5	63,2	60,2	57,6	55,3	53,5

Sources: Oxford Economic Forecasting (release 2.0), and Authors' simulations.

Table 5.2 Inertial Forecast for European Countries

5.2 Alternative Strategies.

Again using the same econometric model, we then attempted to measure what impact could be produced on the European economy and the individual countries as a result of four economic policy alternatives.

The first (**Low Rates**) refers to the traditional use of monetary policy in terms of its expansive effects on the economy, including both the case of a shock reduction in interest rates as well as the case of a gradual downward movement.

The second (**Higher Spending, Higher Taxes and No Reforms**) consists of an additional expansion in government spending, which however requires a parallel increase in fiscal pressure to maintain the conditions of financial balance.

We defined, then, a third strategy of economic policy (**Lower Taxes, Lower Spending, Full Employment: the Triangle of Reforms**). This is meant to tie into the theoretical assumptions summarized beforehand, the correlations about the existing link between growth and unemployment as well as the government budget and growth rates as shown for all the European countries in the preceding chapter, and to the positive results obtained in the cited works on the Italian economy (citation). In other words, we measured the impact and effectiveness of a budget policy designed to simultaneously reduce fiscal pressure and government spending with a measure "spread" over four, five years equal to approximately 1% of GDP per year, while at the same time increasing flexibility within the sphere of the labor market. With this third strategy of economic policy, we thus tried to measure if that possible miracle via a strategy of reforms for the Italian economy can also be obtained in the context of other European countries, and if the implementation of a strategy of this type in all the countries can have positive synergetic effects that may strengthen the obtainable results, individually, of every single country. That is, we intend to measure in what way Europe, building "its own and endogenous" path toward growth, can prove itself willing and able to take on the role it deserves in the arena of the global economy.

Finally, the **fourth** policy simulation (**Lower taxes, Lower Spending, and ... Lower Rates**) combines the same fiscal interventions of previous exercise with an expansionary monetary policy. Precisely, it considers a shock reduction of interest rates of 3 points, that is the same size as intervention examined in *Low Rates* simulation. This exercise evaluates the joint impact of fiscal policy with monetary policy in order to verify whether this combination improves the results of the sole fiscal and monetary policy. In other words, we intend to measure if a kind of coordination between single European governments with European Central Bank can improve upon the reallocation of resources generated in absence of that.

6. Easy Monetary Policy: Effectiveness and Limits

6.1 Shock and Gradual Monetary Policy.

We begin the positive part of our analysis with a more expansive monetary policy that pushes the overall level of interest rates toward the low end. The measurements that emerge from this analysis refer, first, to the aggregate data for the 12 countries of the Monetary Union, and then to the "two Europes" (or three, as suggested in Chapter 4 of the book). In this context we evaluate the possibilities that can be offered to the different national realities by a more expansive monetary policy put in place for everyone by the ECB.

Precisely, we will measure the macroeconomic performances in reference in particular to five indicators: the rate of growth, the rate of unemployment, inflation, the government deficit and the government debt.[1] Additional considerations and further details can be obtained from the analytical results reported in the Appendix.[2]

As regards monetary policy, we will take a look at two possible scenarios. In the first case, the European Central Bank "instantly" reduces the entire current system of interest rates by two percentage points (we denote this case as *shock monetary policy* or as a *cold turkey monetary policy*). A second case refers to the possibility in which the

---

[1] The aggregate statistics for the 12 countries of the Monetary Union are defined as follows. The rate of GDP growth is equal to the growth rate of the sum of GDP levels in every country, calculated in Euro. The aggregate inflation rate is defined as the rate of growth of the sum of the consumer price indices in every country, and the rate of unemployment as the relationship between the number of jobless in the 12 countries and the size of the work force in the corresponding countries.
[2] Precisely, the Appendix shows detailed tables containing selected macroeconomic variables concerning the domestic, the foreign, the monetary and the real side of each country economy.

reduction in interest rates, still by 2 points, is put in place gradually over the space of five years (we call this *gradual monetary policy*).

6.2 The Impact on Euroland.

Figure 6.1 and Figure 6.2 show the impact of the two economic policy interventions on all the member countries of the Union, while considering the expansions patterns of aggregate series for GDP and unemployment rate.

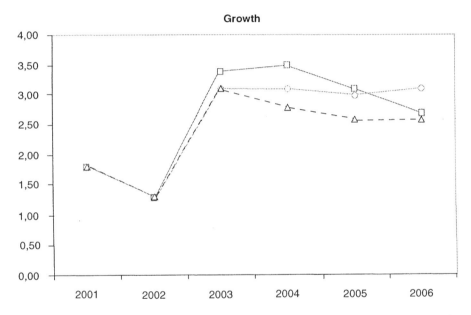

The darker line (with boxes) refers to the *Shock Monetary Policy*, the lighter line (with balls) represents the *Gradualist Monetary Policy*, while the dashed one (with triangles) is the *Baseline* simulation. Source: Authors' Simulation with Oxford Economic Forecasting Model (release 2.0).

Figure 6.1 Easy Monetary Policy: GDP Growth Rate in Euroland

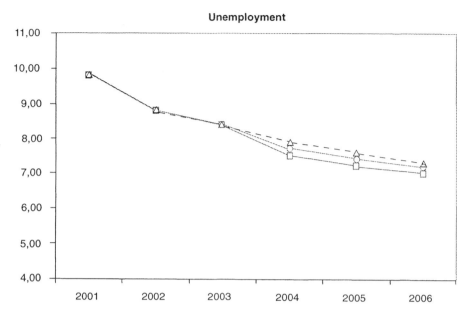

The darker line (with boxes) refers to the *Shock Monetary Policy*, the lighter line (with balls) represents the *Gradualist Monetary Policy*, while the dashed one (with triangles) is the *Baseline* simulation. Source: Authors' Simulation with Oxford Economic Forecasting Model (release 2.0).

Figure 6.2 Easy Monetary Policy: Unemployment Rate in Euroland

A shock monetary policy pushes up growth rate over 3% for the first two years after the intervention, while employment increases by little. Notice, however, that this expansion turns out to be temporary, once the lower rates are incorporated into agent expectations. In fact the forth and the fifth years of simulations present a declining growth rate, while producing a lower impact in reducing unemployment rate.

At contrary, a gradual monetary intervention has, at beginning, a smaller impact, compared with the shock policy, while pushing up Euroland growth rate by more at the end of simulation period. Notice, however, that labor market situation remains unchanged with this second kind of economic policy.

Figure 6.3 and Figure 6.4, then, analyzes the monetary – financial side of the aggregate economy, while focusing on inflation rate and government deficit.

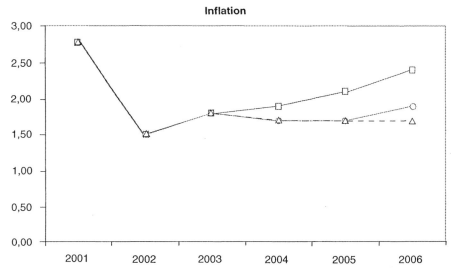

The darker line (with boxes) refers to the *Shock Monetary Policy*, the lighter line (with balls) represents the *Gradualist Monetary Policy*, while the dashed one (with triangles) is the *Baseline* simulation. Source: Authors' Simulation with Oxford Economic Forecasting Model (release 2.0).

Figure 6.3 Easy Monetary Policy: Inflation in Euroland

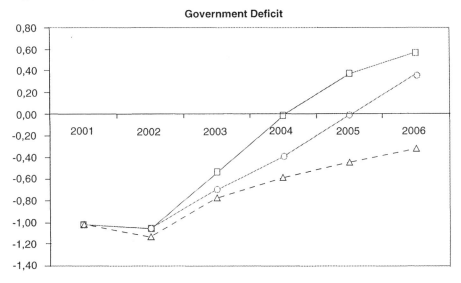

The darker line (with boxes) refers to the *Shock Monetary Policy*, the lighter line (with balls) represents the *Gradualist Monetary Policy*, while the dashed one (with triangles) is the *Baseline* simulation. Source: Authors' Simulation with Oxford Economic Forecasting Model (release 2.0).

Figure 6.4 Easy Monetary Policy: Government Deficit in Euroland

A shock monetary policy leads to an increase in inflation rate of about 1 percentage point *a regime*, while the gradual counterpart leaves it substantially unchanged. The impact on aggregate government deficit is consistent with economic theory, and with our intuition, too. The *cold turkey* policy cancels it in two years, while cutting by the very first day of simulation money borrowing cost by 2 points. The gradual intervention, next, has a qualitatively similar impact, just of smaller size.

Analogously to what has been done in the previous chapter, we then move our attention on macroeconomic patterns of European countries, while separately focusing on Belgium, France, Germany and Italy first, and, on Ireland, Netherlands, Portugal and Spain then. Finally, we consider Finland and Austria. That is in order to investigate different expansion patters of the macroeconomic series we are taking into account.

Figure 6.5 to Figure 6.8 presents the effects of both policy interventions in the first group of countries, that is made of Belgium, France, Germany and Italy. There are presented in the following pages.

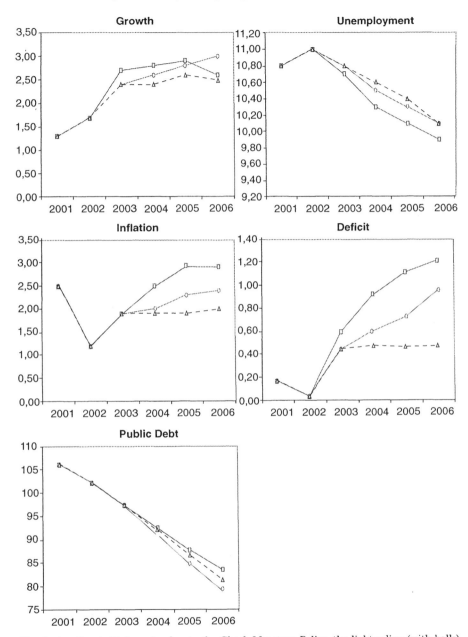

The darker line (with boxes) refers to the *Shock Monetary Policy*, the lighter line (with balls) represents the *Gradualist Monetary Policy*, while the dashed one (with triangles) is the baseline simulation. Source: Authors' Simulation with Oxford Economic Model (release 2.0)

Figure 6.5 Easy Monetary Policy in Belgium

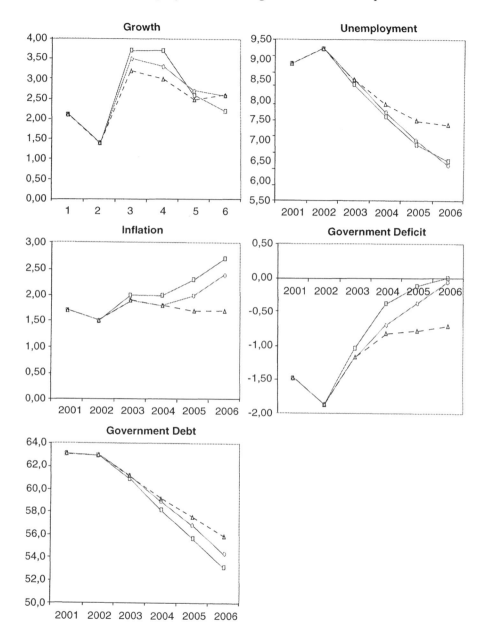

The darker line (with boxes) refers to the *Shock Monetary Policy*, the lighter line (with balls) represents the *Gradualist Monetary Policy*, while the dashed one (with triangles) is the baseline simulation. Source: Authors' Simulation with Oxford Economic Model (release 2.0)

Figure 6.6 Easy Monetary Policy in France

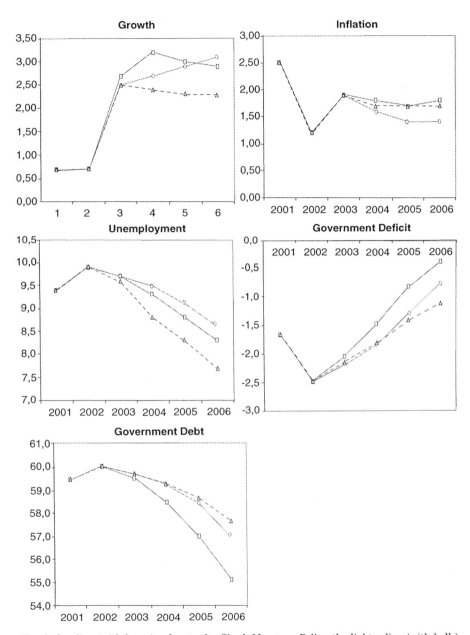

The darker line (with boxes) refers to the *Shock Monetary Policy*, the lighter line (with balls) represents the *Gradualist Monetary Policy*, while the dashed one (with triangles) is the baseline simulation. Source: Authors' Simulation with Oxford Economic Model (release 2.0).

Figure 6.7 Easy Monetary Policy in Germany

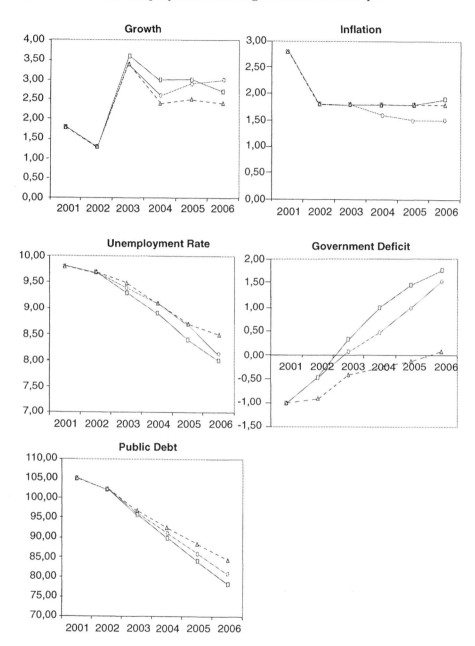

The darker line (with boxes) refers to the *Shock Monetary Policy*, the lighter line (with balls) represents the *Gradualist Monetary Policy*, while the dashed one (with triangles) is the baseline simulation. Source: Authors' Simulation with Oxford Economic Model (release 2.0).

Figure 6.8 Easy Monetary Policy in Italy

For these countries, as already indicated in the inertial tendencies, the rate of annual growth, after the crisis years of 2001-2002, settles around 2-2.5%, inflation stabilizes around 1.5%, unemployment remains high and declines slowly until only in 2006 it reaches 7.5%. Finally, net indebtedness remains far from the target of *zero deficit* for the entire period of the simulation, which means beyond 2006. The policy interventions do not change the picture by much. The growth rate increases about by half percentage point, unemployment profile remains substantially unchanged, while inflation increases and government deficit is reduced because of the lower rates structure. Finally, debt patters follows that of government deficit. Notice that some exceptional elements appears in Germany, where both the shock and the gradual monetary policy leads to an increase, even if small, of unemployment rate.

Next, Figure 6.9 to Figure 6.13 shows how the Netherlands, Ireland, Spain and Portugal response to the two kinds of monetary policy.

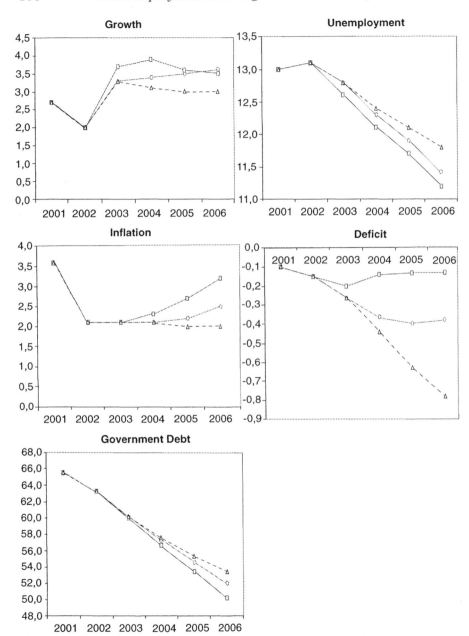

The darker line (with boxes) refers to the *Shock Monetary Policy*, the lighter line (with balls) represents the *Gradualist Monetary Policy*, while the dashed one (with triangles) is the baseline simulation. Source: Authors' Simulation with Oxford Economic Model (release 2.0).

Figure 6.9 Easy Monetary Policy in Spain

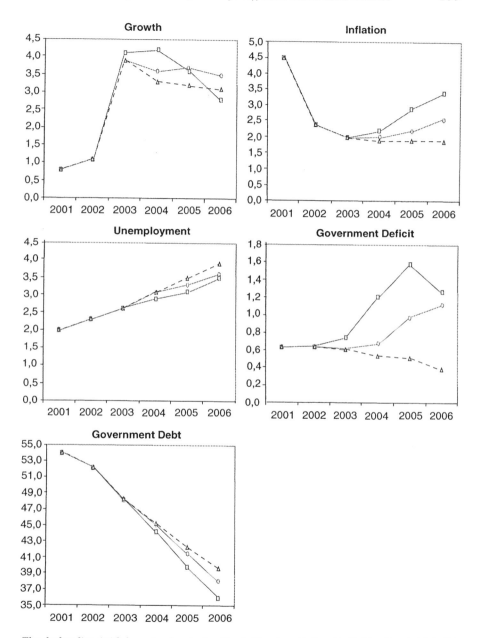

The darker line (with boxes) refers to the *Shock Monetary Policy*, the lighter line (with balls) represents the *Gradualist Monetary Policy*, while the dashed one (with triangles) is the baseline simulation. Source: Authors' Simulation with Oxford Economic Model (release 2.0).

Figure 6.10 Easy Monetary Policy in Netherlands

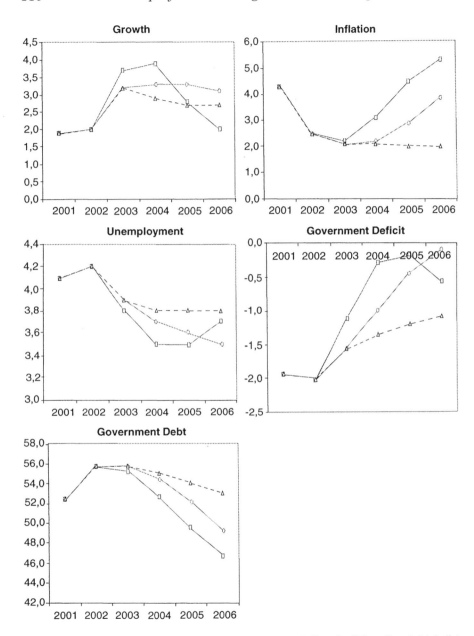

The darker line (with boxes) refers to the *Shock Monetary Policy*, the lighter line (with balls) represents the *Gradualist Monetary Policy*, while the dashed one (with triangles) is the baseline simulation. Source: Authors' Simulation with Oxford Economic Model (release 2.0).

Figure 6.11 Easy Monetary Policy in Portugal

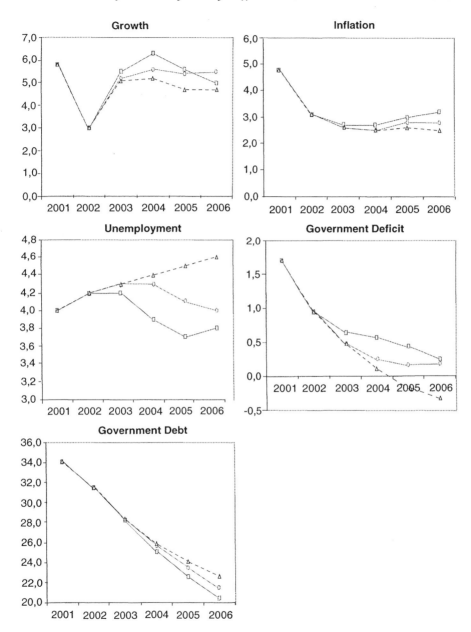

The darker line (with boxes) refers to the *Shock Monetary Policy*, the lighter line (with balls) represents the *Gradualist Monetary Policy*, while the dashed one (with triangles) is the baseline simulation. Source: Authors' Simulation with Oxford Economic Model (release 2.0).

Figure 6.12 Easy Monetary Policy in Ireland

The inertial tendencies for these countries shows a growth rate close to 3%, an unemployment rate close to 5%, with the exception of Spain and Greece, and a good picture of government finance quantities. Notice, however, that Spain labor market significantly improved in the last five years, while reducing its unemployment rate by more than 6 points in 6 years. The annual growth rate pattern induced by a gradual monetary intervention remains close to the inertial one; a shock policy, instead, boosts it up for one or two year, while producing a slump phase in remaining years. Unemployment rate remains substantially unchanged by both monetary interventions, inflation stabilizes around 3%, while government deficit is not a problem for these countries. Some exceptional elements do arise from the impact of monetary policy on unemployment in Spain, where it guarantees a reduction of unemployment of approximately two points, which is a significant development in relative terms compared with the situation in the other countries of the Monetary Union.

Finally, Figure 6.13 and Figure 6.14 show that expansion patterns for Finland and Austria, as generated after the shock and the gradual monetary policies, are not qualitatively different from those of Euroland (as presented in Figure 6.1 - 6.4).

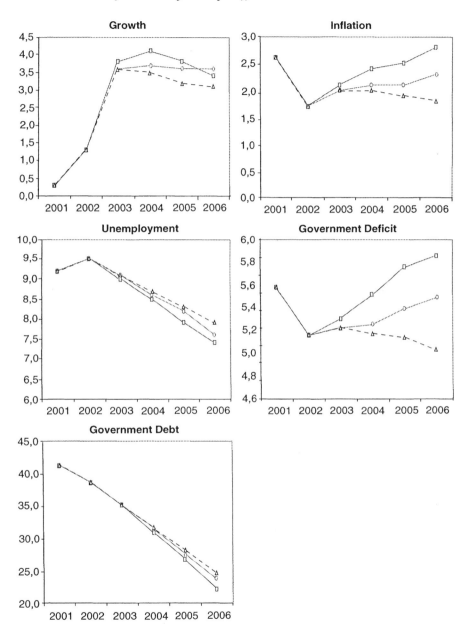

The darker line (with boxes) refers to the *Shock Monetary Policy*, the lighter line (with balls) represents the *Gradualist Monetary Policy*, while the dashed one (with triangles) is the baseline simulation. Source: Authors' Simulation with Oxford Economic Model (release 2.0).

Figure 6.13 Easy Monetary Policy in Finland

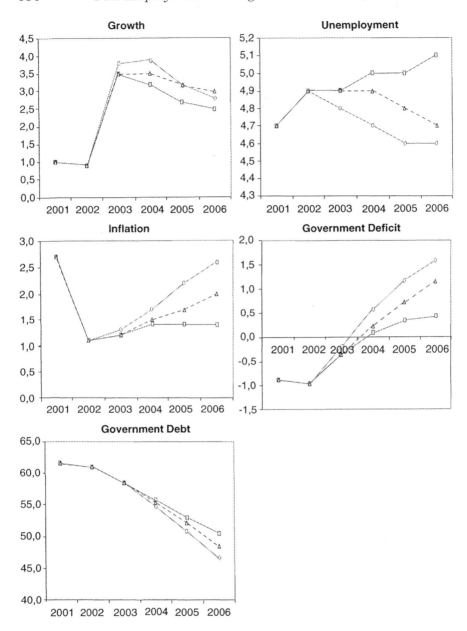

The darker line (with boxes) refers to the *Shock Monetary Policy*, the lighter line (with balls) represents the *Gradualist Monetary Policy*, while the dashed one (with triangles) is the baseline simulation. Source: Authors' Simulation with Oxford Economic Model (release 2.0).

Figure 6.14 Easy Monetary Policy in Austria

The effects of a possible reduction in interest rates, either a *shock reduction* or a *gradual reduction*, carried out on its own without using the other instruments of economic policy, appears to indeed sustain the economic cycle, but in a fragile and non-permanent way. It would in fact give a boost to investments, but not one that would significantly reduce unemployment. On average, the rate of GDP growth would be higher by about a half point, there would be a lower government deficit given the lower spending on interest, but there would also be higher inflation.

Therefore, the monetary policy in itself does not seem to produce substantial effects on the rate of unemployment in the medium to long term. In fact, what's more noticeable is that the monetary policy, which reduces the cost of the capital factor, does not have direct effects on labor demand. *Ceteris paribus*, the relative price of labor increases in respect to capital, therefore not generating incentives for businesses to hire personnel.

Certainly the greater growth there would be would give some push on the employment front, but this would remain an almost entirely transitory effect. In keeping with what has been noted in writings, a *shock* monetary policy would nonetheless be more effective than the *gradual* hypothesis, in as far as the first allows the surprise effect to be used by the markets and by the economic actors.

The results obtained thus do not show there's significant space for an "isolated" reduction in interest rates in Europe. Indeed, there would be a boost to the economic system through the monetary channel, but it would barely even touch the structure of that very system, such as the size and the composition of the government budget and its weight in terms of absorption of national resources, for example.

This is not in fact a case of a structural-type intervention, in other words one to intervene in the medium to long term outlook of the European economy as concerns growth and employment. Given the international framework, all of this does not mean that a reduction in interest rates in Europe is not desirable and useful.[3] Not as a *panacea* for every illness, but used eventually as an element that could accompany more structural economic policy measures.[4] In summary,

---

[3] We reiterate that the first is made up of the biggest countries of continental Europe (Belgium, Germany, Finland and France) plus Italy, and the second, Greece, Ireland, Holland, Portugal and Spain. For solely technical reasons, we don't explicitly take into consideration Luxembourg: in fact the econometric model we've used does not specify the details of Luxembourg's economy, barring a complete analysis of such.

[4] The final chapter of the book explicitly analyzes this exercise.

the monetary policy can be a part of the mix of economic policy, but it cannot replace the entire mix.

It is a fact, however, that specifically for the small European economies a trade-off between participating in the single currency and the ECB and reappropriating monetary sovereignty does not exist. In the latter case, the small currency of a small national economy would recognize even lesser national sovereignty, destined to be overwhelmed by the new international reality.

7. Higher Spending, Higher Taxes and No Reforms

7.1 The Haavelmo Old Way...

The message that emerges from the preceding chapter is quite clear: monetary policy provides a push toward GDP growth by way of investments, but generates inflationary pressures and does not guarantee a steady and permanent reduction in unemployment.

In this chapter, we'll take a look at the possibility of a government budget policy that further expands government spending. Obviously, however, considering the European monetary structure and the constraints of the Stability Pact, it is no longer possible to revert to the old delusion of pure deficit spending. Thus, it is necessary to suppose that an increase in government spending is counterbalanced by an increase in revenues.

It is therefore an issue of testing the impact of a balanced budget intervention ex-ante according to the old and noted theoretical contribution of Haavelmo (1945). In the case, the possible impulse to the economy should thus occur through the transfer of resources from the private sector to the government sector, additionally increasing the weight of the latter on the economy.

7.2 Higher Spending, Higher Taxes and No Reforms.

The maneuver analyzed here hypothesizes that each of the 12 countries of the Monetary Union increases government spending by one percentage point of GDP year after year. Respecting the Stability and Growth Pact, we also assume that the greatest expenses are covered ex-ante by greater tax revenues generated by the increase in fiscal pressure on families and businesses. Finally, we assume that the greater fiscal burden is divided between families and businesses in proportion to the relative weight of each taxable base bracket.[1]

Figure 7.1 to Figure 7.4 present the impact of this policy intervention for Euroland, defined as the aggregate made of the 12 European countries participating the single currency.

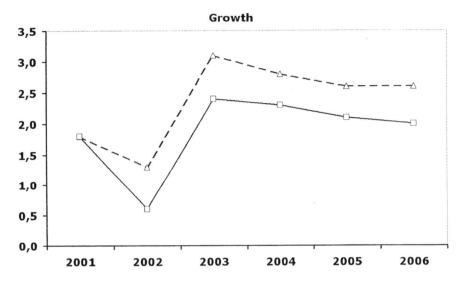

The solid line (with boxes) represents the *Higher Spending, Higher Taxes* ... policy, while the dashed line denotes the *Baseline* simulation. Source: Authors' Simulation with Oxford Economic Model (release 2.0)

Figure 7.1 Higher Spending, Higher Taxes, and No Reforms: Growth Rate in Euroland.

---

[1] The measure we discuss in the next chapter is symmetrical to the one being discussed here.

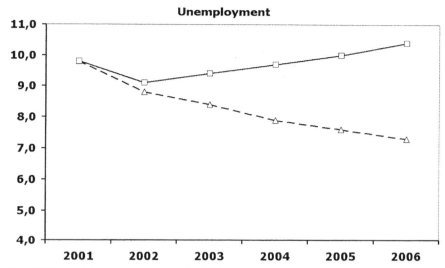

The solid line (with boxes) represents the *Higher Spending, Higher Taxes ...* policy, while the dashed line denotes the *Baseline* simulation. Source: Authors' Simulation with Oxford Economic Model (release 2.0)

Figure 7.2 Higher Spending, Higher Taxes, and No Reforms: Unemployment

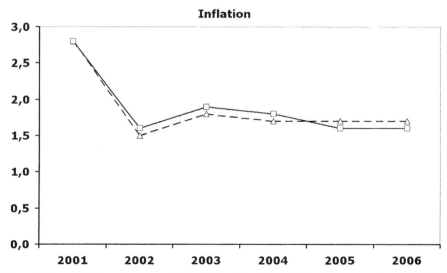

The solid line (with boxes) represents the Higher Spending, Higher Taxes ... policy, while the dashed line denotes the *Baseline* simulation. Source: Authors' Simulation with Oxford Economic Model (release 2.0)

Figure 7.3 Higher Spending, Higher Taxes, and No Reforms: Inflation Rate

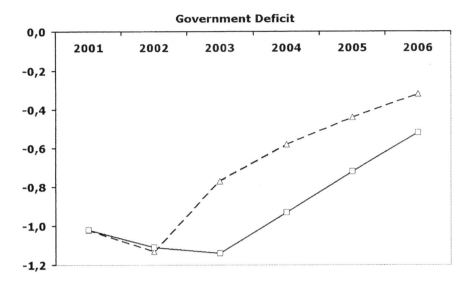

The solid line (with boxes) represents the *Higher Spending, Higher Taxes* ... policy, while the dashed line denotes the *Baseline* simulation. Source: Authors' Simulation with Oxford Economic Model (release 2.0)

Figure 7.4 Higher Spending, Higher Taxes, and No Reforms: Government Deficit

An additional increase in the government budget on the economy would even lead to growth smaller than that which would emerge from a purely inertial process (Figure 7.1), unemployment would increase (Figure 7.2) and inflation would not veer significantly from that same inertial tendency (Figure 7.3). It should be pointed out that there would also be a worsening as far as the government deficit is concerned due to the economy's weaker growth (Figure 7.4).

The results obtained depict a discouraging macroeconomic and government finance situation, for the whole of the Monetary Union and for many of the different countries involved. That worsening would take place despite additional increases in fiscal pressure, and would in turn cause an acceleration in the accumulation of debt.

Interesting differences appear in the results obtained relative to the two Europes. Figure 7.5-7.8 shows the aggregate effects for Italy, France, Germany, and Belgium.

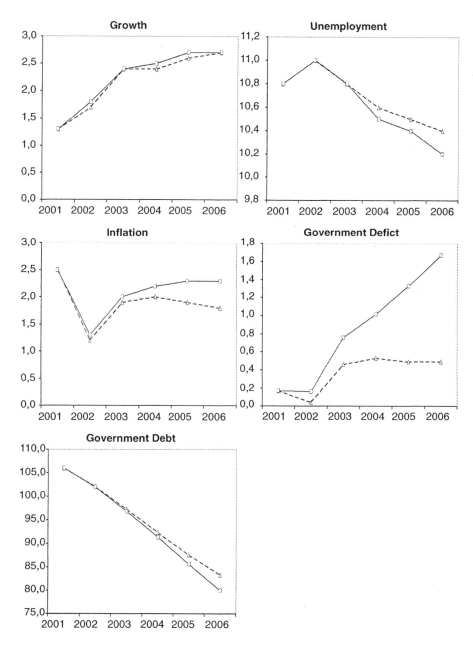

The solid line (with boxes) represents the *Higher Spending, Higher Taxes* ... policy, while the dashed line denotes the *Baseline* simulation. Source: Authors' Simulation with Oxford Economic Model (release 2.0).

Figure 7.5 Higher Spending, Higher Taxes, and No Reforms in Belgium

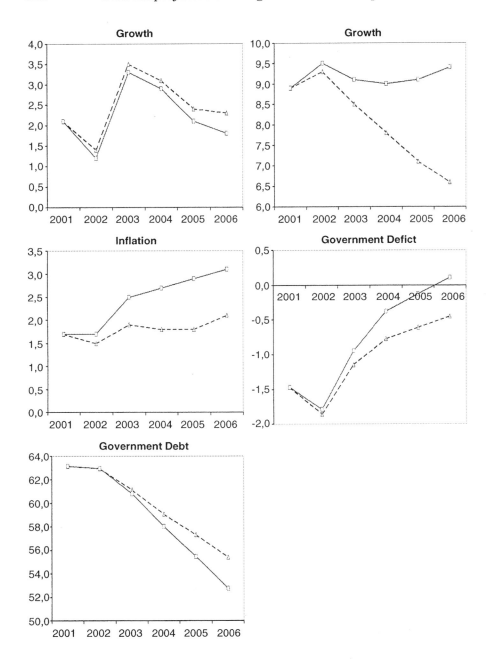

The solid line (with boxes) represents the *Higher Spending, Higher Taxes ...* policy, while the dashed line denotes the *Baseline* simulation. Source: Authors' Simulation with Oxford Economic Model (release 2.0)

Figure 7.6 Higher Spending, Higher Taxes, and No Reforms in France

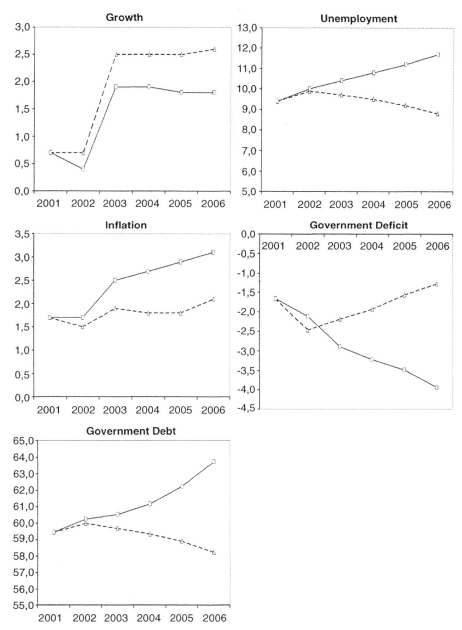

The solid line (with boxes) represents the *Higher Spending, Higher Taxes* ... policy, while the dashed line denotes the *Baseline* simulation. Source: Authors' Simulation with Oxford Economic Model (release 2.0).

Figure 7.7 Higher Spending, Higher Taxes, and No Reforms in Germany

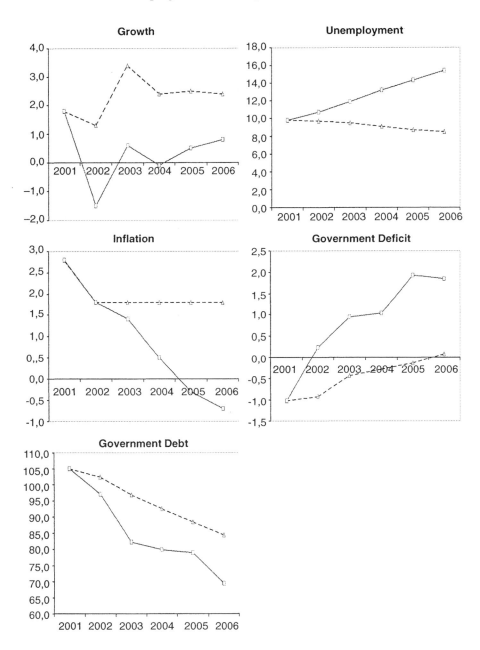

The solid line (with boxes) represents the *Higher Spending, Higher Taxes* ... policy, while the dashed line denotes the *Baseline* simulation. Source: Authors' Simulation with Oxford Economic Model (release 2.0).

Figure 7.8 Higher Spending, Higher Taxes, and No Reforms in Italy

Comparing the profiles with those relating to all the countries of the Monetary Union, in this case the effects of the intervention appear more striking: the negative impact on the rate of growth amounts to about 1 percentage point less with respect to the inertial profile. In Italy this policy has a particularly dramatic effect on growth rate, because it reduces it to a negative value in the first year of simulation, and leaves it lumbering close to the zero line in remaining four ones. The most important aspect, however, is undoubtedly the condition of the unemployment rate, which would grow by some 3 percentage points, in all countries but Belgium, where it remains close to inertial pattern. For France, Germany and Italy, in effect, that would mean reverting back to the unemployment levels of the two years 1997-1998. The response of government finance variables might seems puzzling, because of the reduction of government deficit, and, by this end, of government debt. This response becomes clear looking at the behavior of interest rate, which is reduced by the ECB during recessions.[1]

In summary, government spending would displace investments and private consumption, generating a further regression of the economic system. Thus, given their similar tax structure, Italy, France, and Germany would suffer even more from the added increase in fiscal pressure.

Figures 7.9-7.13 analyzes Ireland, the Netherlands, Portugal, Spain and Greece.

---

[1] Technically speaking, the Taylor rule equation defined for the ECB in the model can be specified more or less *worried* of inflation, and more or less *sensible* to output gap. In our simulation we consider the default setting of the OEF model (as estimated in Spring 2002). It can be showed in a separate exercise that, making the ECB reaction function less sensitive to output gap, interest rate structure does not change at all, or changes by very little. In this case the policy intervention we are considering in these pages becomes even more growth depressing.

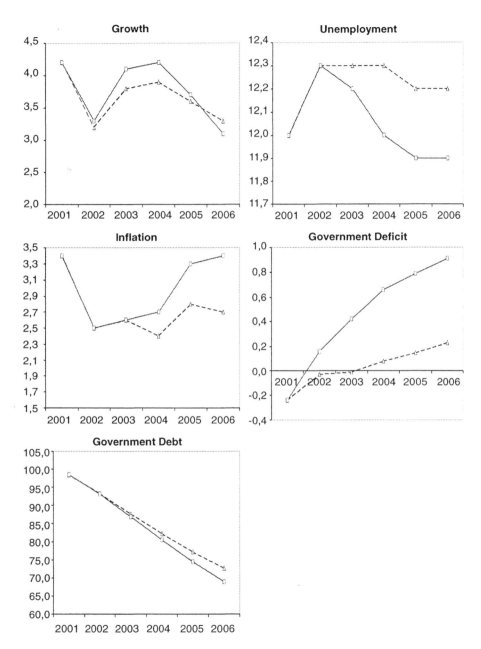

The solid line (with boxes) represents the *Higher Spending, Higher Taxes* ... policy, while the dashed line denotes the *Baseline* simulation. Source: Authors' Simulation with Oxford Economic Model (release 2.0)

Figure 7.9 Higher Spending, Higher Taxes, and No Reforms in Greece

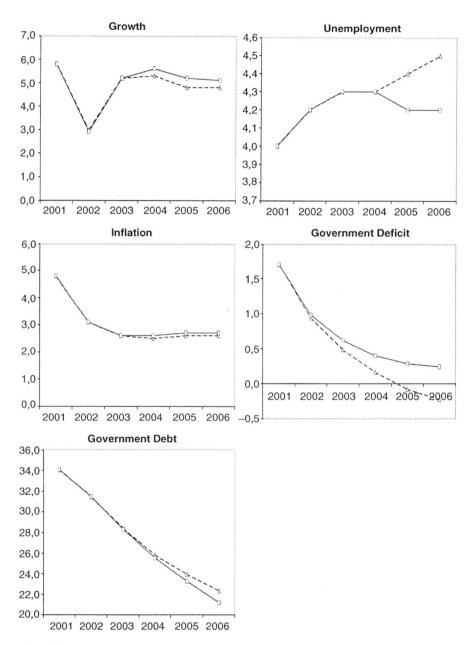

The solid line (with boxes) represents the *Higher Spending, Higher Taxes* ... policy, while the dashed line denotes the *Baseline* simulation. Source: Authors' Simulation with Oxford Economic Model (release 2.0)

Figure 7.10 Higher Spending, Higher Taxes, and No Reforms in Ireland

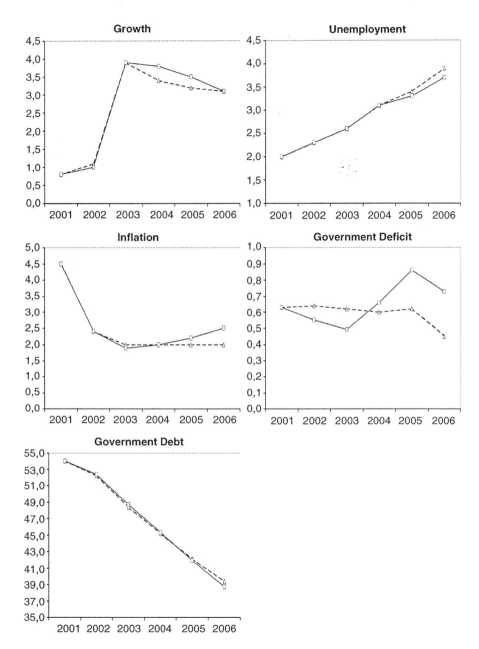

The solid line (with boxes) represents the *Higher Spending, Higher Taxes ...* policy, while the dashed line denotes the *Baseline* simulation. Source: Authors' Simulation with Oxford Economic Model (release 2.0)

Figure 7.11 Higher Spending, Higher Taxes, and No Reforms in Netherlands

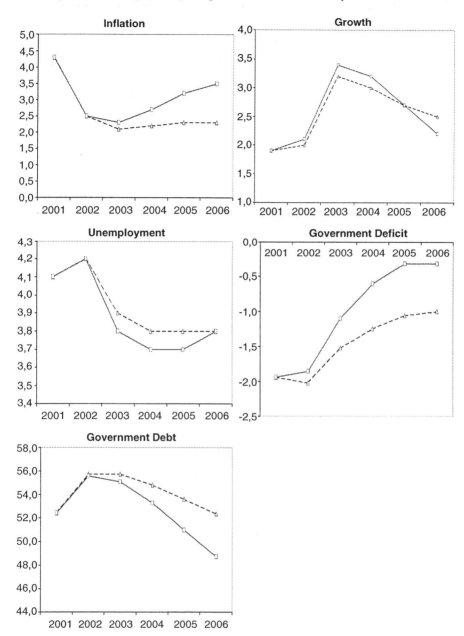

The solid line (with boxes) represents the *Higher Spending, Higher Taxes ...* policy, while the dashed line denotes the *Baseline* simulation. Source: Authors' Simulation with Oxford Economic Model (release 2.0)

Figure 7.12 Higher Spending, Higher Taxes, and No Reforms in Portugal

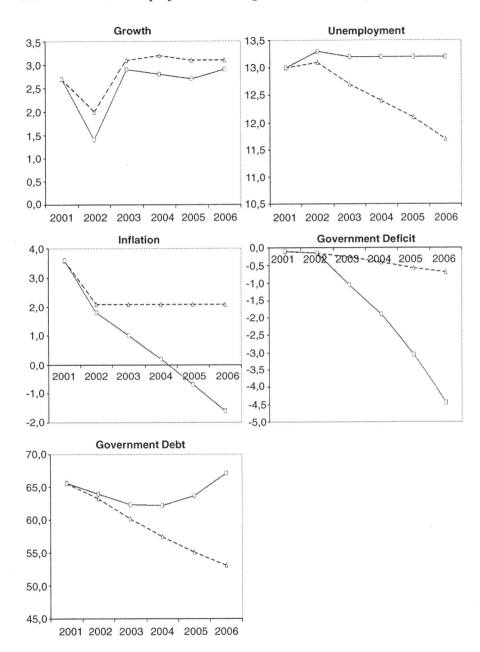

The solid line (with boxes) represents the *Higher Spending, Higher Taxes ...* policy, while the dashed line denotes the *Baseline* simulation. Source: Authors' Simulation with Oxford Economic Model (release 2.0)

Figure 7.13 Higher Spending, Higher Taxes, and No Reforms in Spain

All these countries, but Spain, represent the exception, in which the measure does have an expansive effect. This means that greater fiscal pressure brings about greater growth and a reduction in unemployment in the first two or three years of the simulation, whereas in the end the impact of the intervention is negative in terms of social welfare.

The different results obtained concerning the two Europe and the individual countries would seem to show a non-linearity of the effects described here. In the countries with a lower weight of the government budget, a balanced intervention in the form of a parallel increase in spending and revenues would appear to not produce these negative effects on growth and employment.

Finally, Figures 7.14-7.15 focus their attention on Finland and Austria.

In fact, for these countries the growth rate follows two different patterns. It has a little increase in Austria, while it falls by 1 percentage point in Finland. The inflation rate, then, increases in respect to the inertial evolution in both economies. However, in these countries there would also be an increase in unemployment, albeit limited, which would indicate that the process of job creation via an increase in the weight of the government budget is less than that which is produced when greater levels of resources are left to the private sector. There would also be a slight worsening effect on the equilibrium conditions of the government budget.

Summarizing, we can think it that an upper limit exists above which further increases in the weight of the government budget on the economy, even beyond and in absence of financial imbalances, would produce a sort of real displacement of resources that would lead to a slowing of growth and an increase in unemployment.

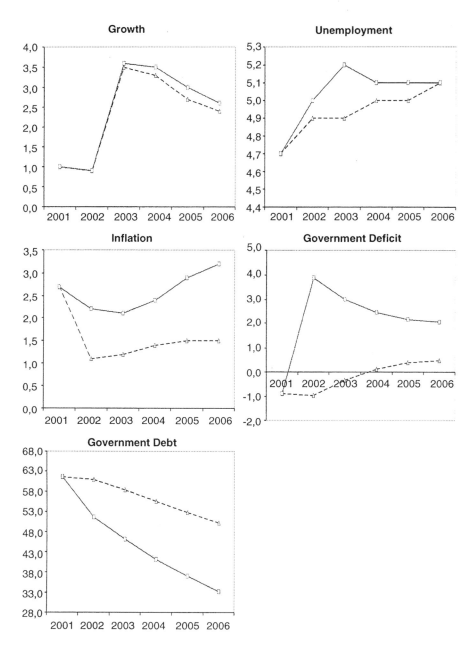

The solid line (with boxes) represents the *Higher Spending, Higher Taxes* ... policy, while the dashed line denotes the *Baseline* simulation. Source: Authors' Simulation with Oxford Economic Model (release 2.0)

Figure 7.14 Higher Spending, Higher Taxes, and No Reforms in Austria

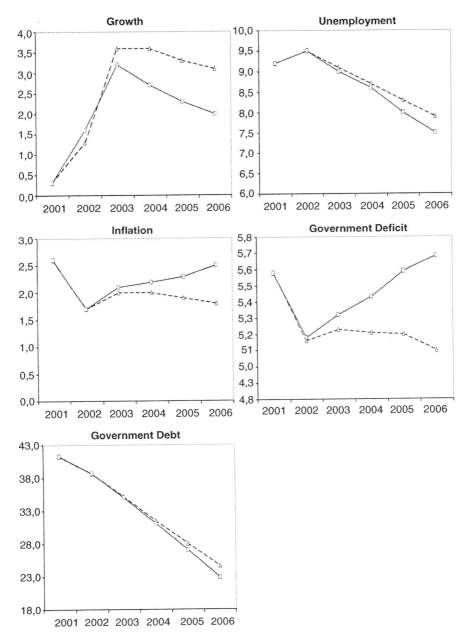

The solid line (with boxes) represents the *Higher Spending, Higher Taxes* ... policy, while the dashed line denotes the *Baseline* simulation. Source: Authors' Simulation with Oxford Economic Model (release 2.0)

Figure 7.15 Higher Spending, Higher Taxes, and No Reforms in Finland

8. Lower Taxes, Lower Spending, Higher Employment

8.1 The Triangle of Reforms.

We showed previously that it is not possible to hope for a reduction in unemployment in Europe, even following a hypothetical international cycle of expansion, without instituting structural reforms. The inertial outlook is characterized by low growth, high unemployment, and non-compliance with the parameters of the Stability Pact. This would happen even amid an international economic cycle that is supposed to tend toward a steady phase of recovery in the years following the strong slowdown of the two years 2001-2002. As we'll see herewith, if the international cycle were to instead extend the slowdown phase that was seen throughout 2002 over a longer time, the inertial prospects would look even worse. Predicting the obtainable results on the basis of this even more negative hypothesis, it is clear straightaway that in this possible eventuality, a structural reform policy would not only be necessary and more urgent, but, in relative terms, would have even more positive results on the economy.

From the analysis of the preceding chapters, its seems clear that the European Monetary Union's goal of full employment cannot be entrusted exclusively to monetary policies or, even less, to government budget policies that increase the weight of the State on the economic system.

Nearly by exclusion, therefore, herein lies the central idea of our work of measuring the effectiveness of a strategy of economic policy based on what we've defined as **the triangle of reforms**: fiscal reform, a reduction of and reforms of current spending, and reforms of the labor and the good and services markets. The whole of these policies is aimed at reinvigorating investments in infrastructure and production, including the aspects of training and improving human capital. We also intend to show how this strategy can and should be linked to the goals of financial equilibrium stipulated by the Stability and Growth Pact. It needs to be clearly pointed out that it is not those very financial constraints that are the true element that hinders growth and employment, but rather the failure to institute structural reforms. On the contrary, in fact, the instituting of those reforms would make the establishment of financial balance more secure, creating a healthy mixture of growth and welfare that is associated with the Stability Pact.

The purpose of our analysis is to measure three different aspects.

The **first** consists of understanding the macroeconomic consequences of a parallel measure of reducing revenues and spending built on two precise pacts (*do ut des*) with families and with businesses. Families would be promised a reduction in personal income tax, a very progressive measure that favors low incomes and large families, against an approximately 3-year increase in the retirement age compared with current regulations, starting first with seniority pensions. Businesses would be proposed a reduction in corporate income tax as well as social contributions, against the elimination of the thousands of streams of subsidies, supports and various transfers from the government budget. This then means measuring the potentials for improvement of each single country via measures decided internally, without relying upon the possible positive effects from interventions carried out in other countries.

The **second** hypothesizes instead that this type of intervention be realized simultaneously in all of the countries. Thus, differently from the first, a measurement of the possible synergic impact of measures "coordinated" at a European level is obtained. This therefore addresses whether positive synergies among the different European countries exist and how important they can be in the event of the widespread institution of structural reforms across Europe under the terms indicated herein.

Finally, the **third** aspect regards the possibility that a country considers so-called "free-riding," which is that that very country were to not effect any reform internally in the hope that reforms initiated in all the other countries can produce positive effects in so as to solve the problem by pushing it to grow more from the outside, and thus reach full employment without confronting the possible political costs of internal reforms.

Previously, we analyzed the macroeconomic conditions of the fifteen European countries of the Union, and we "highlighted" the existence of a Europe with two faces... or maybe three. One is characterized by high growth, low unemployment and low fiscal pressure (Great Britain, Ireland, Holland, Spain, Portugal and Greece), and the other by low growth, high unemployment and high fiscal pressure (Germany, France, Italy and Belgium). Then, added to this latter are the countries that while having a high weight of the government budget on the economy, have nevertheless experienced good paces of growth and low unemployment (Sweden, Denmark, Austria). An exception to the latter is Finland, which shows to have serious problems with unemployment.

For this reason, in the context of the twelve countries of the European Monetary Union, we imagined that the strategy of the triangle of reforms is applied in eight countries (Germany, France, Italy, Belgium, Spain, Portugal, Greece and Finland), both as a single and autonomous strategy of national economic policy and in the event of a coordinated and simultaneous application in all of the countries. In fact, in the other countries (Ireland, Holland and Austria), the rate of unemployment is structurally low, thus linking them to a rate of growth very near their maximum potential.[1] For these same three countries, however, we wanted to measure the possible effect that would be produced as a result of the measures effected by the other eight partners of the Monetary Union.

For each economic system, we addressed five different scenarios.[2]

A first scenario, which we define as *inertial*, represents the evolution of an economic system in absence of any of economic policy intervention whatsoever, taking as a given a framework of international variables. This thus represents the point of reference on the basis of which the effects of different economic policies are measured.[3]

A second scenario refers to the instituting of the economic policy strategy described on the part of each individual country on its own, without the other countries' putting in place any type of economic policy measure.

---

[1] In this context, Luxemburg is not explicitly considered, given is small size.

[2] In this context, we do not consider the possible combinations of the various interventions, in order to avoid weighing down the analysis. In doing so, however, we do not wish to omit these from the list of possible strategies.

[3] The "inertial" simulation, which represents the reference point of our analysis, is obtained from the "base" prepared by Oxford Economic Forecasting for the month of January 2002.

A third scenario measures the effect of this same strategy also being implemented on the part of all of the other countries.

A fourth scenario, which we've called "free-riding", then hypothesizes that a country does not effect any economic policy measure, trusting in the realization of structural reforms in all of the other countries and counting that the positive impact from outside its economy can resolve its own internal problems.

Finally, a fifth scenario combines the same fiscal interventions with an expansionary monetary policy. In other words it put together a reduction in fiscal pressure with an easier access to the credit market, while enhancing, by this end, private investments and consumption.

In Baldassarri et al (1996), the authors studied a similar measure for just the Italian economy, showing how this is effective and guarantees particularly positive performances in terms of growth and employment. In terms of the European Monetary Union, the issue is however more complex, in that structural differences exist among the countries, and nothing implies that similar interventions would generate the same effects in the various countries.

Notwithstanding that and within the limits of possibility, we've defined a measure that's similar for all of the countries.

On the government revenues front, the OEF model specifies up to 5 typologies of revenues for each country, corresponding to taxes on individuals, businesses, on value added, social security payments by employers, and additional taxes paid by the workforce.[4] In our simulation, we tested a gradual reduction of fiscal pressure equal to the value of one percentage point of GDP per year, and we distributed this reduction among all the tax categories, except for value added tax.

This decrease in rates is set against a reduction in the items of current government spending.[5] It is important to reiterate here that

---

[4] It needs to be pointed out how the tax contributions system of some countries, such as Portugal, Greece or Ireland for example, is not specified with the same detail that is characteristic of the "bigger" countries; more precisely, tax revenues are represented by a smaller number of items, and thus fewer brackets. In these cases, being aware of the stylisation, we simulated the measure in question on a structure of "reduced" rates.

[5] We also must emphasize that the intervention we propose in these pages implies a reduction in fiscal pressure for all of the economic actors, families and businesses.

the hypothesized measure is in budget balance ex-ante. It is then evident that the greater growth that would be produced would generate greater proceeds that could be used, ex-post, either for additional fiscal reductions or for additional stimulus for investment.

Furthermore, constraints that limit growth emerge in absence of measures on the supply side, because the boost in demand generates inflationary pressures. In the context of the model, the pressure on the productive sectors would translate into an increase in production capacity: it would thus force the countries of the European Monetary Union to grow "too quickly," without guaranteeing the productive structure the time needed to adjust to the greater demand. In fact, the acceleration in prices would lead to a squeeze on economic growth in the medium to long term, and through the corresponding growth in wages, to again increasing unemployment within the European Monetary Union. A measure that is limited to decreasing revenues and spending generates inflationary tensions, even though reducing the cost of production factors mitigates its impact. For this reason, we need to "close the triangle," hypothesizing that a series of reforms of the labor market are also effected to increase flexibility. As emphasized in the OECD Report on Regulatory Reforms (1997), the reform of regulations within government services and/or within commercial distribution can guarantee, in the medium to long term, an average increase in GDP of between 3 and 6 percent. The theoretical bases of such an argument are quite clear: the greater efficiency of services and regulation of the government sector guarantees a better functioning of the goods market as well as the financial markets, thus improving the productivity of the factors employed and the efficiency of the entire economic system.[6] Technically speaking, in the model we represent this effect as the possibility to increase the degree of production capacity used, without generating inflationary tensions.

---

[6] The concept of efficiency of the financial markets has been the subject of wide economic research: within this extensive literature, it is interesting to look at the seminal paper by Fama (1970).

8.2 Growth and Full Employment: the "Do-It-Yourself" Model.

Here we present the results obtained in the case of the economic policy strategy indicated in the preceding section, implemented individually in every country under the hypothesis that all the other countries continue only along the inertial trend.

In summary, the strategy proposed appears capable of producing the desired effects: more growth, full employment, solid and permanent financial equilibriums. Clearly the different realities of the national economies, just by common sense looking at the results obtained, lead to a measurement of the extent of the obtainable positive effects in the different countries in a sufficiently articulated way.

As can be seen from the comparison of the individual national situations presented in the following, the effects of what we have called the triangle of reforms seem substantial for Germany, France, Italy and Finland, and much more moderate for Spain, Portugal and Belgium. However, the measure does not appear to produce significant effects for Greece.

Given the different conditions of the individual countries, it seems moreover to confirm our intuition about a *non-linearity* of the effects of the measures described previously. In fact, the countries characterized by a high weight of the government sector show important improvements, while the extent of the effects are markedly reduced in the economies that already have a low weight of the government budget within its own economic system. Evidence thus seems to arise that leads to indicate there's a sort of capacity ceiling for the size of the government sector in the economy in which an intervention in the management of its resources can produce positive effects on growth and employment. Moreover, above that threshold the effects reverse, and the weight of the State on the economy becomes excessive in the sense that it hinders both growth and the possibilities for employment.

Also for this reason, it seems appropriate to proceed with a country-by-country analysis aimed at verifying if an economic policy such as the one indicated, decided at a national level and adopted only by that single country, is capable of producing an acceleration in growth and a steady lowering of unemployment. In other words, we're testing the existing room for individual national governments to pursue the goal of a full utilization of the country's production potential via an appropriate economic policy in order to achieve full employment, while abiding by the processes of European integration and respecting the mutual Pacts.

In essence, it's a question of measuring which spaces exist for the "do-it-yourself" model of national economic policies.

8.2.1 Germany

The baseline simulation of the German economy presents a scenario characterized by a very low rate of GDP growth (0.5 percent in 2001 and 2002), price inflation that falls around an average of 2 percent, and an unemployment rate that falls slowly to about 8 percent in 2006. As far as government finance is concerned, it's expected there will be a sizeable deficit markedly above 1% even in 2006.

The application of a triangle of reforms pushes the rate of GDP growth above 3 percent, the increase in prices is fully under control, and the rate of unemployment goes from 10 percent to 5 percent in five years. The condition of net indebtedness improves noticeably with respect to the inertial trend: zero deficit is reached in 2005 (Figure 8.1-8.4).

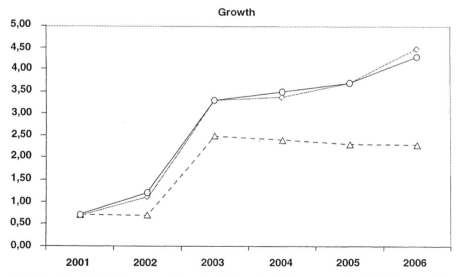

The darker line (with balls) represents the *Fiscal Policy Coordination* case, while the lighter one (with rhombs) denotes the impact of the *"Do it Yourself"* model. The dashed line represents the baseline simulation. Source: Authors' Simulation with Oxford Economic Model (release 2.0)

Figure 8.1 Triangle of Reforms in Germany: GDP Growth Rate

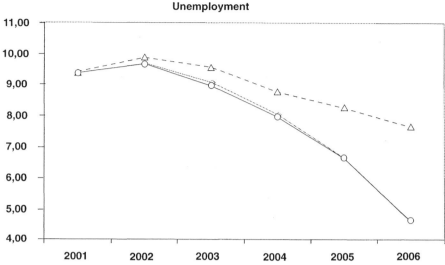

The darker line (with balls) represents the *Fiscal Policy Coordination* case, while the lighter one (with rhombs) denotes the impact of the *"Do it Yourself"* model. The dashed line represents the baseline simulation. Source: Authors' Simulation with Oxford Economic Model (release 2.0)

Figure 8.2 Triangle of Reforms in Germany: Unemployment Rate

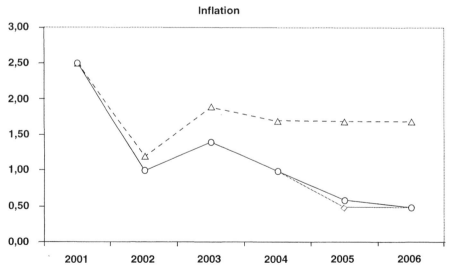

The darker line (with balls) represents the *Fiscal Policy Coordination* case, while the lighter one (with rhombs) denotes the impact of the *"Do it Yourself"* model. The dashed line represents the baseline simulation. Source: Authors' Simulation with Oxford Economic Model (release 2.0)

Figure 8.3 Triangle of Reforms in Germany: Inflation Rate

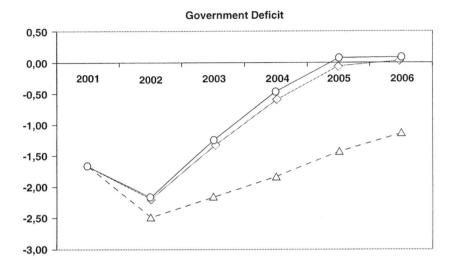

The darker line (with balls) represents the *Fiscal Policy Coordination* case, while the lighter one (with rhombs) denotes the impact of the *"Do it Yourself"* model. The dashed line represents the baseline simulation. Source: Authors' Simulation with Oxford Economic Model (release 2.0)

Figure 8.4 Triangle of Reforms in Germany: Government Deficit

8.2.2 France

The inertial scenario for the French economy is characterized by an average rate of growth of 2.5 percent per year, a steady rate of growth in prices, an unemployment rate above 8 percent, and by non-compliance with the Stability Pact, as evidenced by indebtedness of about 1% still in 2006.

The positive impact of the measures manifests itself in a rate of GDP growth that stabilizes around 3.5%, a slowing in inflation and a rate of unemployment that falls below 4.5%. Also in the simulation, the budget deficit is eliminated in 2003 in accordance with the Stability Pact and maintains a level near zero in the years afterward as well.

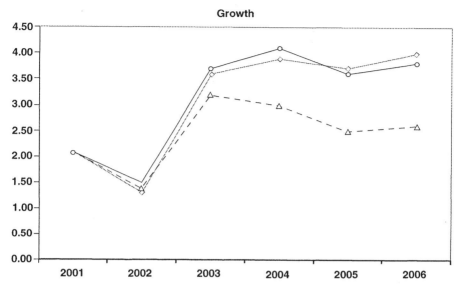

The darker line (with balls) represents the *Fiscal Policy Coordination* case, while the lighter one (with rhombs) denotes the impact of the *"Do it Yourself"* model. The dashed line represents the baseline simulation. Source: Authors' Simulation with Oxford Economic Model (release 2.0)

Figure 8.5 Triangle of Reforms in France: GDP Growth Rate

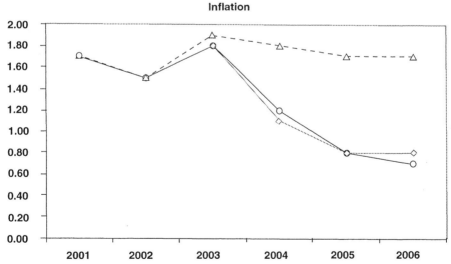

The darker line (with balls) represents the *Fiscal Policy Coordination* case, while the lighter one (with rhombs) denotes the impact of the *"Do it Yourself"* model. The dashed line represents the baseline simulation. Source: Authors' Simulation with Oxford Economic Model (release 2.0)

Figure 8.6 Triangle of Reforms in France: Inflation Rate

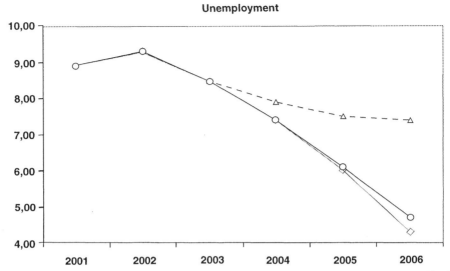

The darker line (with balls) represents the *Fiscal Policy Coordination* case, while the lighter one (with rhombs) denotes the impact of the *"Do it Yourself"* model. The dashed line represents the baseline simulation. Source: Authors' Simulation with Oxford Economic Model (release 2.0)

Figure 8.7 Triangle of Reforms in France: Unemployment Rate

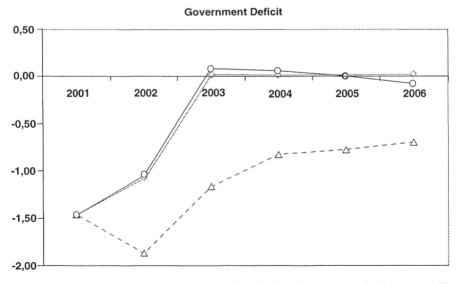

The darker line (with balls) represents the *Fiscal Policy Coordination* case, while the lighter one (with rhombs) denotes the impact of the *"Do it Yourself"* model. The dashed line represents the baseline simulation. Source: Authors' Simulation with Oxford Economic Model (release 2.0)

Figure 8.8 Triangle of Reforms in France: Government Deficit (% GDP)

8.2.3 Italy

The results obtained for Italy confirm those obtained in Baldassarri et al. (1999), despite that at the time of that study, a different econometric model was being used. The average annual rate of growth goes from the 2.5 trend rate to 3.5 percent. Inflation is significantly reduced, and unemployment falls from 10 to about 4 percent. The state of indebtedness, which in the inertial trend does not respect the Stability Pact, falls back in line with the goal of zero deficit.

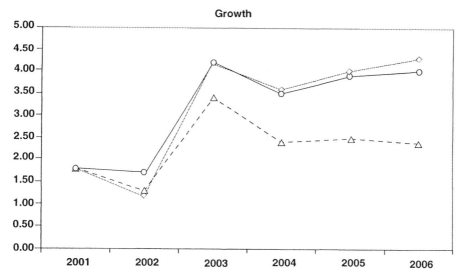

The darker line (with balls) represents the *Fiscal Policy Coordination* case, while the lighter one (with rhombs) denotes the impact of the *"Do it Yourself"* model. The dashed line represents the baseline simulation. Source: Authors' Simulation with Oxford Economic Model (release 2.0)

Figure 8.9 Triangle of Reforms in Italy: GDP Growth Rate

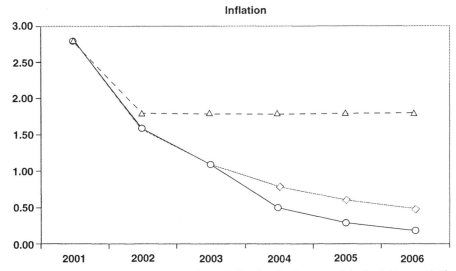

The darker line (with balls) represents the *Fiscal Policy Coordination* case, while the lighter one (with rhombs) denotes the impact of the *"Do it Yourself"* model. The dashed line represents the baseline simulation. Source: Authors' Simulation with Oxford Economic Model (release 2.0)

Figure 8.10 Triangle of Reforms in Italy: Inflation Rate

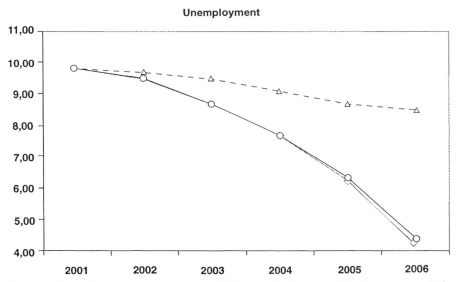

The darker line (with balls) represents the *Fiscal Policy Coordination* case, while the lighter one (with rhombs) denotes the impact of the *"Do it Yourself"* model. The dashed line represents the baseline simulation. Source: Authors' Simulation with Oxford Economic Model (release 2.0)

Figure 8.11 Triangle of Reforms in Italy: Unemployment Rate

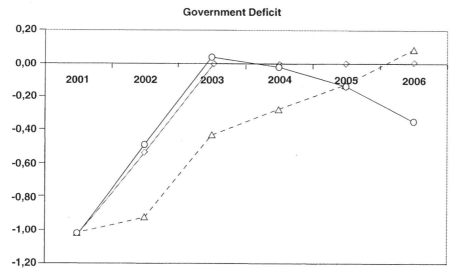

The darker line (with balls) represents the *Fiscal Policy Coordination* case, while the lighter one (with rhombs) denotes the impact of the *"Do it Yourself"* model. The dashed line represents the baseline simulation. Source: Authors' Simulation with Oxford Economic Model (release 2.0)

Figure 8.12 Triangle of Reforms in Italy: Government Deficit (% GDP)

8.2.4 Belgium

In Belgium, in contrast to France, Germany and Italy, there is a budget surplus, albeit of small proportions. Therefore, we reformulated the ensemble of measures in such a way that would reduce government spending by a smaller amount, using the budget surplus for additional spending cuts to guarantee the resources necessary for a reduction in fiscal pressure.[7]

The inertial trend for the Belgian economy indicates an average GDP growth rate of 2% per year, stable inflation of about 2% per year and an unemployment rate that declines toward 10 percent in 2006.

The impact of the economic policy interventions, contrary to what is seen in the other countries, does not seem appreciable. Growth is not triggered, unemployment does not decline, while indebtedness begins to climb again. It must be pointed out, however, that this unsatisfying result could in part depend on a certain limitation in the econometric

---

[7] As for the measures regarding revenues, the interventions are limited to taxes on individuals, businesses and on the level of welfare contributions paid by employers, since the contributions on the part of the workforce are not specified in the model.

fact, in that model a specific variable for welfare contributions is not accounted for. This variable is particularly important in that its reduction acts directly upon the cost of labor, thus activating a greater supply of jobs.

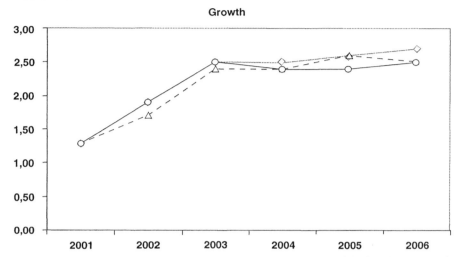

The darker line (with balls) represents the *Fiscal Policy Coordination* case, while the lighter one (with rhombs) denotes the impact of the "*Do it Yourself*" model. The dashed line represents the baseline simulation. Source: Authors' Simulation with Oxford Economic Model (release 2.0)

Figure 8.13 Triangle of Reforms in Belgium: GDP Growth Rate

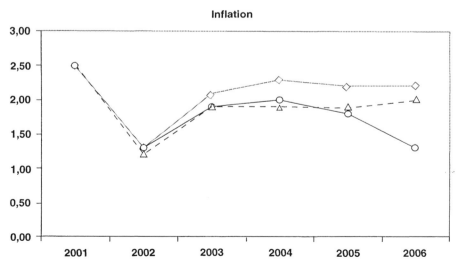

The darker line (with balls) represents the *Fiscal Policy Coordination* case, while the lighter one (with rhombs) denotes the impact of the "*Do it Yourself*" model. The dashed line represents the baseline simulation. Source: Authors' Simulation with Oxford Economic Model (release 2.0)

Figure 8.14 Triangle of Reforms in Belgium: Inflation Rate

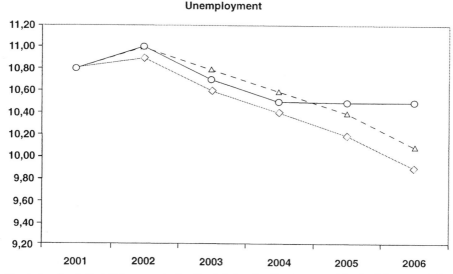

The darker line (with balls) represents the *Fiscal Policy Coordination* case, while the lighter one (with rhombs) denotes the impact of the *"Do it Yourself"* model. The dashed line represents the baseline simulation. Source: Authors' Simulation with Oxford Economic Model (release 2.0)

Figure 8.15 Triangle of Reforms in Belgium: Unemployment Rate

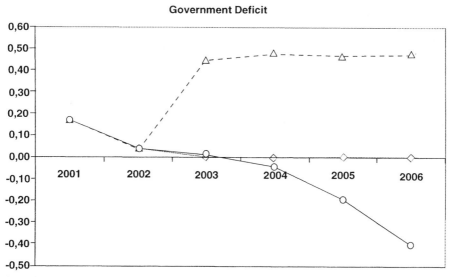

The darker line (with balls) represents the *Fiscal Policy Coordination* case, while the lighter one (with rhombs) denotes the impact of the *"Do it Yourself"* model. The dashed line represents the baseline simulation. Source: Authors' Simulation with Oxford Economic Model (release 2.0)

Figure 8.16 Triangle of Reforms in Belgium: Government Deficit (% GDP)

8.2.5 Spain

The normal outlook for the Spanish economy is characterized by an average annual rate of GDP growth of 3% and inflation of 2%. The rate of unemployment falls to 12% in 5 years, while the budget deficit is estimated to grow until it reaches 0.8% of GDP in 2006.

The application of the economic policy measures described beforehand shows improvements on the standpoint of GDP growth (which surpasses the level of 4 percent), and, as for government finance, the deficit trend is reversed and is eliminated in a short time, generating a small surplus for all the following years. In this scenario, however, unemployment is not reabsorbed in a reasonable timeframe and in sufficient quantities, as can be seen from an unemployment rate that registers at 11% in the last year of the simulation.

Growth

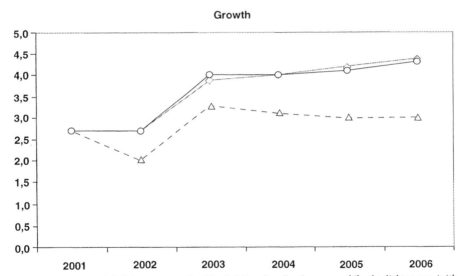

The darker line (with balls) represents the *Fiscal Policy Coordination* case, while the lighter one (with rhombs) denotes the impact of the *"Do it Yourself"* model. The dashed line represents the baseline simulation. Source: Authors' Simulation with Oxford Economic Model (release 2.0)

Figure 8.17 Triangle of Reforms in Spain: GDP Growth Rate

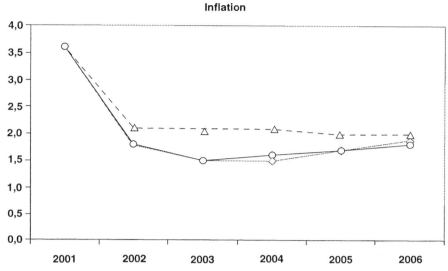

The darker line (with balls) represents the *Fiscal Policy Coordination* case, while the lighter one (with rhombs) denotes the impact of the *"Do it Yourself"* model. The dashed line represents the baseline simulation. Source: Authors' Simulation with Oxford Economic Model (release 2.0)

Figure 8.18 Triangle of Reforms in Spain: Inflation Rate

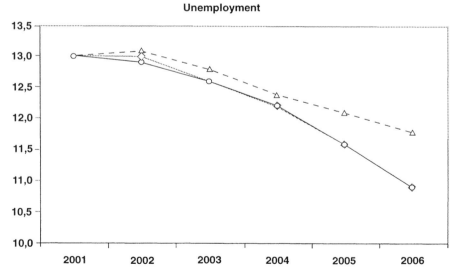

The darker line (with balls) represents the *Fiscal Policy Coordination* case, while the lighter one (with rhombs) denotes the impact of the *"Do it Yourself"* model. The dashed line represents the baseline simulation. Source: Authors' Simulation with Oxford Economic Model (release 2.0))

Figure 8.19 Triangle of Reforms in Spain: Unemployment Rate

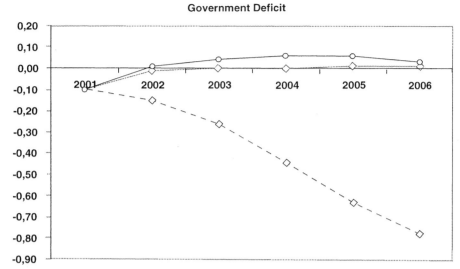

The darker line (with balls) represents the *Fiscal Policy Coordination* case, while the lighter one (with rhombs) denotes the impact of the *"Do it Yourself"* model. The dashed line represents the baseline simulation. Source: Authors' Simulation with Oxford Economic Model (release 2.0)

Figure 8.20 Triangle of Reforms in Spain: Government Deficit (% GDP)

8.2.6 Portugal

After two years marked by a rate of growth of approximately 2%, the inertial simulation for Portugal shows an increase in growth to a level of about 3%. At the same time, the unemployment rate remains below 4%. Finally, inflation lodges at 2%, and the budget deficit falls toward 1% in 2006. In these conditions, the effects of our mix of economic policies are practically negligible, as we can see from the following figure.

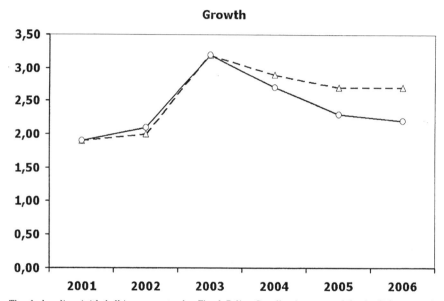

The darker line (with balls) represents the *Fiscal Policy Coordination* case, while the lighter one (with rhombs) denotes the impact of the *"Do it Yourself"* model. The dashed line represents the baseline simulation. Source: Authors' Simulation with Oxford Economic Model (release 2.0)

Figure 8.21 Triangle of Reforms in Portugal: GDP Growth Rate

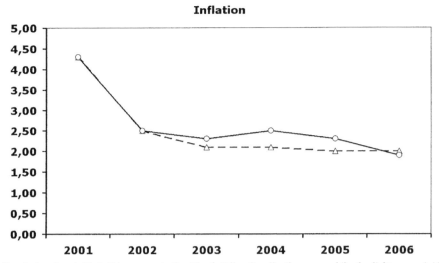

The darker line (with balls) represents the *Fiscal Policy Coordination* case, while the lighter one (with rhombs) denotes the impact of the "*Do it Yourself*" model. The dashed line represents the baseline simulation. Source: Authors' Simulation with Oxford Economic Model (release 2.0)

Figure 8.22 Triangle of Reforms in Portugal: Inflation

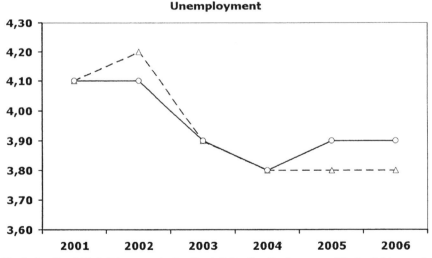

The darker line (with balls) represents the *Fiscal Policy Coordination* case, while the lighter one (with rhombs) denotes the impact of the "*Do it Yourself*" model. The dashed line represents the baseline simulation. Source: Authors' Simulation with Oxford Economic Model (release 2.0)

Figure 8.23 Triangle of Reforms in Portugal: Unemployment

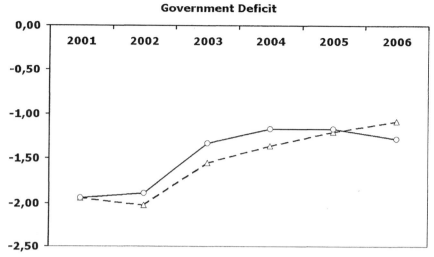

The darker line (with balls) represents the *Fiscal Policy Coordination* case, while the lighter one (with rhombs) denotes the impact of the *"Do it Yourself"* model. The dashed line represents the baseline simulation. Source: Authors' Simulation with Oxford Economic Model (release 2.0)

Figure 8.24 Triangle of Reforms in Portugal: Government Deficit (% GDP)

8.2.7 Greece

The analysis of the principal real and financial aspects characterizing the baseline simulation for the Greek economy presents mixed results: on one hand, the country shows a high rate of GDP growth (an average annual rate of about 3.5%), inflation stabilizes around 2.5% per year and, on the other hand, there's a high rate of unemployment, rooted at about 12%. Lastly, as regards government finance, the deficit is eliminated in 2004 and remains above this value for the following years.

The response to the mix of economic policies differs from that seen in Italy, France, Germany. Similarly to what was seen for Spain and Portugal, the Greek economy draws only a small advantage from enacting the mix of economic policies. The impact of the interventions on the rate of GDP growth and the effects on the rate of unemployment and inflation reflect the trend in the growth rate itself. The reduction in the cost of labor allows a rebound, though modest, in employment.

Growth

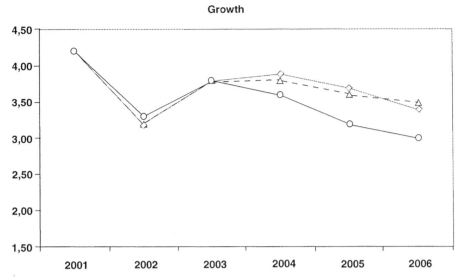

The darker line (with balls) represents the *Fiscal Policy Coordination* case, while the lighter one (with rhombs) denotes the impact of the *"Do it Yourself"* model. The dashed line represents the baseline simulation. Source: Authors' Simulation with Oxford Economic Model (release 2.0)

Figure 8.25 Triangle of Reforms in Greece: GDP Growth Rate

Inflation

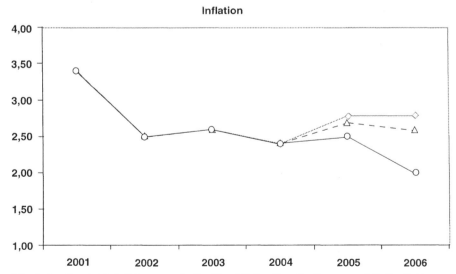

The darker line (with balls) represents the *Fiscal Policy Coordination* case, while the lighter one (with rhombs) denotes the impact of the *"Do it Yourself"* model. The dashed line represents the baseline simulation. Source: Authors' Simulation with Oxford Economic Model (release 2.0)

Figure 8.26 Triangle of Reforms in Greece: Inflation Rate

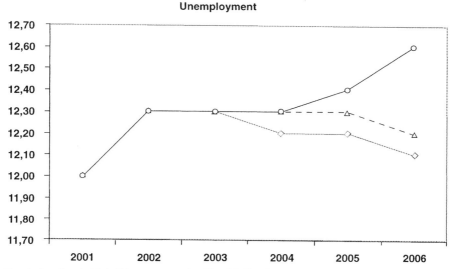

The darker line (with balls) represents the *Fiscal Policy Coordination* case, while the lighter one (with rhombs) denotes the impact of the *"Do it Yourself"* model. The dashed line represents the baseline simulation. Source: Authors' Simulation with Oxford Economic Model (release 2.0)

Figure 8.27 Triangle of Reforms in Greece: Unemployment Rate

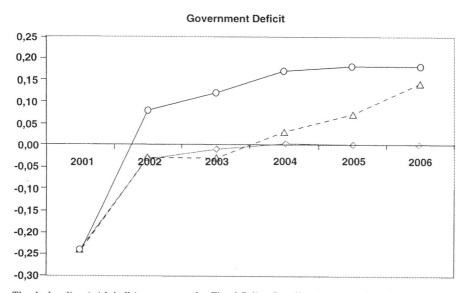

The darker line (with balls) represents the *Fiscal Policy Coordination* case, while the lighter one (with rhombs) denotes the impact of the *"Do it Yourself"* model. The dashed line represents the baseline simulation. Source: Authors' Simulation with Oxford Economic Model (release 2.0)

Figure 8.28 Triangle of Reforms in Greece: Government Deficit (% GDP)

8.2.8 Finland

The Finnish economy offers a positive inertial-trend picture, characterized by a good rate of GDP growth (average 2.5% per year), a contained growth in price levels and a budget surplus of about 5 percent of GDP. Compared with this, however, an average unemployment rate of about 9% persists.

Given the circumstances of a budget surplus, it was not necessary for us to account for containments from the standpoint of government spending. Therefore, in this case we limited the interventions to reducing fiscal pressure and instituting measures on the supply side. The rate of growth reaches and surpasses 4%, the inflationary situation remains largely unchanged and unemployment falls to 6.5% in 2006. Financial balance is maintained with a surplus that registers at about 1% in the final year of the simulation.

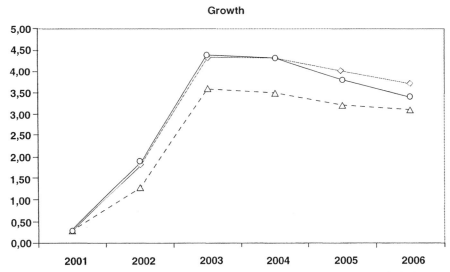

The darker line (with balls) represents the *Fiscal Policy Coordination* case, while the lighter one (with rhombs) denotes the impact of the *"Do it Yourself"* model. The dashed line represents the baseline simulation. Source: Authors' Simulation with Oxford Economic Model (release 2.0).

Figure 8.29 Triangle of Reforms in Finland: GDP Growth Rate

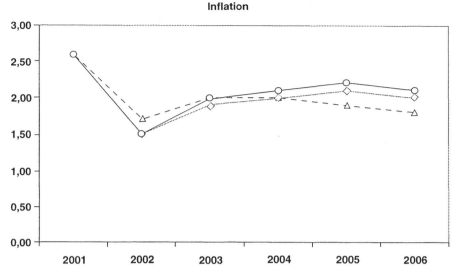

The darker line (with balls) represents the *Fiscal Policy Coordination* case, while the lighter one (with rhombs) denotes the impact of the *"Do it Yourself"* model. The dashed line represents the baseline simulation. Source: Authors' Simulation with Oxford Economic Model (release 2.0).

Figure 8.30 Triangle of Reforms in Finland: Inflation Rate

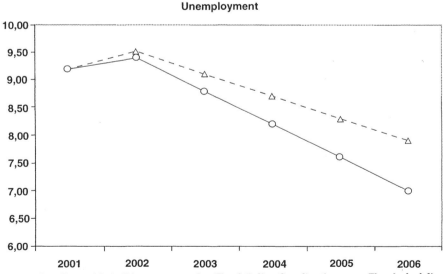

The darker line (with balls) represents the *Fiscal Policy Coordination* case. The dashed line represents the baseline simulation. Source: Authors' Simulation with Oxford Economic Model (release 2.0).

Figure 8.31 Triangle of Reforms in Finland: Unemployment Rate

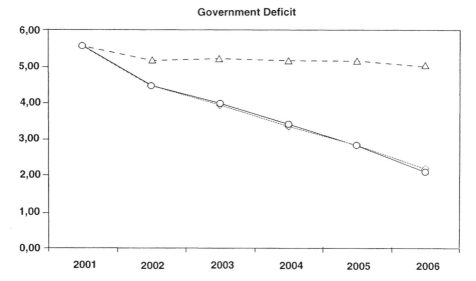

The darker line (with balls) represents the *Fiscal Policy Coordination* case, while the lighter one (with rhombs) denotes the impact of the *"Do it Yourself"* model. The dashed line represents the baseline simulation. Source: Authors' Simulation with Oxford Economic Model (release 2.0).

Figure 8.32 Triangle of Reforms in Finland: Government Deficit (% GDP)

8.3 Better Off Alone and in Bad Company... Or in Good Company?

8.3.1 The Impact on Countries Implementing Our Policy Strategy.

We've therefore addressed the effects of applying the triangle of reforms in different European countries under the hypothesis that this strategy of economic policy is adopted individually in a single country and not by all of the others.

Meanwhile, in this section we record the results obtained in the instance that the measure is adopted simultaneously in all of the countries. We thus intend to verify if positive synergies exist among the various countries that would be able to reinforce and improve the obtainable results of each single national state individually.

As such, we ask ourselves the question if it's better to act alone even if the others let themselves be guided by inertia (alone and in poor company) or if it's not better to produce a common and coordinated effort (which is to say, in good company).

Still referring to the individual countries' graphs presented in the previous section, here we show the trend of the different economies expressed in a coordinated hypothesis (indicated with the darker line, with triangles).

In general, it's shown that the effect of a concurrent application of this specific economic policy in all of the countries is almost negligible. And this result shouldn't be surprising. The economic policy strategy in case aims to relaunch internal demand and to regain levels of competitiveness. The first action, besides making the individual national economic system grow internally, can also certainly result in giving the other countries an impetus toward growth. However, the second action, in creating greater competitiveness in that single country, tends to counterbalance the positive effect that could be produced for the other countries, that by following their inertial trend would see a relative loss of competitiveness. In addition, the country's gain in competitiveness with respect to other European countries is obviously reinforced by the gain it would have in the rest of the world.

Therefore, when all of the countries simultaneously effect the measure, the spur in demand would be reciprocal and the gain in competitiveness would be nearly canceled out in the countries undertaking the measure. Thus the competitive gain would only be in respect to the rest of the world, one that nonetheless would be obtained in the case of a measure effected just in a single country as well.

Surely, given the integration process among the European countries, it is better to be in good company, rather than in poor company. But it is even more certain that the responsibility for the decisions should be assumed individually. This condition seems moreover to be in line with Europe's actual institutional structures, which assign the ECB the sole responsibility for monetary policy, but leave the individual national governments with the responsibility for budget policy. It is true that the latter is bound in terms of financial balances by the Stability Pact, but it is just as true that the levels and compositions of the government budget completely fall within the responsibility of the national governments.

8.3.2 The effect of measures taken elsewhere on countries that don't need to institute them: Ireland, Netherlands and Austria

A consideration of the effects produced when applying this economic policy to the other three countries participating in the Euro (Ireland, Holland and Austria) can be added to the conclusions regarding the eight countries mentioned beforehand. In other words, Netherlands do not implement any fiscal policy in this exercise. Hence, the Fiscal Policy Coordination represents the externality generate in Netherlands by the fiscal intervention undertaken by other countries (see previous section)

As can be seen from the following figures, their inertial trend would not be changed by the effects of the economic policies' possibly being implemented in the other countries.

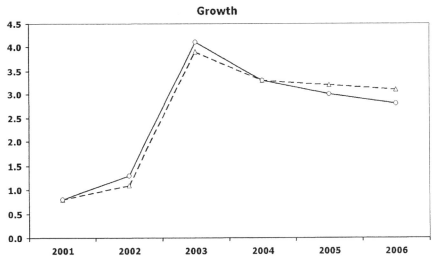

The darker line (with balls) represents the *Fiscal Policy Coordination* case. The dashed line represents the baseline simulation. Source: Authors' Simulation with Oxford Economic Model (release 2.0).

Figure 8.33 Triangle of Reforms in Netherlands: GDP Growth

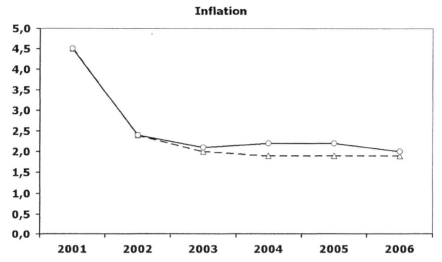

The darker line (with balls) represents the *Fiscal Policy Coordination* case. The dashed line represents the baseline simulation. Source: Authors' Simulation with Oxford Economic Model (release 2.0).

Figure 8.34 Triangle of Reforms in Netherlands: Inflation Rate

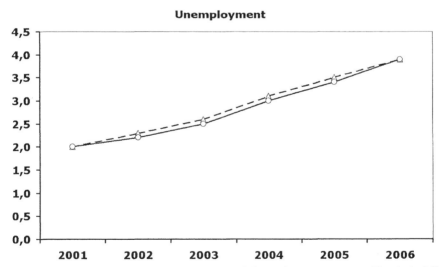

The darker line (with balls) represents the *Fiscal Policy Coordination* case. The dashed line represents the baseline simulation. Source: Authors' Simulation with Oxford Economic Model (release 2.0).

Figure 8.35 Triangle of Reforms in Netherlands: Unemployment Rate

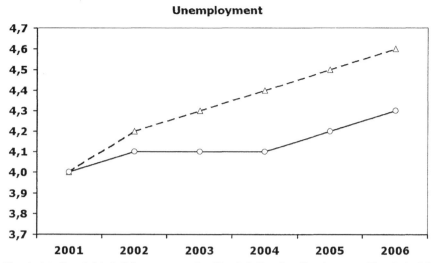

The darker line (with balls) represents the *Fiscal Policy Coordination* case. The dashed line represents the baseline simulation. Source: Authors' Simulation with Oxford Economic Model (release 2.0).

Figure 8.36 Triangle of Reforms in Netherlands: Unemployment Rate

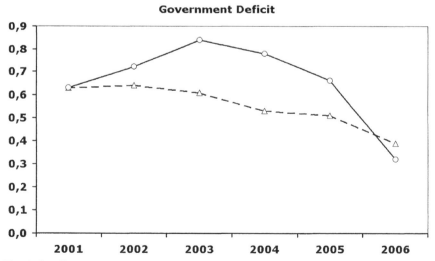

The darker line (with balls) represents the *Fiscal Policy Coordination* case. The dashed line represents the baseline simulation. Source: Authors' Simulation with Oxford Economic Model (release 2.0).

Figure 8.37 Triangle of Reforms in Netherlands: Government Deficit (% GDP)

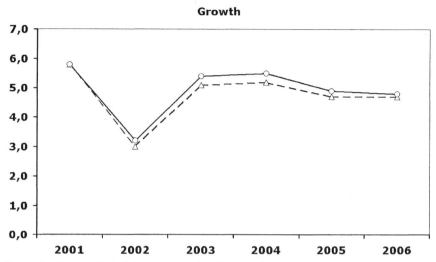

The darker line (with balls) represents the *Fiscal Policy Coordination* case. The dashed line represents the baseline simulation. Source: Authors' Simulation with Oxford Economic Model (release 2.0).

Figure 8.38 Triangle of Reforms in Ireland: GDP Growth Rate

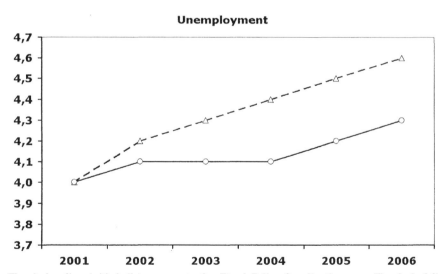

The darker line (with balls) represents the *Fiscal Policy Coordination* case. The dashed line represents the baseline simulation. Source: Authors' Simulation with Oxford Economic Model (release 2.0).

Figure 8.39 Triangle of Reforms in Ireland: Unemployment Rate

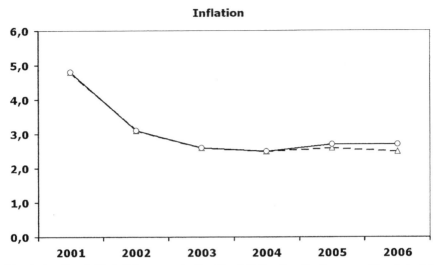

The darker line (with balls) represents the *Fiscal Policy Coordination* case. The dashed line represents the baseline simulation. Source: Authors' Simulation with Oxford Economic Model (release 2.0).

Figure 8.40 Triangle of Reforms in Ireland: Inflation Rate

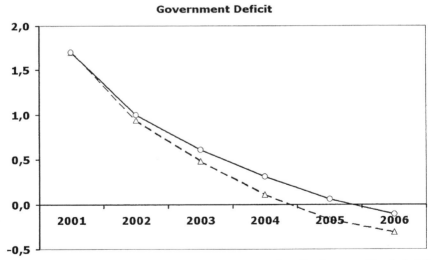

The darker line (with balls) represents the *Fiscal Policy Coordination* case. The dashed line represents the baseline simulation. Source: Authors' Simulation with Oxford Economic Model (release 2.0).

Figure 8.41 Triangle of Reforms in Ireland: Government Deficit (% GDP)

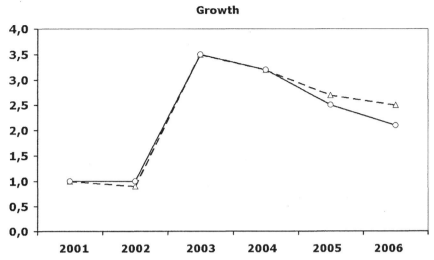

The darker line (with balls) represents the *Fiscal Policy Coordination* case. The dashed line represents the baseline simulation. Source: Authors' Simulation with Oxford Economic Model (release 2.0).

Figure 8.42 Triangle of Reforms in Austria: GDP Growth Rate

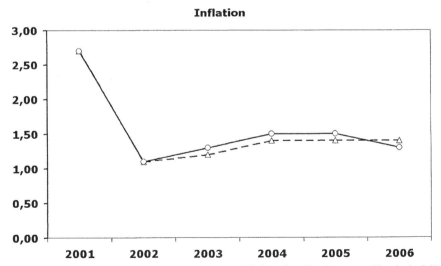

The darker line (with balls) represents the *Fiscal Policy Coordination* case. The dashed line represents the baseline simulation. Source: Authors' Simulation with Oxford Economic Model (release 2.0).

Figure 8.43 Triangle of Reforms in Austria: Inflation Rate

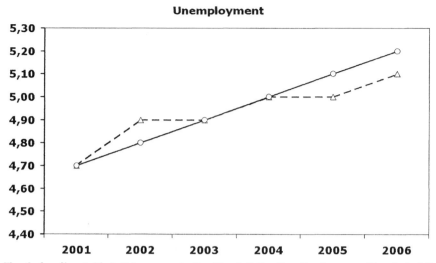

The darker line (with balls) represents the *Fiscal Policy Coordination* case. The dashed line represents the baseline simulation. Source: Authors' Simulation with Oxford Economic Model (release 2.0).

Figure 8.44 Triangle of Reforms in Austria: Unemployment Rate

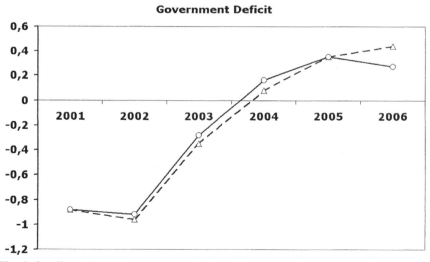

The darker line (with balls) represents the *Fiscal Policy Coordination* case. The dashed line represents the baseline simulation. Source: Authors' Simulation with Oxford Economic Model (release 2.0).

Figure 8.45 Triangle of Reforms in Austria: Government Deficit (% GDP)

In fact, over the last decade these three countries have already shown their autonomous capacity to produce solid rates of growth, low unemployment and budget balance. And thus toward them the aforementioned banal observation can be applied: better off in good company than in poor company. On the other hand, however, in their case those national responsibilities of economic policymaking already seem to have been resolved.

An important message thus seems to emerge for Europe.

Of course the coordination of budget policy can be "politically useful" to deepen the process of institutional integration, but in and of itself it does not appear to produce "additional" important economic results in comparison with those that can be obtained based on rigorous and bold national decision-making.

More than coordination within the European countries, what seems to be much more important for the growth outlook and welfare of the Old Continent is the question of European competitiveness as compared with the rest of the world.

8.4 Lower Spending, Lower Taxes, and ... Lower Interest Rates.

The two policy exercises presented in previous sections focus on the sole fiscal policy. In other words, the possibility of reviving European economy is left, in this analysis, to the governments of individual countries.

As we've already seen previously, this is not the only alternative that policymakers have at their disposal. Indeed, in chapter 6, we studied the impact of expansionary monetary policies on the European economy, and we showed how a reduction in interest rates provides a stimulating boost to the system, though only for a short time. We shouldn't be surprised by this kind of result, however, since the monetary policy interventions do not entail structural changes within the economic system.

At the end of the analysis, however, we did emphasize how an improvement in conditions in the credit market could guarantee an additional impetus for interventions of a structural nature. This is the hypothesis that we will test with this economic policy exercise.

In the preceding pages, we showed that in the context of the European Union, the coordination of fiscal policies does not generate externalities to redistribute among the participants in the economic policy game. To put it another way, there are no significant differences in the patterns of growth generated by fiscal interventions, coordinated or not.

Based on this result, we thus looked to verify if by coupling the structural reforms described beforehand with a more relaxed monetary policy, the macroeconomic scenario can effectively be improved. Technically speaking, we used the case of fiscal coordination for all the EU member countries except Ireland, Spain and Portugal as our basis, and to this we "added" the shock expansionary monetary policy.

The following figures illustrate the impact of the monetary policy on all the countries of the Monetary Union, when added to the triangle of reforms described in the previous sections. It is obvious that the performances of the economic systems improves in terms of both economic growth and employment. The former grows by about 1 percentage point with respect to the case without the easier monetary policy, while the latter reaches levels close to 4 percent, nearly the same value as the structural rate of unemployment. Inflation remains under control, even if in some countries (Portugal and Spain, for example) it tends to grow in the last two years of the simulation.

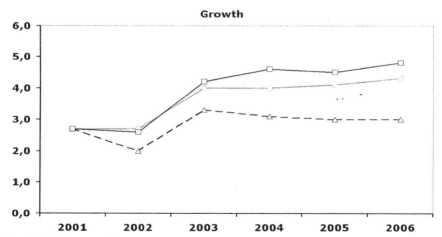

The darker line (with boxes) represents the *Lower Spending, Lower Taxes and Lower Rates Policy*, while the lighter one (with balls) denotes the impact of the same policy fiscal policy, *without* the additional easing of the monetary conditions. The dashed line (with triangles) represents the baseline simulation. Source: Authors' Simulation with Oxford Economic Model (release 2.0)

Figure 8.46 Lower Taxes, Lower Spending, ... and Lower Rates in Spain: GDP Growth Rate

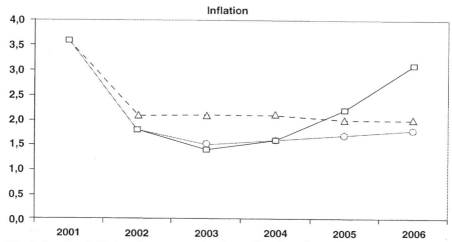

The darker line (with boxes) represents the *Lower Spending, Lower Taxes and Lower Rates Policy*, while the lighter one (with balls) denotes the impact of the same policy fiscal policy, *without* the additional easing of the monetary conditions. The dashed line (with triangles) represents the baseline simulation. Source: Authors' Simulation with Oxford Economic Model (release 2.0)

Figure 8.47 Lower Taxes, Lower Spending, ... and Lower Rates in Spain: Inflation Rate

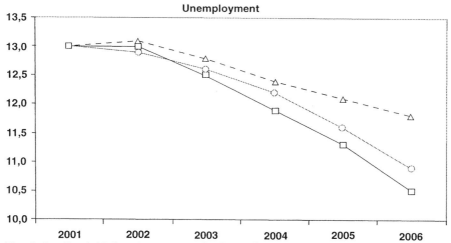

The darker line (with boxes) represents the *Lower Spending, Lower Taxes and Lower Rates Policy*, while the lighter one (with balls) denotes the impact of the same policy fiscal policy, *without* the additional easing of the monetary conditions. The dashed line (with triangles) represents the baseline simulation. Source: Authors' Simulation with Oxford Economic Model (release 2.0)

Figure 8.48 Lower Taxes, Lower Spending, ... and Lower Rates in Spain: Unemployment Rate

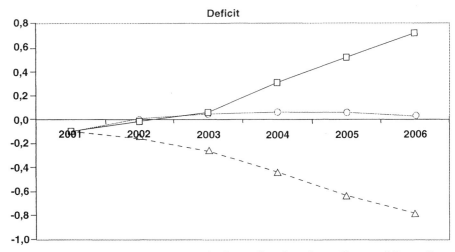

The darker line (with boxes) represents the *Lower Spending, Lower Taxes and Lower Rates Policy,* while the lighter one (with balls) denotes the impact of the same policy fiscal policy, *without* the additional easing of the monetary conditions. The dashed line (with triangles) represents the baseline simulation. Source: Authors' Simulation with Oxford Economic Model (release 2.0)

Figure 8.49 Lower Taxes, Lower Spending, ... and Lower Rates in Spain: Government Deficit (as a % of GDP)

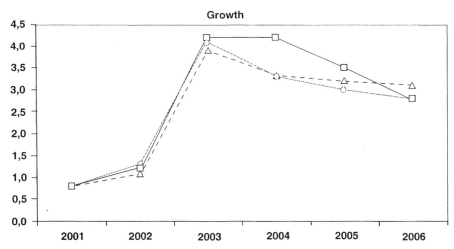

The darker line (with boxes) represents the *Lower Spending, Lower Taxes and Lower Rates Policy,* while the lighter one (with balls) denotes the impact of the same policy fiscal policy, *without* the additional easing of the monetary conditions. The dashed line (with triangles) represents the baseline simulation. Source: Authors' Simulation with Oxford Economic Model (release 2.0)

Figure 8.50 Lower Taxes, Lower Spending, ... and Lower Rates in Portugal: GDP Growth Rate

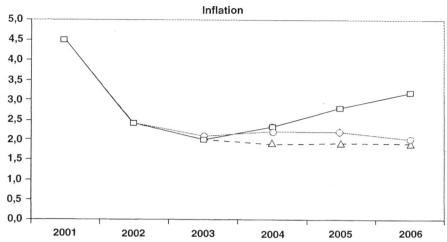

The darker line (with boxes) represents the *Lower Spending, Lower Taxes and Lower Rates Policy,* while the lighter one (with balls) denotes the impact of the same policy fiscal policy, *without* the additional easing of the monetary conditions. The dashed line (with triangles) represents the baseline simulation. Source: Authors' Simulation with Oxford Economic Model (release 2.0)

Figure 8.51 Lower Taxes, Lower Spending, ... and Lower Rates in Portugal: Inflation Rate

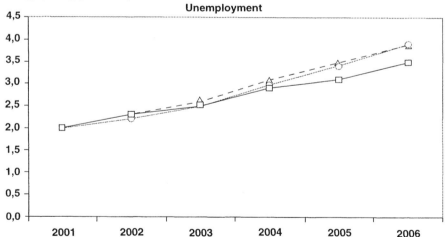

The darker line (with boxes) represents the *Lower Spending, Lower Taxes and Lower Rates Policy,* while the lighter one (with balls) denotes the impact of the same policy fiscal policy, *without* the additional easing of the monetary conditions. The dashed line (with triangles) represents the baseline simulation. Source: Authors' Simulation with Oxford Economic Model (release 2.0)

Figure 8.52 Lower Taxes, Lower Spending, ... and Lower Rates in Portugal: Unemployment Rate

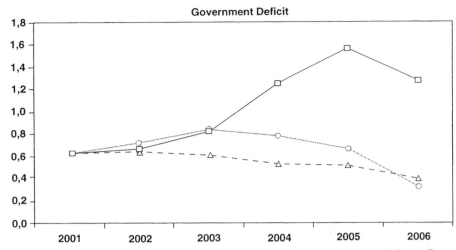

The darker line (with boxes) represents the *Lower Spending, Lower Taxes and Lower Rates Policy*, while the lighter one (with balls) denotes the impact of the same policy fiscal policy, *without* the additional easing of the monetary conditions. The dashed line (with triangles) represents the baseline simulation. Source: Authors' Simulation with Oxford Economic Model (release 2.0)

Figure 8.53 Lower Taxes, Lower Spending, ... and Lower Rates in Portugal: Government Deficit (as a % of GDP)

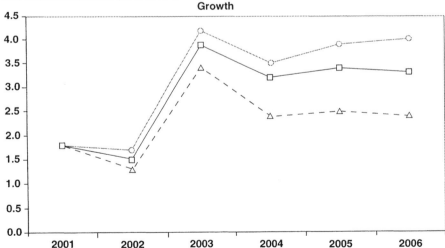

The darker line (with boxes) represents the *Lower Spending, Lower Taxes and Lower Rates Policy*, while the lighter one (with balls) denotes the impact of the same policy fiscal policy, *without* the additional easing of the monetary conditions. The dashed line (with triangles) represents the baseline simulation. Source: Authors' Simulation with Oxford Economic Model (release 2.0)

Figure 8.54 Lower Taxes, Lower Spending, ... and Lower Rates in Italy: GDP Growth Rate

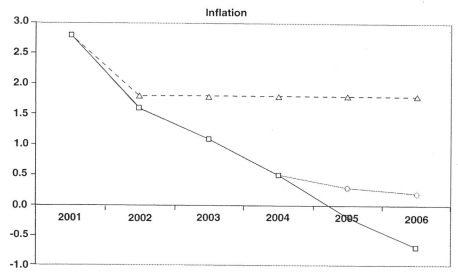

The darker line (with boxes) represents the *Lower Spending, Lower Taxes and Lower Rates Policy*, while the lighter one (with balls) denotes the impact of the same policy fiscal policy, *without* the additional easing of the monetary conditions. The dashed line (with triangles) represents the baseline simulation. Source: Authors' Simulation with Oxford Economic Model (release 2.0)

Figure 8.55 Lower Taxes, Lower Spending, ... and Lower Rates in Italy: Inflation Rate

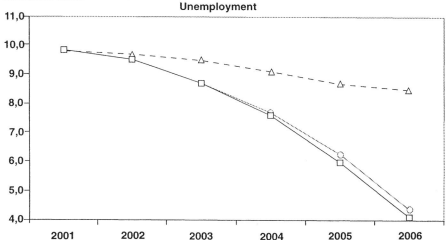

The darker line (with boxes) represents the *Lower Spending, Lower Taxes and Lower Rates Policy*, while the lighter one (with balls) denotes the impact of the same policy fiscal policy, *without* the additional easing of the monetary conditions. The dashed line (with triangles) represents the baseline simulation. Source: Authors' Simulation with Oxford Economic Model (release 2.0)

Figure 8.56 Lower Taxes, Lower Spending, ... and Lower Rates in Italy: Unemployment Rate

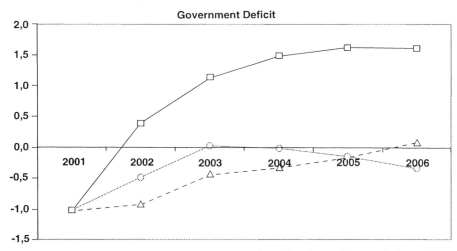

The darker line (with boxes) represents the *Lower Spending, Lower Taxes and Lower Rates Policy*, while the lighter one (with balls) denotes the impact of the same policy fiscal policy, *without* the additional easing of the monetary conditions. The dashed line (with triangles) represents the baseline simulation. Source: Authors' Simulation with Oxford Economic Model (release 2.0)

Figure 8.57 Lower Taxes, Lower Spending, ... and Lower Rates in Italy: Government Deficit (as a % of GDP)

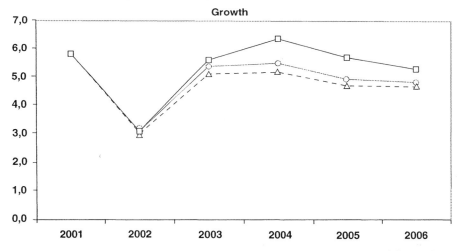

The darker line (with boxes) represents the *Lower Spending, Lower Taxes and Lower Rates Policy*, while the lighter one (with balls) denotes the impact of the same policy fiscal policy, *without* the additional easing of the monetary conditions. The dashed line (with triangles) represents the baseline simulation. Source: Authors' Simulation with Oxford Economic Model (release 2.0)

Figure 8.58 Lower Taxes, Lower Spending, ... and Lower Rates in Ireland: GDP Growth Rate

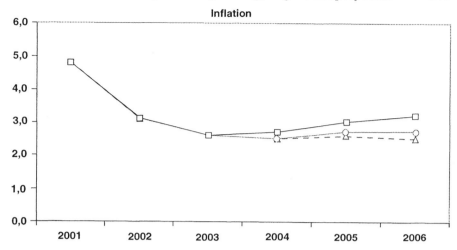

The darker line (with boxes) represents the *Lower Spending, Lower Taxes and Lower Rates Policy*, while the lighter one (with balls) denotes the impact of the same policy fiscal policy, *without* the additional easing of the monetary conditions. The dashed line (with triangles) represents the baseline simulation. Source: Authors' Simulation with Oxford Economic Model (release 2.0)

Figure 8.59 Lower Taxes, Lower Spending, ... and Lower Rates in Ireland: Inflation Rate

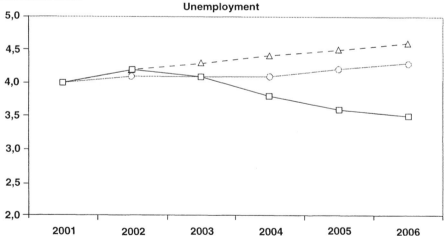

The darker line (with boxes) represents the *Lower Spending, Lower Taxes and Lower Rates Policy*, while the lighter one (with balls) denotes the impact of the same policy fiscal policy, *without* the additional easing of the monetary conditions. The dashed line (with triangles) represents the baseline simulation. Source: Authors' Simulation with Oxford Economic Model (release 2.0)

Figure 8.60 Lower Taxes, Lower Spending, ... and Lower Rates in Ireland: Unemployment Rate

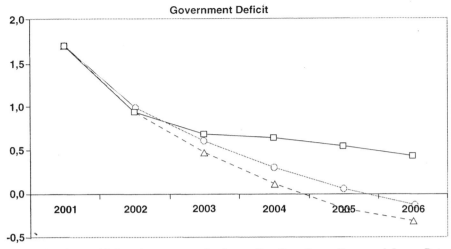

The darker line (with boxes) represents the *Lower Spending, Lower Taxes and Lower Rates Policy,* while the lighter one (with balls) denotes the impact of the same policy fiscal policy, *without* the additional easing of the monetary conditions. The dashed line (with triangles) represents the baseline simulation. Source: Authors' Simulation with Oxford Economic Model (release 2.0)

Figure 8.61 Lower Taxes, Lower Spending, ... and Lower Rates in Ireland: Government Deficit (as a % of GDP)

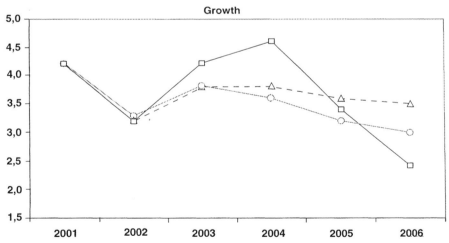

The darker line (with boxes) represents the *Lower Spending, Lower Taxes and Lower Rates Policy,* while the lighter one (with balls) denotes the impact of the same policy fiscal policy, *without* the additional easing of the monetary conditions. The dashed line (with triangles) represents the baseline simulation. Source: Authors' Simulation with Oxford Economic Model (release 2.0)

Figure 8.62 Lower Taxes, Lower Spending, ... and Lower Rates in Greece: GDP Growth Rate

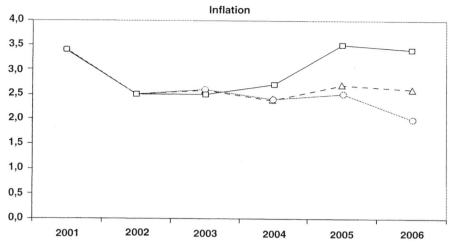

The darker line (with boxes) represents the *Lower Spending, Lower Taxes and Lower Rates Policy*, while the lighter one (with balls) denotes the impact of the same policy fiscal policy, *without* the additional easing of the monetary conditions. The dashed line (with triangles) represents the baseline simulation. Source: Authors' Simulation with Oxford Economic Model (release 2.0)

Figure 8.63 Lower Taxes, Lower Spending, ... and Lower Rates in Greece: Inflation Rate

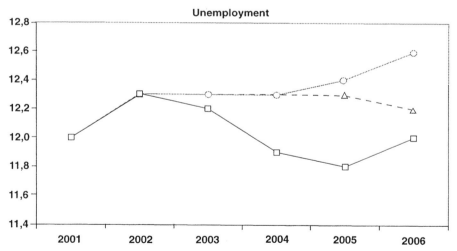

The darker line (with boxes) represents the *Lower Spending, Lower Taxes and Lower Rates Policy*, while the lighter one (with balls) denotes the impact of the same policy fiscal policy, *without* the additional easing of the monetary conditions. The dashed line (with triangles) represents the baseline simulation. Source: Authors' Simulation with Oxford Economic Model (release 2.0)

Figure 8.64 Lower Taxes, Lower Spending, ... and Lower Rates in Greece: Unemployment Rate

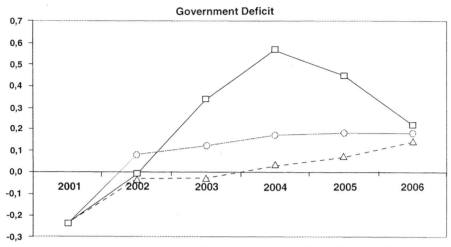

The darker line (with boxes) represents the *Lower Spending, Lower Taxes and Lower Rates Policy*, while the lighter one (with balls) denotes the impact of the same policy fiscal policy, *without* the additional easing of the monetary conditions. The dashed line (with triangles) represents the baseline simulation. Source: Authors' Simulation with Oxford Economic Model (release 2.0)

Figure 8.65 Lower Taxes, Lower Spending, ... and Lower Rates in Greece: Government Deficit (as a % of GDP)

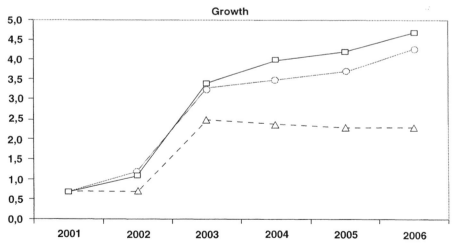

The darker line (with boxes) represents the *Lower Spending, Lower Taxes and Lower Rates Policy*, while the lighter one (with balls) denotes the impact of the same policy fiscal policy, *without* the additional easing of the monetary conditions. The dashed line (with triangles) represents the baseline simulation. Source: Authors' Simulation with Oxford Economic Model (release 2.0)

Figure 8.66 Lower Taxes, Lower Spending, ... and Lower Rates in Germany: GDP Growth Rate

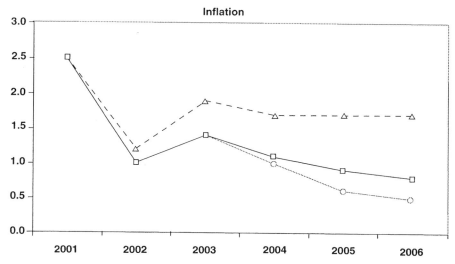

The darker line (with boxes) represents the *Lower Spending, Lower Taxes and Lower Rates Policy*, while the lighter one (with balls) denotes the impact of the same policy fiscal policy, *without* the additional easing of the monetary conditions. The dashed line (with triangles) represents the baseline simulation. Source: Authors' Simulation with Oxford Economic Model (release 2.0)

Figure 8.67 Lower Taxes, Lower Spending, ... and Lower Rates in Germany: Inflation Rate

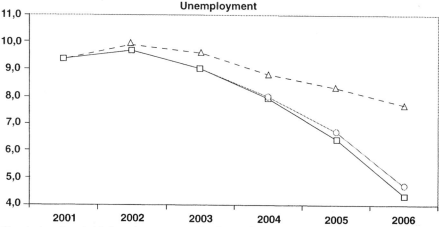

The darker line (with boxes) represents the *Lower Spending, Lower Taxes and Lower Rates Policy*, while the lighter one (with balls) denotes the impact of the same policy fiscal policy, *without* the additional easing of the monetary conditions. The dashed line (with triangles) represents the baseline simulation. Source: Authors' Simulation with Oxford Economic Model (release 2.0)

Figure 8.68 Lower Taxes, Lower Spending, ... and Lower Rates in Germany: Unemployment Rate

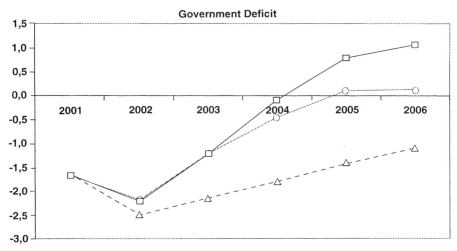

The darker line (with boxes) represents the *Lower Spending, Lower Taxes and Lower Rates Policy*, while the lighter one (with balls) denotes the impact of the same policy fiscal policy, *without* the additional easing of the monetary conditions. The dashed line (with triangles) represents the baseline simulation. Source: Authors' Simulation with Oxford Economic Model (release 2.0)

Figure 8.69 Lower Taxes, Lower Spending, ... and Lower Rates in Germany: Government Deficit (as a % of GDP)

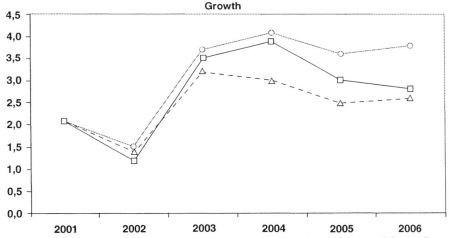

The darker line (with boxes) represents the *Lower Spending, Lower Taxes and Lower Rates Policy*, while the lighter one (with balls) denotes the impact of the same policy fiscal policy, *without* the additional easing of the monetary conditions. The dashed line (with triangles) represents the baseline simulation. Source: Authors' Simulation with Oxford Economic Model (release 2.0)

Figure 8.70 Lower Taxes, Lower Spending, ... and Lower Rates in France: GDP Growth Rate

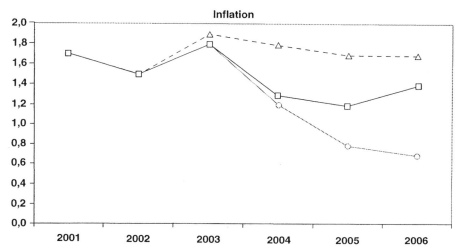

The darker line (with boxes) represents the *Lower Spending, Lower Taxes and Lower Rates Policy*, while the lighter one (with balls) denotes the impact of the same policy fiscal policy, *without* the additional easing of the monetary conditions. The dashed line (with triangles) represents the baseline simulation. Source: Authors' Simulation with Oxford Economic Model (release 2.0)

Figure 8.71 Lower Taxes, Lower Spending, ... and Lower Rates in France: Inflation Rate

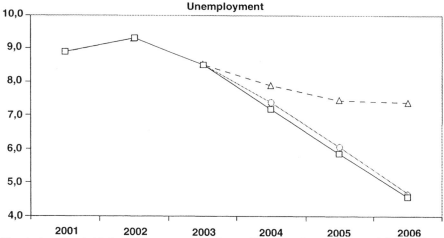

The darker line (with boxes) represents the *Lower Spending, Lower Taxes and Lower Rates Policy*, while the lighter one (with balls) denotes the impact of the same policy fiscal policy, *without* the additional easing of the monetary conditions. The dashed line (with triangles) represents the baseline simulation. Source: Authors' Simulation with Oxford Economic Model (release 2.0)

Figure 8.72 Lower Taxes, Lower Spending, ... and Lower Rates in France: Unemployment Rate

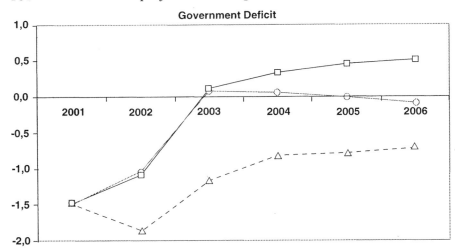

The darker line (with boxes) represents the *Lower Spending, Lower Taxes and Lower Rates Policy*, while the lighter one (with balls) denotes the impact of the same policy fiscal policy, *without* the additional easing of the monetary conditions. The dashed line (with triangles) represents the baseline simulation. Source: Authors' Simulation with Oxford Economic Model (release 2.0)

Figure 8.73 Lower Taxes, Lower Spending, ... and Lower Rates in France: Government Deficit (as a % of GDP)

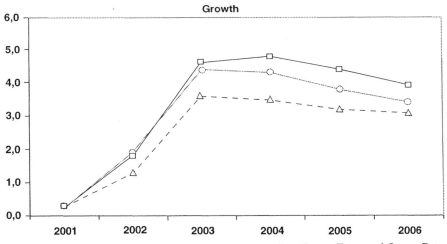

The darker line (with boxes) represents the *Lower Spending, Lower Taxes and Lower Rates Policy*, while the lighter one (with balls) denotes the impact of the same policy fiscal policy, *without* the additional easing of the monetary conditions. The dashed line (with triangles) represents the baseline simulation. Source: Authors' Simulation with Oxford Economic Model (release 2.0)

Figure 8.74 Lower Taxes, Lower Spending, ... and Lower Rates in Finland: GDP Growth Rate

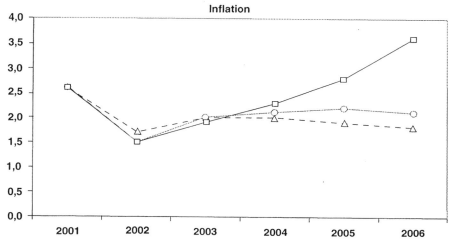

The darker line (with boxes) represents the *Lower Spending, Lower Taxes and Lower Rates Policy*, while the lighter one (with balls) denotes the impact of the same policy fiscal policy, *without* the additional easing of the monetary conditions. The dashed line (with triangles) represents the baseline simulation. Source: Authors' Simulation with Oxford Economic Model (release 2.0)

Figure 8.75 Lower Taxes, Lower Spending, ... and Lower Rates in Finland: Inflation Rate

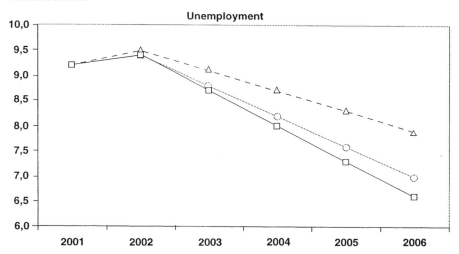

The darker line (with boxes) represents the *Lower Spending, Lower Taxes and Lower Rates Policy*, while the lighter one (with balls) denotes the impact of the same policy fiscal policy, *without* the additional easing of the monetary conditions. The dashed line (with triangles) represents the baseline simulation. Source: Authors' Simulation with Oxford Economic Model (release 2.0)

Figure 8.76 Lower Taxes, Lower Spending, ... and Lower Rates in Finland: Unemployment Rate

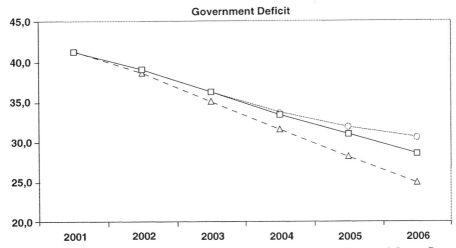

The darker line (with boxes) represents the *Lower Spending, Lower Taxes and Lower Rates Policy*, while the lighter one (with balls) denotes the impact of the same policy fiscal policy, *without* the additional easing of the monetary conditions. The dashed line (with triangles) represents the baseline simulation. Source: Authors' Simulation with Oxford Economic Model (release 2.0)

Figure 8.77 Lower Taxes, Lower Spending, ... and Lower Rates in Finland: Government Deficit (as a % of GDP)

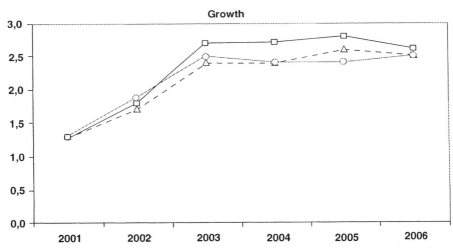

The darker line (with boxes) represents the *Lower Spending, Lower Taxes and Lower Rates Policy*, while the lighter one (with balls) denotes the impact of the same policy fiscal policy, *without* the additional easing of the monetary conditions. The dashed line (with triangles) represents the baseline simulation. Source: Authors' Simulation with Oxford Economic Model (release 2.0)

Figure 8.78 Lower Taxes, Lower Spending, ... and Lower Rates in Belgium: GDP Growth Rate

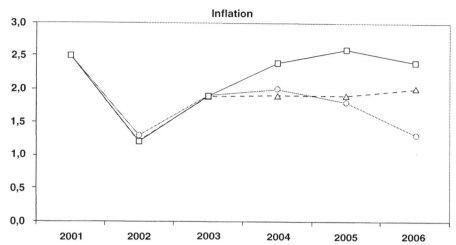

The darker line (with boxes) represents the *Lower Spending, Lower Taxes and Lower Rates Policy*, while the lighter one (with balls) denotes the impact of the same policy fiscal policy, *without* the additional easing of the monetary conditions. The dashed line (with triangles) represents the baseline simulation. Source: Authors' Simulation with Oxford Economic Model (release 2.0)

Figure 8.79 Lower Taxes, Lower Spending, ... and Lower Rates in Belgium: Inflation Rate

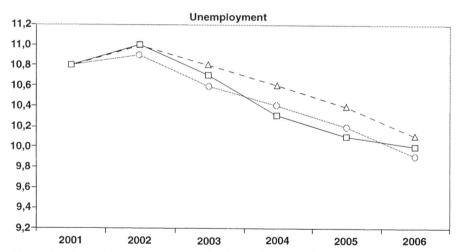

The darker line (with boxes) represents the *Lower Spending, Lower Taxes and Lower Rates Policy*, while the lighter one (with balls) denotes the impact of the same policy fiscal policy, *without* the additional easing of the monetary conditions. The dashed line (with triangles) represents the baseline simulation. Source: Authors' Simulation with Oxford Economic Model (release 2.0)

Figure 8.80 Lower Taxes, Lower Spending, ... and Lower Rates in Belgium: Unemployment Rate

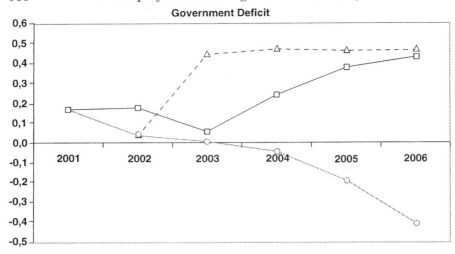

The darker line (with boxes) represents the *Lower Spending, Lower Taxes and Lower Rates Policy*, while the lighter one (with balls) denotes the impact of the same policy fiscal policy, *without* the additional easing of the monetary conditions. The dashed line (with triangles) represents the baseline simulation. Source: Authors' Simulation with Oxford Economic Model (release 2.0)

Figure 8.81 Lower Taxes, Lower Spending, ... and Lower Rates in Belgium: Government Debt (% GDP)

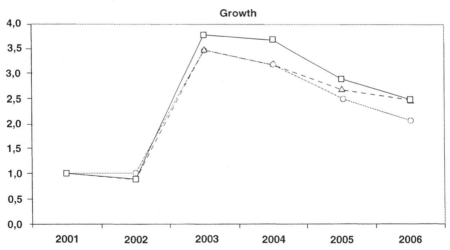

The darker line (with boxes) represents the *Lower Spending, Lower Taxes and Lower Rates Policy*, while the lighter one (with balls) denotes the impact of the same policy fiscal policy, *without* the additional easing of the monetary conditions. The dashed line (with triangles) represents the baseline simulation. Source: Authors' Simulation with Oxford Economic Model (release 2.0)

Figure 8.82 Lower Taxes, Lower Spending, ... and Lower Rates in Austria: GDP Growth Rate

Inflation

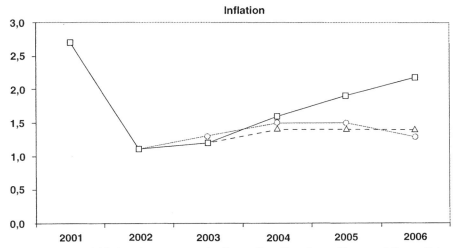

The darker line (with boxes) represents the *Lower Spending, Lower Taxes and Lower Rates Policy*, while the lighter one (with balls) denotes the impact of the same policy fiscal policy, *without* the additional easing of the monetary conditions. The dashed line (with triangles) represents the baseline simulation. Source: Authors' Simulation with Oxford Economic Model (release 2.0)

Figure 8.83 Lower Taxes, Lower Spending, ... and Lower Rates in Austria: Inflation Rate

Unemployment

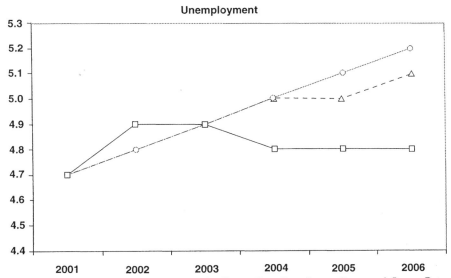

The darker line (with boxes) represents the *Lower Spending, Lower Taxes and Lower Rates Policy*, while the lighter one (with balls) denotes the impact of the same policy fiscal policy, *without* the additional easing of the monetary conditions. The dashed line (with triangles) represents the baseline simulation. Source: Authors' Simulation with Oxford Economic Model (release 2.0)

Figure 8.84 Lower Taxes, Lower Spending, ... and Lower Rates in Austria: Unemployment Rate

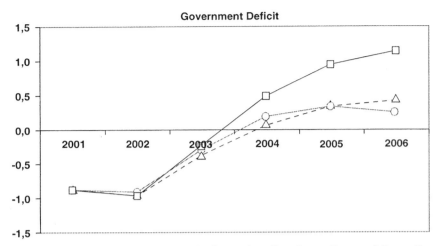

The darker line (with boxes) represents the *Lower Spending, Lower Taxes and Lower Rates Policy*, while the lighter one (with balls) denotes the impact of the same policy fiscal policy, *without* the additional easing of the monetary conditions. The dashed line (with triangles) represents the baseline simulation. Source: Authors' Simulation with Oxford Economic Model (release 2.0)

Figure 8.85 Lower Taxes, Lower Spending, ... and Lower Rates in Austria: Government Deficit (% GDP)

8.5 No Room For Foul Play: the Illusion of Free-Riding.

What has been said so far implies that national governments want to assume the responsibility of identifying and adopting an economic policy strategy capable of noticeably changing their unsatisfactory inertial trends, thus setting themselves the goal of leading their countries toward higher paths of growth and toward full employment.

Economic theory teaches us, however, that a number of market failures exist, and among these is one called free-riding. Wherewith, in a multilateral context like the European one, the hypothesis of a free-riding of State could also be outlined and applied to the behavior of national governments.

We have therefore hypothesized a scenario in which a country, counting on/ hoping for the structural reforms undertaken by the other member countries of the European Monetary Union, delays or does not effect any reform, imitating the behavior of the famous petty thief that after having entered the jewelry store gets a punch in the teeth from the attentive jeweler who was waiting inside, comes out with a hand over his mouth and tells his accomplice, "you go in first, since I feel like laughing".

It should be emphasized, however, in a different way from the anecdote that was just told, which has empirical bases, this possible choice is based on plausible theoretical foundations. In this context, the free-rider reinterprets the export-led model, based on the European economies' being propelled by global demand (and especially the United States) in a domestic-European style. In this instance, the external push to this country would be given by that group of countries that have effected the structural reforms, despite the difficulties and political and social risks that this could entail within their own borders.

We've thus asked ourselves about the convenience or inconvenience of this strategy, quantifying the benefits in terms of growth and unemployment; we've tested these hypotheses setting in place a series of simulations, one for each member country of the European Monetary Union. Technically speaking, we repeated the simulation of coordination described beforehand, excluding one country one by one (the free-rider) from the realization of these very economic policy interventions.

The results obtained are indicated, country by country, from Figure 8.22 to 8.29. The question posed in this section (is free-riding possible?) can get a clear response from a simple look at these same graphs.

There is no room for a possible sit-and-wait attitude that leaves the necessary decision-making to other countries in order to resolve one's own internal problems. In this sense, therefore, the export-led model that is no longer practicable for the whole of Europe, which after monetary union has become a large, closed economy similar to the United States is not even practicable on a level of single national economies. Not only Europe as a whole must show itself capable of building conditions for growth, employment and welfare internally, without waiting for miraculous recoveries and pushes from the rest of the world, but also every country of the Union has to know how to tap its "national" capacities without waiting for the rest of Europe to resolve its own internal problems.

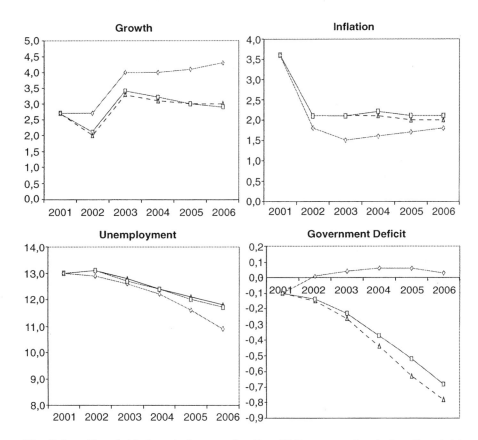

The lighter line (with boxes) denotes the *Free Riding* case, the darker line (with rhombs) represents the *Triangle of Reforms* case. The dashed line (with triangles) is the *Baseline* simulation. Source: Authors' Simulation with Oxford Economic Model (release 2.0)

Figure 8.86 The Illusion of Free Riding in Spain.

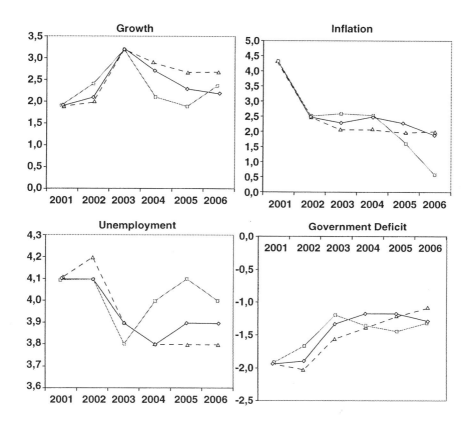

The lighter line (with boxes) denotes the *Free Riding* case, the darker line (with rhombs) represents the *Triangle of Reforms* case. The dashed line (with triangles) is the *Baseline* simulation. Source: Authors' Simulation with Oxford Economic Model (release 2.0)

Figure 8.87 The Illusion of Free Riding in Portugal

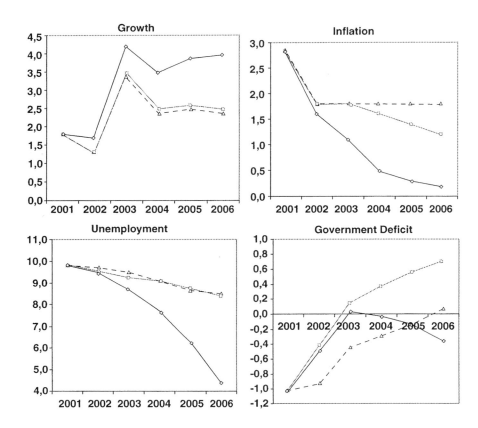

The lighter line (with boxes) denotes the *Free Riding* case, the darker line (with rhombs) represents the *Triangle of Reforms* case. The dashed line (with triangles) is the *Baseline* simulation. Source: Authors' Simulation with Oxford Economic Model (release 2.0)

Figure 8.88 The Illusion of Free Riding in Italy

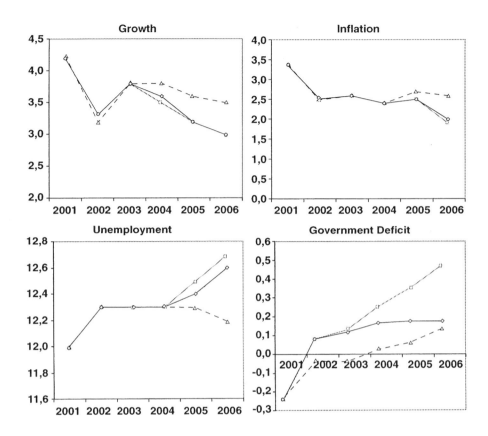

The lighter line (with boxes) denotes the *Free Riding* case, the darker line (with rhombs) represents the *Triangle of Reforms* case. The dashed line (with triangles) is the *Baseline* simulation. Source: Authors' Simulation with Oxford Economic Model (release 2.0)

Figure 8.89 The Illusion of Free Riding in Greece.

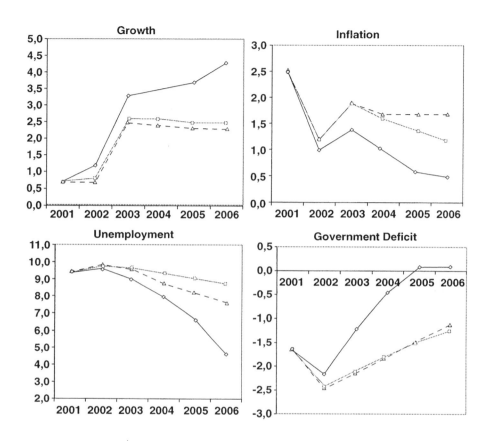

The lighter line (with boxes) denotes the *Free Riding* case, the darker line (with rhombs) represents the *Triangle of Reforms* case. The dashed line (with triangles) is the *Baseline* simulation. Source: Authors' Simulation with Oxford Economic Model (release 2.0)

Figure 8.90 The Illusion of Free Riding in Germany.

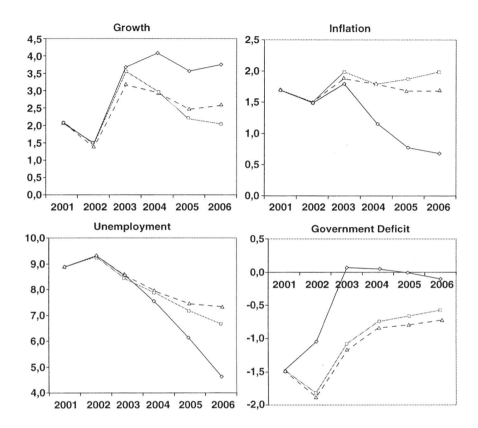

The lighter line (with boxes) denotes the *Free Riding* case, the darker line (with rhombs) represents the *Triangle of Reforms* case. The dashed line (with triangles) is the *Baseline* simulation. Source: Authors' Simulation with Oxford Economic Model (release 2.0)

Figure 8.91 The Illusion of Free Riding in France.

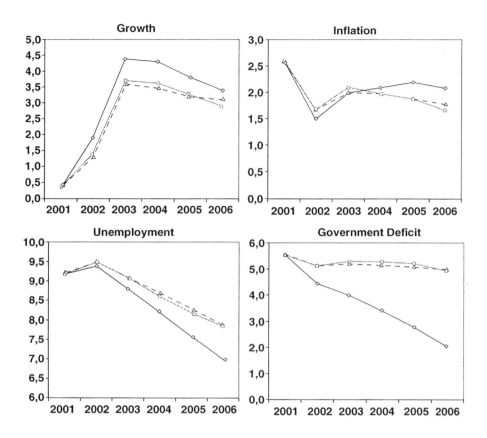

The lighter line (with boxes) denotes the *Free Riding* case, the darker line (with rhombs) represents the *Triangle of Reforms* case. The dashed line (with triangles) is the *Baseline* simulation. Source: Authors' Simulation with Oxford Economic Model (release 2.0)

Figure 8.92 The Illusion of Free Riding in Finland.

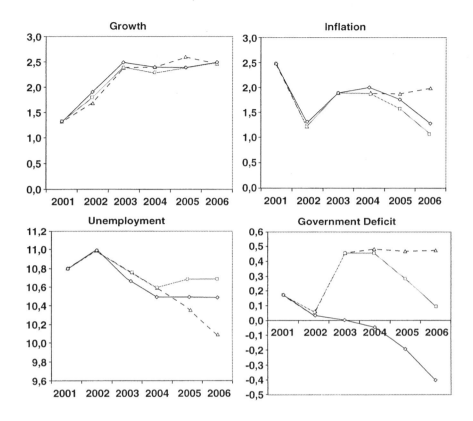

The lighter line (with boxes) denotes the *Free Riding* case, the darker line (with rhombs) represents the *Triangle of Reforms* case. The dashed line (with triangles) is the *Baseline* simulation. Source: Authors' Simulation with Oxford Economic Model (release 2.0)

Figure 8.93 The Illusion of Free Riding in Belgium.

8.6 And If the World Slows Down.... More Reforms in Europe.

Up until this point, we've tried to show that the state of the European economy mostly depends... on Europe and that each European economy depends on the decisions and behaviors... of the same single countries.

However, all of us are surrounded by the environment of a more globalized world economy that is constantly becoming more and more competitive.

As we've said many times before, all of the results obtained in this work are necessarily based on a vision of developments in the world economy that, for technical reasons in the econometric simulations, are considered "exogenous." It should be stated, however, that the proportions that an integrated European economy now assumes within the context of the world economy should make it understood that the status of the latter is also based on what happens in the economy of the Old Continent. This means that Europe has to begin to be aware of the fact that not only the rest of the world cannot solve its problems, but also and more so that the very evolution of the rest of the world is dependent on the capacity for self-propelling growth of the European economy.

The international setting used in our work and elaborated beforehand shows a comforting and solid recovery in the world economy after the sharp downturn of the last two years.

It therefore seemed necessary and fair to us to also verify the results obtained under an alternative hypothesis of a less favorable international framework with a slowdown of the world economy that could extend further over time.

Obviously with a worse international picture, the inertial trend of the European economies also worsens. And it is on this "worse" point of reference that the economic policy alternatives considered in this work would have to produce their effects.

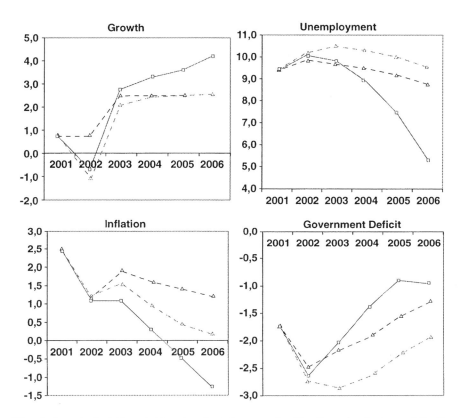

The darker dashed line (with triangles) denotes the *Baseline* simulation, while the lighter dashed line (with triangles, too) denotes the *Baseline simulation in a worsened macroeconomic scenario*. The solid line (with boxes) represents the *Fiscal Policy Coordination* case, when the policy is applied to the worsened scenario. Source: Authors' Simulation with Oxford Economic Model (release 2.0)

Figure 8.94 Panel A: Sensitivity Analysis for Germany.

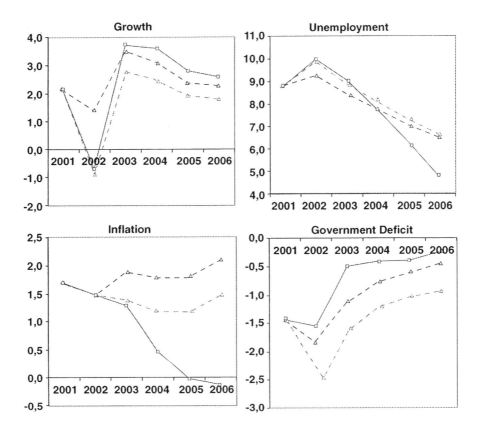

The darker dashed line (with triangles) denotes the *Baseline* simulation, while the lighter dashed line (with triangles, too) denotes the *Baseline simulation in a worsened macroeconomic scenario*. The solid line (with boxes) represents the *Fiscal Policy Coordination* case, when the policy is applied to the worsened scenario. Source: Authors' Simulation with Oxford Economic Model (release 2.0)

Figure 8.95 Sensitivity Analysis for France.

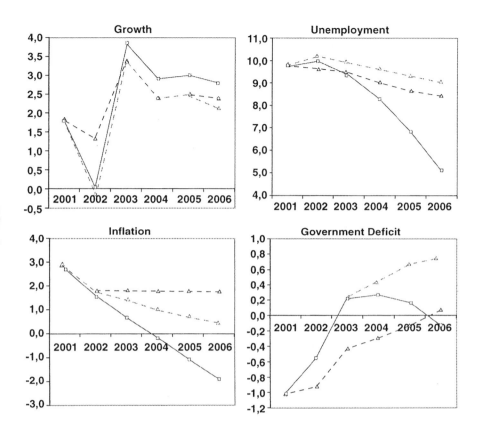

The darker dashed line (with triangles) denotes the *Baseline* simulation, while the lighter dashed line (with triangles, too) denotes the *Baseline simulation in a worsened macroeconomic scenario*. The solid line (with boxes) represents the *Fiscal Policy Coordination* case, when the policy is applied to the worsened scenario. Source: Authors' Simulation with Oxford Economic Model (release 2.0)

Figure 8.96 Sensitivity Analysis for Italy.

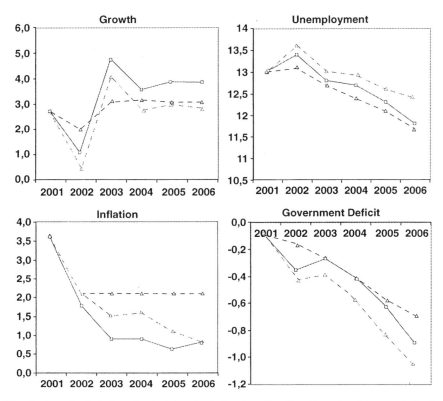

The darker dashed line (with triangles) denotes the *Baseline* simulation, while the lighter dashed line (with triangles, too) denotes the *Baseline simulation in a worsened macroeconomic scenario*. The solid line (with boxes) represents the *Fiscal Policy Coordination* case, when the policy is applied to the worsened scenario. Source: Authors' Simulation with Oxford Economic Model (release 2.0)

Figure 8.97 Sensitivity Analysis for Spain.

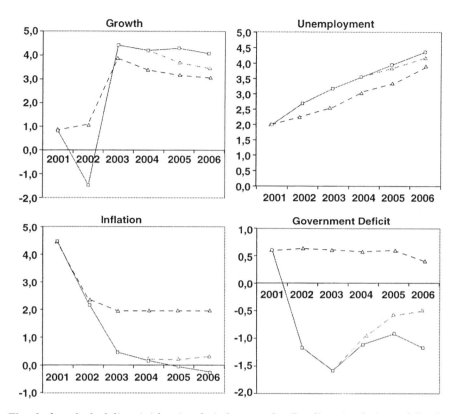

The darker dashed line (with triangles) denotes the *Baseline* simulation, while the lighter dashed line (with triangles, too) denotes the *Baseline simulation in a worsened macroeconomic scenario*. The solid line (with boxes) represents the *Fiscal Policy Coordination* case, when the policy is applied to the worsened scenario. Source: Authors' Simulation with Oxford Economic Model (release 2.0)

Figure 8.98 Sensitivity Analysis for Netherlands.

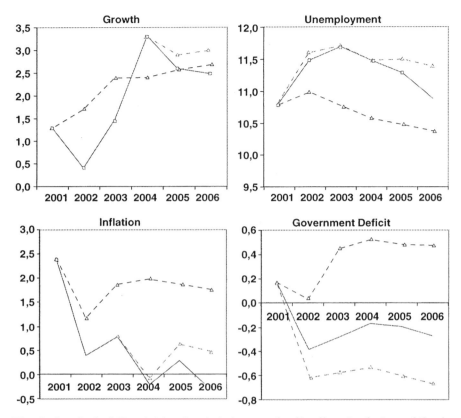

The darker dashed line (with triangles) denotes the *Baseline* simulation, while the lighter dashed line (with triangles, too) denotes the *Baseline simulation in a worsened macroeconomic scenario*. The solid line (with boxes) represents the *Fiscal Policy Coordination* case, when the policy is applied to the worsened scenario. Source: Authors' Simulation with Oxford Economic Model (release 2.0)

Figure 8.99 Sensitivity Analysis for Belgium.

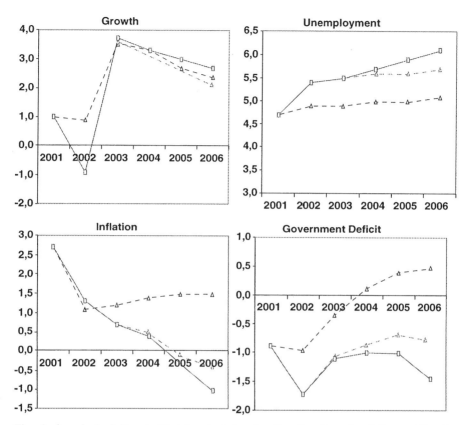

The darker dashed line (with triangles) denotes the *Baseline* simulation, while the lighter dashed line (with triangles, too) denotes the *Baseline simulation in a worsened macroeconomic scenario*. The solid line (with boxes) represents the *Fiscal Policy Coordination* case, when the policy is applied to the worsened scenario. Source: Authors' Simulation with Oxford Economic Model (release 2.0)

Figure 8.100 Sensitivity Analysis for Austria.

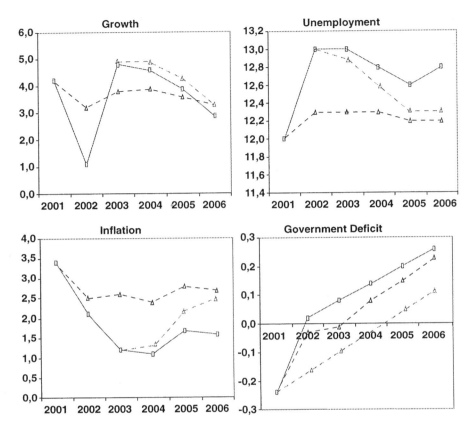

The darker dashed line (with triangles) denotes the *Baseline* simulation, while the lighter dashed line (with triangles, too) denotes the *Baseline simulation in a worsened macroeconomic scenario*. The solid line (with boxes) represents the *Fiscal Policy Coordination* case, when the policy is applied to the worsened scenario. Source: Authors' Simulation with Oxford Economic Model (release 2.0)

Figure 8.101 Sensitivity Analysis for Greece.

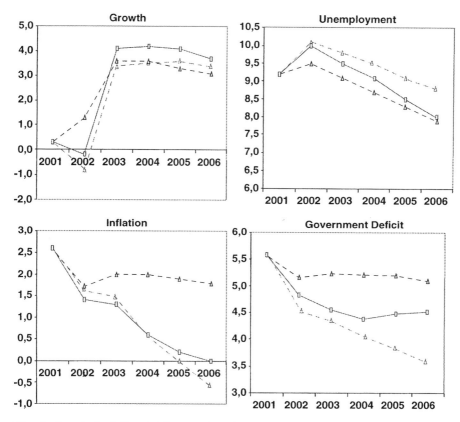

The darker dashed line (with triangles) denotes the *Baseline* simulation, while the lighter dashed line (with triangles, too) denotes the *Baseline simulation in a worsened macroeconomic scenario.* The solid line (with boxes) represents the *Fiscal Policy Coordination* case, when the policy is applied to the worsened scenario. Source: Authors' Simulation with Oxford Economic Model (release 2.0)

Figure 8.102 Sensitivity Analysis for Finland.

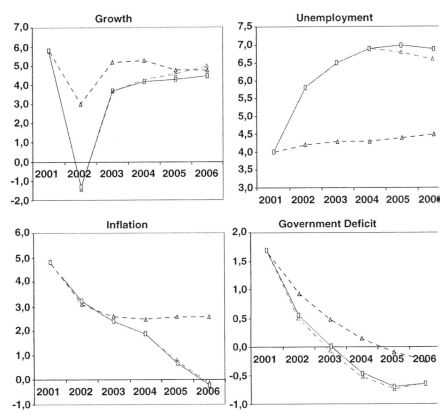

The darker dashed line (with triangles) denotes the *Baseline* simulation, while the lighter dashed line (with triangles, too) denotes the *Baseline simulation in worsened macroeconomic scenario*. The solid line (with boxes) represents the *Fiscal Policy Coordination* case, when the policy is applied to the worsened scenario. Source Authors' Simulation with Oxford Economic Model (release 2.0)

Figure 8.103 Sensitivity Analysis for Ireland.

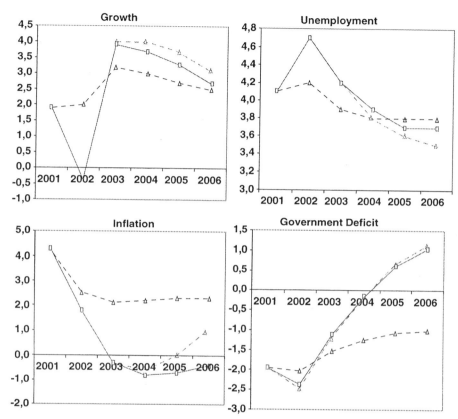

The darker dashed line (with triangles) denotes the *Baseline* simulation, while the lighter dashed line (with triangles, too) denotes the *Baseline simulation in a worsened macroeconomic scenario*. The solid line (with boxes) represents the *Fiscal Policy Coordination* case, when the policy is applied to the worsened scenario. Source: Authors' Simulation with Oxford Economic Model (release 2.0)

Figure 8.104 Sensitivity Analysis for Portugal.

To summarize, the results we obtained show that the strategy of structural reforms seems equally necessary to counterbalance the more negative impact of the supposedly worse international economic conditions, although producing less significant effects in percentage terms. In other words, the depressed conditions of the international cycle reduce the overall impact of the measure, but the new planned trend is positioned above the two inertial trends, the original one and the one taken into consideration for sensitivity analysis.

Here we limit ourselves to present the inertial trends and the trends that would occur upon implementing the triangle of reforms compared with the hypotheses, more favorable or less favorable, regarding the developments in the world economy and, limitedly, with the developments in the rate of growth, the rate of unemployment and the government deficit in the eight countries on which we've focused this work.

The sensitivity analysis presented in this section is meant to validate the robustness of our results with respect scenarios alternative to the one on which all simulations are based. This has a technical interpretation, which is to verify that the obtained results does not depend significantly from the baseline of the econometric model. In addition, there exist an economic interpretation of a sensitivity analysis exercise. It is meant to offer the possibility of generalizing the results of a simulation, once the economic environment changes from the one incorporated into the original model.

The worsened macroeconomic scenario we consider in the sensitivity analysis exercise can be interpreted as representing the consequences of the Iraqi war of March-April 2003.

The economic effects of the Iraq war could be summarized in a higher government spending, a higher oil price, a negative effects on business and consumer confidence, on equity prices, and on risk spread, together with a significantly negative effects on tourism. In particular, oil price increased significantly in the months before the beginning of the war, for descending after the first weeks of war. Notice, moreover, that investments and equities were damaged by the sole war related uncertainty.

The sectorial impact of the war should not be overlooked, since supply in some sectors is more exposed to effects of oil prices (like for example Agriculture, Non-metallic minerals, Utilities and Transport), and the demand in some sectors is more exposed to confidence effects. For example, tourism is likely to be hit hard, especially to Middle East and also to far East, due to the other very different cause, given by the SARS disease.[8]

---

[8] Domestic tourism probably would go up, but not enough to offset reduction in international tourism.

In conclusion, the model itself, and the results obtained via simulations appear to be robust to the worsening of macroeconomic scenario. We hope, however, that the analysis and the comments would be based on a better scenario with no war, and no terrorism of any kind. Obviously, a more optimistic scenario would improve upon our results, but whatever it would be, we think to be proven that fir Europe the way of structural reforms is a must to *play a leading role* in the *New World Economy*, and in the *Institutional and Political framework*.

9. Appendix

Institutional Meetings in Europe.

The **European Council** met in **Barcelona on March 15th and 16th 2002** for the second annual spring meeting dedicated to the Union's economic, social, and environmental situation. During the council, various subjects were thoroughly discussed. Regarding the fiscal aspects, it was reaffirmed that the coordination of fiscal policies hinges on a commitment to assuring healthy government finances and on the rules set in place by the Stability and Growth Pact. As it stands now, the euro-zone forms a monetary union in which a single, independent monetary policy and decentralized but coordinated fiscal policies are in force. For this reason, it is necessary to achieve additional progress by operating on various points. The first is the harmonization of the methodologies used for the elaboration of statistics and indicators relative to the euro-zone. The second is to create a systematic analysis of the whole of the euro-zone's "policy mix" to measure the coherence of the monetary and fiscal policies in relation to economic developments. In essence, this strengthens the present mechanisms for coordination of fiscal policies. In this vein, the Commission will present proposals geared toward reinforcing the coordination of economic policies in time for the Summit in the spring of 2003. Additionally, the European Council has been invited to continue the examination of the long-term sustainability of government finances as part of its annual monitoring exercise, paying particular attention to the financial challenges connected with demographic aging. (Source: Presidency Document, Barcelona, 15 and 16 March 2002).

In **Santa Maria da Feira on the 19th and 20th of June 2000**, an important step forward was made as regards taxation of savings. The European Council adjourned with the unanimous agreement of the Fifteen that provides for the exchange of information among the member States pertaining to financial earnings of non-resident European citizens. The new proposal entails no change until 2003, when the directive that will introduce a mixed regime into the EU should enter into force: sharing of information among fiscal administrations via the paying agent entity, or, for Luxembourg, Austria and Belgium, the enforcement of a withholding at origin on capital gains of non-residents (at a rate of 15% for the first three years and 20% until the end of the transitional period); at the same time, those countries would receive information on incomes received by their own residents in other countries of the Union. The withholding tax does not prevent the beneficiary's State of residence from subjecting him or her to taxes in accordance with its national law. During such a transitional period, it is planned that the States with an at source withholding tax should transfer 75% of revenues to the beneficiary Country, which once effected will guarantee the elimination of double taxation that can result from such a withholding, while the remaining 25% will be due to the member State of the paying agent. This temporary arrangement will be applicable for a maximum period of 7 years, after which, in 2010, the entire EU will have to adopt the final structure of the information exchange, with the abolition of banking secrecy, though only for non-residents, and ordinary taxation in the recipient's country of residence. In this way, the implementation of Capital Export Neutrality will be assured. The 2000-2002 period has been set aside by the Commission to involve third Countries (Switzerland, Liechtenstein, the Principality of Monaco, Andorra, USA) and dependent and associated territories in negotiations (the Channel Islands, the Isle of Man, Caribbean countries) to adopt equivalent measures in the former and the same measures in the latter on the exchange of information. At the Ecofin Council of June 2002, the Commission showed the state of progress of the negotiations with third countries; of these, all except Switzerland have expressed their commitment to cooperate with the EU in applying equivalent measures on taxation of savings. For dependent and associated territories, Holland informed the Ecofin Council that an agreement had been reached with the Dutch Antilles and Aruba concerning the commitment of those territories to adopt the same measures foreseen in the future EU directive, while Great Britain communicated that discussions are under way with all the associated and dependent territories, with Jersey and Guernsey having already announced their commitment to the exchange of information.

As far as Switzerland is concerned, Commissioner Frists Bolkestein only recently told the **Ecofin Council that gathered in Brussels on November 5, 2002**, about the process of negotiations in that country. The Swiss government refuses to ease the mesh of banking secrecy and proposed the imposition of a withholding tax (at a rate of 35%, applicable from the 1st of January, 2004), on income that EU citizens receive from financial investments transacted within its territory, and then dividing the yield with the EU countries involved. Brussels, however, does not consider this to be a measure equivalent to the system of information exchange, which will be set in place for the Members of the Union. Therefore the negotiations will be extended in order to obtain appreciable results by the end of the year, the last possibility before the approval of the directive on taxation of savings. Without an agreement with Switzerland, it will be difficult to have the unanimity necessary in fiscal matters, and in fact a veto from Luxembourg or Austria is possible.

This very lack of unanimity was the principal cause of the foundering of the previous proposal for a directive on the taxation of savings included in the so-called "**Monti Package**" (**Ecofin Council December 1, 1997**) that was based on the "coexistence model," or the possibility conceded to each State of the Union to choose between the two models outlined, that of applying a withholding tax at source (the rate established was 20%) or that of the information exchange on savings income received by non-residents in another country of the Union. Besides this proposal for a directive, which was later replaced by the one set out during the Ecofin Council of Feira noted above, the "Monti Package" also consisted of a "Code of conduct" to standardize corporate taxation and of a directive proposal concerning the common tax regime applied to interest payments and rights among companies associated in different member States. The code of conduct represents a political commitment for the States of the Union to prevent requirements or mechanisms from being introduced that favor some players or support certain operations, such as investments from non-resident companies, for example, or that may constitute true and bona fide State assistance for specific national sectors. The code stipulates a commitment from States to avoid introducing new prejudicial (standstill) fiscal measures and to "dismantle" those already in existence (rollback) by means of a sort of internal monitoring of their own regulations and existing procedures. A "code of conduct" group of high-level representatives was instituted and presided over by Dawn Primarolo, charged with assessing the fiscal measures that can be included in applying the code and to control the communication of information important to the fiscal measures adopted by the different States. The group reports periodically to the Ecofin Council as regards progress made in the three work areas: standstill, rollback, transparency and information exchange relative to the practice of transfer pricing. During the Council of the European Union on June 20, 2002, note is made of the Group's progress regarding the legislative and administrative measures meant to dismantle the damaging effects identified in the "code of conduct" Group report (annex C) presented during the Ecofin Council of November 23, 1999. It then concludes by inviting the Group to complete its work program relating to transparency and the sharing of information in the area of transfer pricing in accordance with what was laid out in Annex I of the Group report presented to the Ecofin Council on 5 June 2001.

Lastly, as relates to the proposal for a directive about the handling of interest and royalties, the goal is to introduce a total exemption for interest and payments received from a community business within a member State in which it is not resident, with interest being taxed directly in the State of residence. From the conclusions of the Ecofin Council of 20 June 2002, it is understood that the Swedish Presidency drafted a new version of the directive proposal (8697/01 FISC 82) reflecting the conclusions of the Ecofin Council of the 26th and 27th November 2000.

By the end of 2002, when an agreement is reached about the edited proposals and the opinions of the European Parliament and the Economic and Social Commission have been heard, the Ecofin Council will unanimously adopt: the directive on taxation of savings and the Directive on interest and royalty payments among associated companies of different Member States.

The **Stability and Growth Pact (June, 1997)** is a part of the groundwork of the third phase of the Economic and Monetary Union (EMU) begun on January 1, 1999. The objective is to guarantee that the discipline employed by the member States regarding budget balances be maintained, even after the single currency is introduced. Actually, the Stability and Growth Pact is made up of a package of provisions, including the European Council resolution adopted in Amsterdam on June 17, 1997, and two regulations from the Council of July 7, 1997 (regulation (CE) n. 1466/97 and 1467/97), that specify the Pact's technical requirements. The Pact is born of the fear that since the criteria of the Maastricht Treaty (maximum limits of 3% on deficit/GDP and 60% on national debt/GDP) were necessary for entry into the third phase of Economic and Monetary Union, the States, once having gained entry, could revert to "easy" fiscal policies, compromising the monetary stability and credibility of the EMU, having inevitable repercussions on the exchange rate of the new currency. The goal of the pact is to achieve a balanced budget, with a close to zero or positive balance, that will be able to permit Member States to deal with the normal cyclical fluctuations, maintaining the national deficit within the reference value of 3% of GDP. The European Council's 1997 Amsterdam resolution emphasizes "the importance of sound government finances as a means of strengthening the conditions for price stability and for strong sustainable growth conducive to employment creation." The Pact provides that member States present the Council and the Commission with multi-year stability programs containing information about the process of moving toward the goal of "close to balance" of the government Administration's budget, as well as the estimated state of the national debt/GDP ratio. The document contains forecasts about the state of the economy, as well as about most important macroeconomic variables (investments, real GDP growth, employment, inflation) and the description of economic policy measures adopted and proposed in order to achieve the objectives of the program, with an estimate of the effects of the budget intervention on the government accounts. The stability program is then examined by the Council on the basis of the assessments expressed by the Commission and the Monetary Committee; in particular the expected progress toward achieving the goal of budget balance is closely examined, as well as the credibility and adequateness of the measures put into motion. In case there's a noticeable deviation from the desired budget balances in the medium term, the Council forwards a recommendation to the State concerned that it adopt the necessary adjusting measures, and then keeps watch to ensure they are carried out.

In regulation 1467/97 the conditions are specified for implementing the excessive deficit procedure, which is initiated when the reference value for the government deficit is surpassed. Only one situation described in article 2 of the same regulation would not trigger the "excessive deficit" procedure, which is when the amount in excess of the 3% threshold is considered exceptional and temporary, caused by an unusual event not subject to the control of the State involved or when a serious economic recession occurs that makes real GDP drop by at least 2% year-on-year. In all the other cases, when an excessive deficit is foreseen, the Council sends a recommendation to the State in question so that it adopt all the necessary measures to reduce the budget deficit. The next move, if it's noted that the first recommendation has not been followed through and the 3% deficit/GDP limit has been infringed, there is an injunction to reduce the deficit to within the permissible limits. If the deficit continues, and the State concerned has not complied with the Council's decisions, then the latter can opt to implement or intensify sanctions. Based on article 104C, paragraph 11 of the Treaty of Maastricht, the planned sanctions include inviting the European Investment Bank to reconsider its policy of lending to the member State in question, to requesting that a non-interest-bearing deposit for an adequate amount (which is established in article 12 of reg. 1467/97) be lodged with the Commission until the excessive deficit is corrected, up to the extreme case of transforming the deposit into a penalty if still, two years after the decision to create the deposit, the excessive deficit is not corrected.

The Treaty of Maastricht

In order to guarantee the lasting convergence that is necessary for the establishment of the Economic and Monetary Union (EMU) the treaty set in place the following convergence criteria that have to be respected by the member States to be able to participate in the third phase of the EMU.

1. Price stability

The treaty requires that "the achievement of a high degree of price stability [...] will be apparent from a rate of inflation which is close to that of, at most, the three best performing Member States in terms of price stability. In concrete terms, the inflation rate of one member State must not go more than 1.5% higher than the rate of the three member States that have performed the best in terms of price stability in the year prior to examination of the situation of the member State in question.

2. Government Finances

The treaty stipulates that "the sustainability of the government financial position [...] will be apparent from having achieved a government budgetary position without a deficit that is excessive...". In practice, when it is time for the Commission to detail its yearly recommendation to the Council of the ministers of finance, it evaluates whether financial discipline has been respected based on the two following parameters: the annual national deficit: the ratio between annual national deficit and gross domestic product (GDP) must not be more than 3% for the period of the last complete fiscal year. If this is not the case, the ratio should however be decreasing on a considerable and constant basis, attaining a level near 3% (tendential interpretation) or alternatively, register around 3% only having surpassed that value in an exceptional and temporary way; the national debt: the ration between gross national debt and GDP must not, for the period of the last complete fiscal year, rise above 60%. If this is not the case, the ratio should however be decreased by a sufficient amount, tending to fall toward 60% at a satisfactory pace (tendential interpretation).

3. Exchange Rates

The treaty stipulates "the observance of the normal fluctuation margins provided for by the exchange rate mechanism of the European Monetary System, for at least two years, without devaluing against the currency of any other Member State." In other words, the member State has to have participated in the mechanism of the European monetary exchange system without interruption over the course of the two years leading up to the assessment of the situation, without moreover having been subject to serious strains. In addition, the member State cannot have devalued its national currency (or rather the central bilateral rate of its value with respect to the currency of another member State) on purpose, over the course of that same period.

4. Interest Rates

The treaty stipulates that "the long-term interest rate levels [...] reflect the durability of convergence achieved by the member State." In practice, the nominal rates of interest over the long term should not surpass by more than 2% the rates of the three member States, at most, that will have performed best in terms of price stability (in fact they are the same countries taken into consideration for the price stability parameter). The period to consider is the year preceding the assessment of the situation in the member State in question (for more details, see the website *www.europa.eu.int*).

The Process Toward Fiscal Harmonization

Fiscal Harmonization is the process of convergence and coordination in fiscal matters of the countries of the European Community, having the final goal of jointly creating the single market. The evolutionary process toward complete fiscal harmonization is supposed to have been carried out in three phases: abolishment of customs tariffs, harmonization of VAT and excises, harmonization of direct taxes. The harmonization of direct taxes in the European Community still seems far off, especially since it implies the reorganization of the most important instrument of economic intervention presently available to the national governments, fiscal policy. The sector in which there's been a however minimal harmonization is in taxation of corporate profits, so as to avoid the double taxation of those same profits in different countries. Another sector that has been regulated is that of mergers, divisions and transfer of assets between companies that belong to different States. The goal is to institute a single fiscal regime for cross-border transactions in cases where capital gains result (directive 90/434). Another measure effected is the reorganization of the fiscal regime applied to "parent and subsidiary" companies operating in different States. The Aim is to prevent profits from the same company from being taxed two times: once in the State in which they were made and a second time in the State to which they are transferred, when they've been conferred to the controlling company. (directive 90/435). The rule specifies that the profits of the controlled company (subsidiary) be taxed at source, while the State in which the controlling company (parent) has its seat can a) not tax the dividends received by the subsidiary company; b) concede a tax credit for the profits recorded by the controlled company. A third provision (not issued by the Community institutions, but the product of an intergovernmental agreement) introduces an arbitrational procedure to resolve the conflicts between the different tax administrations, whenever disputes arise regarding to whom to assign the profits of parent and subsidiary companies.

Tables

Chapter 6

Euroland – Baseline

GDP AT CONSTANT PRICES						
	2001	2002	2003	2004	2005	2006
Gross Domestic Product	1.8	1.3	3.1	2.8	2.6	2.6
Private Consumption	1.5	1.1	2.6	2.6	2.5	2.5
Public Consumption	0.9	0.7	1.1	1.2	1.2	1.3
Total Fixed Investment	1.3	0.3	4.3	4.1	3.4	3.3
Exp. of Goods and Serv	5.6	2.0	7.5	7.0	6.2	5.9
Imp. of goods and serv.	4.1	1.3	7.7	6.9	6.1	5.9
PRICES, % CHANGE						
Consumer Prices	2.8	1.5	1.8	1.7	1.7	1.7
Wholesale Prices	2.1	1.5	2.1	2.0	1.9	1.9
EMPLOYMENT, % CHANGE						
Unemployment Rate (%)	9.8	8.8	8.4	7.9	7.6	7.3
Employment	1.7	-0.3	0.6	0.5	0.5	0.5
Labour Force	0.6	0.2	0.2	0.0	0.1	0.1
EXTERNAL TRADE (BOP)						
Visible Trade Balance	7317.0	53.8	63.7	75.7	85.5	96.7
Curr Acc and Cap Mov	-9332.8	-33.9	-23.3	-19.0	-18.4	-18.3
As % GDP	-0.4	-0.5	-0.3	-0.2	-0.2	-0.2
GOVERNMENT ACCOUNTS						
Government Revenues % of GDP	44.0	46.3	45.8	45.3	45.0	44.7
Government Expend % of GDP	45.0	46.6	45.7	45.2	44.7	44.3
Net Lending As % GDP	-1.0	-1.1	-0.8	-0.6	-0.4	-0.3
Gross Debt % of GDP	105.0	67.0	64.5	62.1	59.8	57.5
INTERNATIONAL INDICATORS						
Exch. Rate Euro vs US$	0.9	0.9	1.0	1.0	1.1	1.1
World Trade Index	1.4	3.8	7.5	7.3	6.6	6.4
World Price of Raw Materials	-13.7	-1.8	2.6	0.6	0.7	0.4
World Price of Oil	24.6	20.6	23.4	25.4	26.2	26.8
Capacity Utilization	75.6	81.2	82.0	82.8	83.1	83.5

Euroland – Gradualist Monetary Policy

GDP AT CONSTANT PRICES						
	2001	2002	2003	2004	2005	2006
Gross Domestic Product	1.8	1.3	3.4	3.5	3.1	2.7
Private Consumption	1.5	1.1	2.9	3.3	3.0	2.7
Public Consumption	0.9	0.7	1.1	1.2	1.2	1.3
Total Fixed Investment	1.3	0.3	4.7	5.4	4.4	3.7
Exp. of Goods and Serv	5.6	2.0	8.0	8.4	6.8	5.7
Imp. of goods and serv.	4.1	1.3	8.3	8.6	6.8	5.6
PRICES, % CHANGE						
Consumer Prices	2.8	1.5	1.8	1.9	2.1	2.4
Wholesale Prices	2.1	1.5	2.1	2.1	2.3	2.5
EMPLOYMENT, % CHANGE						
Unemployment Rate (%)	9.8	8.8	8.4	7.5	7.2	7.0
Employment	1.7	-0.3	0.7	0.8	0.7	0.6
Labour Force	0.6	0.2	0.3	0.3	0.2	0.2
EXTERNAL TRADE (BOP)						
Visible Trade Balance	7317.0	53.8	59.3	64.0	74.6	87.3
Curr Acc and Cap Mov	-9332.8	-33.9	-25.7	-26.9	-26.7	-27.7
As % GDP	-0.4	-0.5	-0.3	-0.3	-0.3	-0.3
GOVERNMENT ACCOUNTS						
Government Revenues % of GDP	44.0	46.3	45.7	45.3	44.9	44.6
Government Expend % of GDP	45.0	46.5	45.5	44.5	43.8	43.4
Net Lending As % GDP	-1.0	-1.1	-0.5	0.0	0.4	0.6
Gross Debt % of GDP	105.0	67.0	64.1	60.8	57.4	54.0
INTERNATIONAL INDICATORS						
Exch. Rate Euro vs US$	0.9	0.9	1.0	1.0	1.1	1.1
World Trade Index	1.4	3.8	7.6	8.0	7.0	6.3
World Price of Raw Materials	-13.7	-1.8	2.1	0.2	0.5	0.5
World Price of Oil	24.6	20.6	23.4	25.4	26.2	26.8
Capacity Utilization	75.6	81.2	82.3	83.7	84.5	85.0

Euroland – Shock Monetary Policy

GDP AT CONSTANT PRICES	2001	2002	2003	2004	2005	2006
Gross Domestic Product	1.8	1.3	3.1	3.1	3.0	3.1
Private Consumption	1.5	1.1	2.7	2.9	2.9	3.0
Public Consumption	0.9	0.7	1.1	1.2	1.2	1.3
Total Fixed Investment	1.3	0.3	4.3	4.5	4.2	4.2
Exp. of Goods and Serv	5.6	2.0	7.5	7.5	7.0	6.7
Imp. of goods and serv.	4.1	1.3	7.7	7.6	7.1	6.7
PRICES, % CHANGE						
Consumer Prices	2.8	1.5	1.8	1.7	1.7	1.9
Wholesale Prices	2.1	1.5	2.1	1.9	1.9	2.0
EMPLOYMENT, % CHANGE						
Unemployment Rate (%)	9.8	8.8	8.4	7.7	7.4	7.2
Employment	1.7	-0.3	0.6	0.6	0.7	0.7
Labour Force	0.6	0.2	0.3	0.2	0.2	0.2
EXTERNAL TRADE (BOP)						
Visible Trade Balance	7317.0	53.8	63.3	70.2	75.5	82.4
Curr Acc and Cap Mov	-9332.8	-33.9	-23.6	-22.9	-25.6	-29.3
As % GDP	-0.4	-0.5	-0.3	-0.3	-0.3	-0.3
GOVERNMENT ACCOUNTS						
Government Revenues % of GDP	44.0	46.3	45.8	45.3	45.0	44.6
Government Expend % of GDP	45.0	46.5	45.7	45.0	44.2	43.6
Net Lending As % GDP	-1.0	-1.1	-0.7	-0.4	0.0	0.4
Gross Debt % of GDP	105.0	67.0	64.3	61.7	58.9	55.7
INTERNATIONAL INDICATORS						
Exch. Rate Euro vs US$	0.9	0.9	1.0	1.0	1.1	1.1
World Trade Index	1.4	3.8	7.5	7.5	7.1	6.8
World Price of Raw Materials	-13.7	-1.8	2.5	0.3	0.4	0.0
World Price of Oil	24.6	20.6	23.4	25.4	26.2	26.8
Capacity Utilization	75.6	81.2	82.0	82.9	83.7	84.6

Chapter 7

Euroland – Baseline

GDP AT CONSTANT PRICES						
	2001	2002	2003	2004	2005	2006
Gross Domestic Product	1.8	1.3	3.1	2.8	2.6	2.6
Private Consumption	1.5	1.1	2.6	2.6	2.5	2.5
Public Consumption	0.9	0.7	1.1	1.2	1.2	1.3
Total Fixed Investment	1.3	0.3	4.3	4.1	3.4	3.3
Exp. of Goods and Serv	5.6	2.0	7.5	7.0	6.2	5.9
Imp. of goods and serv.	4.1	1.3	7.7	6.9	6.1	5.9
PRICES, % CHANGE						
Consumer Prices	2.8	1.5	1.8	1.7	1.7	1.7
Wholesale Prices	2.1	1.5	2.1	2.0	1.9	1.9
EMPLOYMENT, % CHANGE						
Unemployment Rate (%)	9.8	8.8	8.4	7.9	7.6	7.3
Employment	1.7	-0.3	0.6	0.5	0.5	0.5
Labour Force	0.6	0.2	0.2	0.0	0.1	0.1
EXTERNAL TRADE (BOP)						
Visible Trade Balance	7317.0	53.8	63.7	75.7	85.5	96.7
Curr Acc and Cap Mov	-9332.8	-33.9	-23.3	-19.0	-18.4	-18.3
As % GDP	-0.4	-0.5	-0.3	-0.2	-0.2	-0.2
GOVERNMENT ACCOUNTS						
Government Revenues % of GDP	44.0	46.3	45.8	45.3	45.0	44.7
Government Expend % of GDP	45.0	46.6	45.7	45.2	44.7	44.3
Net Lending As % GDP	-1.0	-1.1	-0.8	-0.6	-0.4	-0.3
Gross Debt % of GDP	105.0	67.0	64.5	62.1	59.8	57.5
INTERNATIONAL INDICATORS						
Exch. Rate Euro vs US$	0.9	0.9	1.0	1.0	1.1	1.1
World Trade Index	1.4	3.8	7.5	7.3	6.6	6.4
World Price of Raw Materials	-13.7	-1.8	2.6	0.6	0.7	0.4
World Price of Oil	24.6	20.6	23.4	25.4	26.2	26.8
Capacity Utilization	75.6	81.2	82.0	82.8	83.1	83.5

Euroland – More Taxes, …

GDP AT CONSTANT PRICES						
	2001	2002	2003	2004	2005	2006
Gross Domestic Product	1.8	0.6	2.4	2.3	2.1	2.0
Private Consumption	1.5	-0.1	1.3	1.4	1.3	1.3
Public Consumption	0.9	0.7	1.1	1.2	1.2	1.3
Total Fixed Investment	1.3	-0.3	3.6	3.9	3.4	3.2
Exp. of Goods and Serv	5.6	1.3	7.0	7.1	6.2	5.7
Imp. of goods and serv.	4.1	0.0	6.5	6.6	5.7	5.2
PRICES, % CHANGE						
Consumer Prices	2.8	1.6	1.9	1.8	1.6	1.6
Wholesale Prices	2.1	1.5	2.2	1.9	1.8	1.6
EMPLOYMENT, % CHANGE						
Unemployment Rate (%)	9.8	9.1	9.4	9.7	10.0	10.4
Employment	1.7	-0.7	0.0	-0.1	-0.2	-0.2
Labour Force	0.6	0.2	0.3	0.2	0.2	0.2
EXTERNAL TRADE (BOP)						
Visible Trade Balance	7317.0	69.4	93.4	114.4	134.9	156.6
Curr Acc and Cap Mov	-9332.8	-14.7	16.7	36.9	54.8	71.8
As % GDP	-0.4	-0.2	0.2	0.5	0.7	0.9
GOVERNMENT ACCOUNTS						
Government Revenues % of GDP	45.0	45.7	45.9	46.4	47.0	47.7
Government Expend % of GDP	44.0	46.8	47.0	47.3	47.7	48.2
Net Lending As % GDP	-1.0	-1.1	-1.1	-0.9	-0.7	-0.5
Gross Debt % of GDP	105.0	66.1	61.9	58.4	55.4	53.0
INTERNATIONAL INDICATORS						
Exch. Rate Euro vs US$	0.9	0.9	1.0	1.0	1.0	1.1
World Trade Index	1.4	3.6	7.3	7.7	7.0	6.5
World Price of Raw Materials	-13.7	-2.6	2.3	0.3	0.2	-0.3
World Price of Oil	24.6	20.6	23.4	25.4	26.2	26.8
Capacity Utilization	75.6	80.3	80.5	80.6	80.5	80.5

Chapter 8
Italy
Baseline

GDP AT CONSTANT PRICES

	2001	2002	2003	2004	2005	2006
Gross Domestic Product	1.8	1.3	3.4	2.4	2.5	2.4
Private Consumption	1.5	1.4	3.1	2.2	2.4	2.3
Public Consumption	0.9	1.7	2.2	2.4	2.3	2.3
Total Fixed Investment	1.3	1.6	3.1	3.4	3.3	2.9
Exp. of Goods and Serv	5.6	3.5	7.3	5.3	5.4	5.0
Imp. of goods and serv.	4.1	3.9	7.8	6.0	5.5	5.1
PRICES, % CHANGE						
Consumer Prices	2.8	1.8	1.8	1.8	1.8	1.8
Wholesale Prices	2.1	1.1	1.4	1.1	1.0	1.0
EMPLOYMENT, % CHANGE						
Unemployment Rate (%)	9.8	9.7	9.5	9.1	8.7	8.5
Employment	1.7	0.2	0.1	0.2	0.2	0.2
Labour Force	0.6	0.3	0.0	0.0	0.0	0.0
EXTERNAL TRADE (BOP)						
Visible Trade Balance	7317.0	9510.0	11093.3	18336.9	22478.7	27585.0
Curr Acc and Cap Mov	-9332.8	-21936.6	-3305.0	-1050.5	-421.7	-126.5
As % GDP	-0.4	-0.9	-0.1	0.0	0.0	0.0
GOVERNMENT ACCOUNTS						
Government Revenues % of GDP	44.0	43.9	42.6	42.0	41.6	41.2
Government Expend % of GDP	45.0	44.8	43.0	42.3	41.8	41.2
Net Lending As % GDP	-1.0	-0.9	-0.4	-0.3	-0.1	0.1
Gross Debt % of GDP	105.0	102.3	96.8	92.5	88.4	84.4
INTERNATIONAL INDICATORS						
Exch. Rate Euro vs US$	0.9	0.9	1.0	1.0	1.1	1.1
World Trade Index	1.4	2.7	7.7	7.6	6.7	6.4
World Price of Raw Materials	-13.7	-1.8	2.6	0.6	0.7	0.4
World Price of Oil	24.6	20.6	23.4	25.4	26.2	26.8
Capacity Utilization	75.6	74.5	75.2	75.7	75.9	75.9

"Do it yourself" model

GDP AT CONSTANT PRICES

	2001	2002	2003	2004	2005	2006
Gross Domestic Product	1.8	1.2	4.2	3.6	4.0	4.3
Private Consumption	1.5	1.7	3.7	2.8	3.2	3.1
Public Consumption	0.9	1.7	2.2	2.4	2.3	2.3
Total Fixed Investment	1.3	2.1	4.0	4.6	4.8	4.5
Exp. of Goods and Serv	5.6	3.7	7.6	5.9	6.1	5.8
Imp. of goods and serv.	4.1	4.1	8.2	6.4	5.8	5.2
PRICES, % CHANGE						
Consumer Prices	2.8	1.6	1.1	0.8	0.6	0.5
Wholesale Prices	2.1	0.9	0.8	0.8	0.5	0.4
EMPLOYMENT, % CHANGE						
Unemployment Rate (%)	9.8	9.5	8.7	7.7	6.2	4.2
Employment	1.7	0.4	0.7	1.2	1.6	2.1
Labour Force	0.6	0.3	-0.1	0.0	0.0	0.0
EXTERNAL TRADE (BOP)						
Visible Trade Balance	7317.0	9480.2	11075.7	19499.2	26098.9	35390.5
Curr Acc and Cap Mov	-9332.8	-21795.5	-2974.2	1024.0	4426.3	9310.0
As % GDP	-0.4	-0.9	-0.1	0.0	0.2	0.3
GOVERNMENT ACCOUNTS						
Government Revenues % of GDP	44.0	42.9	40.6	38.7	36.7	34.4
Government Expend % of GDP	45.0	43.5	40.6	38.7	36.7	34.4
Net Lending As % GDP	-1.0	-0.5	0.0	0.0	0.0	0.0
Gross Debt % of GDP	105.0	102.0	96.4	92.6	89.6	87.3
INTERNATIONAL INDICATORS						
Exch. Rate Euro vs US$	0.9	0.9	1.0	1.0	1.1	1.1
World Trade Index	1.4	2.7	7.7	7.6	6.7	6.4
World Price of Raw Materials	-13.7	-1.8	2.5	0.4	0.6	0.2
World Price of Oil	24.6	20.6	23.4	25.4	26.2	26.8
Capacity Utilization	75.6	74.7	75.7	76.6	77.2	77.8

Appendix

Lower Spending and Lower Taxes

GDP AT CONSTANT PRICES

	2001	2002	2003	2004	2005	2006
Gross Domestic Product	1.8	1.7	4.2	3.5	3.9	4.0
Private Consumption	1.5	1.8	3.7	2.8	3.0	2.8
Public Consumption	0.9	1.7	2.2	2.4	2.3	2.3
Total Fixed Investment	1.3	2.1	4.0	4.5	4.5	4.1
Exp. of Goods and Serv	5.6	3.7	7.5	5.7	6.0	5.6
Imp. of goods and serv.	4.1	4.2	8.3	6.4	5.8	5.1

PRICES, % CHANGE

Consumer Prices	2.8	1.6	1.1	0.5	0.3	0.2
Wholesale Prices	2.1	0.9	0.7	0.5	0.3	0.2

EMPLOYMENT, % CHANGE

Unemployment Rate (%)	9.8	9.5	8.7	7.7	6.3	4.4
Employment	1.7	0.4	0.7	1.1	1.5	2.0
Labour Force	0.6	0.3	-0.1	0.0	0.0	0.0

EXTERNAL TRADE (BOP)

Visible Trade Balance	7317.0	8798.5	9332.2	16792.6	22556.5	31280.7
Curr Acc and Cap Mov	-9332.8	-21516.0	-3830.5	-1206.2	362.4	3028.5
As % GDP	-0.4	-0.9	-0.1	0.0	0.0	0.1

GOVERNMENT ACCOUNTS

Government Revenues % of GDP	44.0	42.9	40.6	38.7	36.7	34.4
Government Expend % of GDP	45.0	43.4	40.6	38.7	36.8	34.7
Net Lending As % GDP	-1.0	-0.5	0.0	0.0	-0.1	-0.4
Gross Debt % of GDP	105.0	102.0	96.3	92.6	89.9	88.2

INTERNATIONAL INDICATORS

Exch. Rate Euro vs US$	0.9	0.9	1.0	1.0	1.1	1.1
World Trade Index	1.4	2.7	7.7	7.6	6.7	6.4
World Price of Raw Materials	-13.7	-1.9	2.6	0.5	0.8	0.6
World Price of Oil	24.6	20.6	23.4	25.4	26.2	26.8
Capacity Utilization	75.6	74.7	75.7	76.5	77.0	77.4

Lower spending, lower taxes, lower interest rates

GDP AT CONSTANT PRICES

	2001	2002	2003	2004	2005	2006
Gross Domestic Product	1.8	1.5	3.9	3.2	3.4	3.3
Private Consumption	1.5	1.7	3.8	3.3	3.5	3.2
Public Consumption	0.9	1.7	2.2	2.4	2.3	2.3
Total Fixed Investment	1.3	1.8	3.7	4.5	4.2	3.5
Exp. of Goods and Serv	5.6	3.6	7.7	6.1	6.1	5.8
Imp. of goods and serv.	4.1	4.1	8.4	7.0	6.1	5.3

PRICES, % CHANGE

Consumer Prices	2.8	1.6	1.1	0.5	-0.2	-0.7
Wholesale Prices	2.1	0.9	0.7	0.1	-0.7	-1.2

EMPLOYMENT, % CHANGE

Unemployment Rate (%)	9.8	9.5	8.7	7.6	6.0	4.1
Employment	1.7	0.4	0.7	1.3	1.7	2.1
Labour Force	0.6	0.3	-0.1	0.0	0.0	0.0

EXTERNAL TRADE (BOP)

Visible Trade Balance	7317.0	9156.6	9245.6	13831.1	17994.6	26383.3
Curr Acc and Cap Mov	-9332.8	-22319.3	-1426.1	2924.2	3433.7	5038.5
As % GDP	-0.4	-0.9	-0.1	0.1	0.1	0.2

GOVERNMENT ACCOUNTS

Government Revenues % of GDP	44.0	42.9	40.6	38.7	36.7	34.4
Government Expend % of GDP	45.0	42.5	39.5	37.2	35.1	32.8
Net Lending As % GDP	-1.0	0.4	1.1	1.5	1.6	1.6
Gross Debt % of GDP	105.0	100.6	94.0	88.7	83.9	80.0

INTERNATIONAL INDICATORS

Exch. Rate Euro vs US$	0.9	0.9	1.0	1.0	1.1	1.1
World Trade Index	1.4	2066.9	1985.1	1909.0	1820.5	1781.5
World Price of Raw Materials	-13.7	2.7	7.7	7.8	6.8	6.5
World Price of Oil	24.6	-1.8	2.1	0.3	0.6	0.6
Capacity Utilization	75.6	20.6	23.4	25.4	26.2	26.8
		74.7	75.8	76.8	77.6	78.1

Germany

Baseline

GDP AT CONSTANT PRICES

	2001	2002	2003	2004	2005	2006
Gross Domestic Product	0.7	0.7	2.5	2.4	2.3	2.3
Private Consumption	1.4	0.4	2.1	2.4	2.3	2.3
Public Consumption	1.1	-0.9	0.3	0.7	0.8	0.8
Total Fixed Investment	-3.9	-1.2	2.7	3.1	2.7	3.0
Exp. of Goods and Serv	5.4	2.2	6.6	6.7	6.3	6.0
Imp. of goods and serv.	1.6	0.8	6.9	6.6	6.4	6.1

PRICES, % CHANGE

	2001	2002	2003	2004	2005	2006
Consumer Prices	2.5	1.2	1.9	1.7	1.7	1.7
Wholesale Prices	3.2	0.4	1.4	1.5	1.6	1.6

EMPLOYMENT, % CHANGE

	2001	2002	2003	2004	2005	2006
Unemployment Rate (%)	9.4	9.9	9.6	8.8	8.3	7.7
Employment	0.2	0.2	0.3	0.2	0.2	0.2
Labour Force	0.3	0.9	0.5	0.5	0.5	0.5

EXTERNAL TRADE (BOP)

	2001	2002	2003	2004	2005	2006
Visible Trade Balance	71.6	82.2	89.5	96.2	97.5	99.5
Curr Acc and Cap Mov	-15.2	-3.4	-3.5	-2.2	-4.0	-5.3
As % GDP	-0.4	-0.1	-0.1	0.0	-0.1	-0.1

GOVERNMENT ACCOUNTS

	2001	2002	2003	2004	2005	2006
Current Revenues % of GDP	45.7	45.5	44.9	44.5	44.3	44.1
Current Expend % of GDP	47.3	47.9	47.1	46.4	45.7	45.2
Net Lending As % GDP	-1.7	-2.5	-2.1	-1.8	-1.4	-1.1
Gross Debt % of GDP	59.4	60.0	59.7	59.2	58.6	57.6

INTERNATIONAL INDICATORS

	2001	2002	2003	2004	2005	2006
Exch. Rate Euro vs US$	0.9	0.9	1.0	1.0	1.1	1.1
World Trade Index	2.3	3.0	8.4	7.8	6.7	6.5
World Price of Raw Materials	-13.7	-1.8	2.6	0.6	0.7	0.4
World Price of Oil	24.6	20.6	23.4	25.4	26.2	26.8
Capacity Utilization	86.5	84.2	84.9	85.8	86.5	87.2

"Do it yourself" model

GDP AT CONSTANT PRICES

	2001	2002	2003	2004	2005	2006
Gross Domestic Product	0.7	1.1	3.3	3.4	3.7	4.5
Private Consumption	1.4	1.2	3.5	4.2	4.7	6.0
Public Consumption	1.1	-0.9	0.3	0.7	0.8	0.8
Total Fixed Investment	-3.9	-1.0	3.5	4.1	4.0	4.7
Exp. of Goods and Serv	5.4	2.6	7.2	7.4	7.2	7.4
Imp. of goods and serv.	1.6	1.8	8.3	8.0	8.1	8.9

PRICES, % CHANGE

	2001	2002	2003	2004	2005	2006
Consumer Prices	2.5	1.0	1.4	1.0	0.5	0.5
Wholesale Prices	3.2	0.3	1.1	1.0	0.8	0.5

EMPLOYMENT, % CHANGE

	2001	2002	2003	2004	2005	2006
Unemployment Rate (%)	9.4	9.7	9.1	8.1	6.7	4.7
Employment	0.2	0.4	0.8	1.1	1.5	2.2
Labour Force	0.3	0.9	0.5	0.5	0.5	0.5

EXTERNAL TRADE (BOP)

	2001	2002	2003	2004	2005	2006
Visible Trade Balance	71.6	73.8	70.2	65.3	52.9	28.8
Curr Acc and Cap Mov	-15.2	-12.1	-24.2	-36.4	-54.6	-86.5
As % GDP	-0.4	-0.3	-0.6	-0.8	-1.2	-1.8

GOVERNMENT ACCOUNTS

	2001	2002	2003	2004	2005	2006
Current Revenues % of GDP	45.7	44.5	43.1	41.7	39.8	37.1
Current Expend % of GDP	47.3	46.7	44.5	42.3	39.8	37.0
Net Lending As % GDP	-1.7	-2.2	-1.3	-0.6	0.0	0.1
Gross Debt % of GDP	59.4	59.7	58.7	57.1	55.1	52.9

INTERNATIONAL INDICATORS

	2001	2002	2003	2004	2005	2006
Exch. Rate Euro vs US$	0.9	0.9	1.0	1.0	1.1	1.1
World Trade Index	2.3	3.2	8.6	7.9	6.8	6.7
World Price of Raw Materials	-13.7	-1.7	2.6	0.5	0.7	0.5
World Price of Oil	24.6	20.6	23.4	25.4	26.2	26.8
Capacity Utilization	86.5	84.6	86.0	87.6	89.5	92.4

Lower Spending and Lower Taxes

GDP AT CONSTANT PRICES

	2001	2002	2003	2004	2005	2006
Gross Domestic Product	0.7	1.2	3.3	3.5	3.7	4.3
Private Consumption	1.4	1.3	3.6	4.2	4.7	5.9
Public Consumption	1.1	-0.9	0.3	0.7	0.8	0.8
Total Fixed Investment	-3.9	-1.0	3.7	4.2	4.0	4.6
Exp. of Goods and Serv	5.4	2.7	7.4	7.5	7.3	7.4
Imp. of goods and serv.	1.6	2.0	8.5	8.2	8.3	9.0

PRICES, % CHANGE

	2001	2002	2003	2004	2005	2006
Consumer Prices	2.5	1.0	1.4	1.0	0.6	0.5
Wholesale Prices	3.2	0.3	1.1	1.1	0.9	0.5

EMPLOYMENT, % CHANGE

	2001	2002	2003	2004	2005	2006
Unemployment Rate (%)	9.4	9.7	9.0	8.0	6.7	4.7
Employment	0.2	0.4	0.9	1.1	1.5	2.1
Labour Force	0.3	0.9	0.5	0.5	0.5	0.5

EXTERNAL TRADE (BOP)

	2001	2002	2003	2004	2005	2006
Visible Trade Balance	71.6	72.7	68.7	63.3	50.2	24.8
Curr Acc and Cap Mov	-15.2	-13.1	-25.6	-38.3	-57.2	-90.3
As % GDP	-0.4	-0.3	-0.6	-0.8	-1.2	-1.8

GOVERNMENT ACCOUNTS

	2001	2002	2003	2004	2005	2006
Current Revenues % of GDP	45.7	44.5	43.2	41.7	39.8	37.0
Current Expend % of GDP	47.3	46.7	44.4	42.2	39.7	36.9
Net Lending As % GDP	-1.7	-2.2	-1.2	-0.5	0.1	0.1
Gross Debt % of GDP	59.4	59.7	58.5	56.8	54.6	52.4

INTERNATIONAL INDICATORS

	2001	2002	2003	2004	2005	2006
Exch. Rate Euro vs US$	0.9	0.9	1.0	1.0	1.1	1.1
World Trade Index	2.3	3.2	8.8	8.3	7.2	7.1
World Price of Raw Materials	-13.7	-1.9	2.6	0.5	0.8	0.6
World Price of Oil	24.6	20.6	23.4	25.4	26.2	26.8
Capacity Utilization	86.5	84.6	86.1	87.8	89.7	92.4

Lower spending, lower taxes, lower interest rates

GDP AT CONSTANT PRICES

	2001	2002	2003	2004	2005	2006
Gross Domestic Product	0.7	1.1	3.4	4.0	4.2	4.7
Private Consumption	1.4	1.2	3.8	4.7	5.1	6.3
Public Consumption	1.1	-0.9	0.3	0.7	0.8	0.8
Total Fixed Investment	-3.9	-1.0	3.7	5.0	5.0	5.2
Exp. of Goods and Serv	5.4	2.5	7.7	8.8	8.0	7.5
Imp. of goods and serv.	1.6	1.8	9.0	9.6	8.7	8.9

PRICES, % CHANGE

	2001	2002	2003	2004	2005	2006
Consumer Prices	2.5	1.0	1.4	1.1	0.9	0.8
Wholesale Prices	3.2	0.2	1.2	1.3	1.4	1.4

EMPLOYMENT, % CHANGE

	2001	2002	2003	2004	2005	2006
Unemployment Rate (%)	9.4	9.7	9.0	7.9	6.4	4.3
Employment	0.2	0.4	0.9	1.3	1.6	2.2
Labour Force	0.3	0.9	0.1	0.0	0.0	0.0

EXTERNAL TRADE (BOP)

	2001	2002	2003	2004	2005	2006
Visible Trade Balance	71.6	73.1	66.6	60.7	52.7	33.2
Curr Acc and Cap Mov	-15.2	-12.8	-27.4	-40.5	-54.8	-82.4
As % GDP	-0.4	-0.3	-0.6	-0.9	-1.1	-1.6

GOVERNMENT ACCOUNTS

	2001	2002	2003	2004	2005	2006
Current Revenues % of GDP	45.7	44.5	43.2	41.8	39.9	37.2
Current Expend % of GDP	47.3	46.7	44.4	41.9	39.1	36.1
Net Lending As % GDP	-1.7	-2.2	-1.2	-0.1	0.8	1.1
Gross Debt % of GDP	59.4	59.7	58.6	56.3	53.2	49.7

INTERNATIONAL INDICATORS

	2001	2002	2003	2004	2005	2006
Exch. Rate Euro vs US$	0.9	0.9	1.0	1.0	1.1	1.1
World Trade Index	2.3	3.1	9.0	9.3	7.8	7.2
World Price of Raw Materials	-13.7	-1.8	2.1	0.3	0.6	0.6
World Price of Oil	24.6	20.6	23.4	25.4	26.2	26.8
Capacity Utilization	86.5	84.6	86.2	88.6	91.3	94.5

Spain

Baseline

GDP AT CONSTANT PRICES

	2001	2002	2003	2004	2005	2006
Gross Domestic Product	2.7	2.0	3.3	3.1	3.0	3.0
Private Consumption	2.5	1.4	2.9	3.1	2.9	3.2
Public Consumption	2.0	2.1	2.0	1.9	1.9	2.0
Total Fixed Investment	3.4	2.2	3.7	4.3	4.0	3.9
Exp. of Goods and Serv	5.8	6.0	7.0	7.7	7.2	6.9
Imp. of goods and serv.	5.2	4.5	6.6	7.4	7.1	6.9

PRICES, % CHANGE

	2001	2002	2003	2004	2005	2006
Consumer Prices	3.6	2.1	2.1	2.1	2.0	2.0
Wholesale Prices	1.8	1.5	3.1	2.7	2.1	1.8

EMPLOYMENT, % CHANGE

	2001	2002	2003	2004	2005	2006
Unemployment Rate (%)	13.0	13.1	12.8	12.4	12.1	11.8
Employment	2.0	1.4	1.5	1.2	1.2	1.2
Labour Force	0.8	1.5	1.1	0.8	0.8	0.8

EXTERNAL TRADE (BOP)

	2001	2002	2003	2004	2005	2006
Visible Trade Balance	-6404.0	-7020.6	-7232.7	-7429.9	-7736.4	-7861.8
Curr Acc and Cap Mov	-3183.8	-4098.0	-4177.1	-4225.1	-4335.4	-4468.6
As % GDP	-3.0	-3.7	-3.5	-3.4	-3.3	-3.3

GOVERNMENT ACCOUNTS

	2001	2002	2003	2004	2005	2006
Current Revenues % of GDP	38.4	38.6	38.1	37.7	37.4	37.1
Current Expend % of GDP	38.1	38.3	38.0	37.8	37.7	37.5
Net Lending As % GDP	-0.1	-0.2	-0.3	-0.4	-0.6	-0.8
Gross Debt % of GDP	65.5	63.2	60.2	57.6	55.3	53.5

INTERNATIONAL INDICATORS

	2001	2002	2003	2004	2005	2006
Exch. Rate Euro vs US$	0.9	0.9	1.0	1.0	1.1	1.1
World Trade Index	1.8	2.5	7.9	7.5	6.4	6.1
World Price of Raw Materials	-13.7	-1.8	2.6	0.6	0.7	0.4
World Price of Oil	24.6	20.6	23.4	25.4	26.2	26.8
Capacity Utilization	79.4	79.3	80.1	80.2	80.2	80.2

"Do it yourself" model

GDP AT CONSTANT PRICES

	2001	2002	2003	2004	2005	2006
Gross Domestic Product	2.7	2.7	3.9	4.0	4.2	4.4
Private Consumption	2.5	2.7	4.8	5.1	5.5	6.3
Public Consumption	2.0	2.1	2.0	1.9	1.9	2.0
Total Fixed Investment	3.4	2.3	3.7	4.7	5.0	5.6
Exp. of Goods and Serv	5.8	6.2	7.3	8.2	7.5	6.9
Imp. of goods and serv.	5.2	5.5	8.5	9.0	9.1	9.3

PRICES, % CHANGE

	2001	2002	2003	2004	2005	2006
Consumer Prices	3.6	1.8	1.5	1.5	1.7	1.9
Wholesale Prices	1.8	1.1	2.5	2.2	1.9	2.1

EMPLOYMENT, % CHANGE

	2001	2002	2003	2004	2005	2006
Unemployment Rate (%)	13.0	13.0	12.6	12.2	11.6	10.9
Employment	2.0	1.6	1.5	1.4	1.5	1.6
Labour Force	0.8	1.5	1.1	0.9	0.8	0.8

EXTERNAL TRADE (BOP)

	2001	2002	2003	2004	2005	2006
Visible Trade Balance	-6404.0	-7340.9	-8224.6	-8994.9	-10168.1	-11508.7
Curr Acc and Cap Mov	-3183.8	-4456.5	-5280.6	-6033.4	-7222.3	-8908.6
As % GDP	-3.0	-4.0	-4.5	-4.8	-5.5	-6.3

GOVERNMENT ACCOUNTS

	2001	2002	2003	2004	2005	2006
Current Revenues % of GDP	38.4	37.5	36.1	34.6	33.1	31.5
Current Expend % of GDP	38.1	37.2	35.7	34.3	32.8	31.2
Net Lending As % GDP	-0.1	0.0	0.0	0.0	0.0	0.0
Gross Debt % of GDP	65.5	63.0	59.7	56.6	53.5	50.2

INTERNATIONAL INDICATORS

	2001	2002	2003	2004	2005	2006
Exch. Rate Euro vs US$	0.89	0.93	0.98	1.04	1.08	1.1
World Trade Index	1.8	2.6	8.1	7.7	6.5	6.2
World Price of Raw Materials	-13.7	-1.8	2.6	0.5	0.7	0.4
World Price of Oil	24.58	20.61	23.43	25.36	26.17	26.84
Capacity Utilization	79.37	77.68	79.14	80.27	81.62	83.27

Lower Spending and Lower Taxes

GDP AT CONSTANT PRICES

	2001	2002	2003	2004	2005	2006
Gross Domestic Product	2.7	2.6	4.2	4.6	4.5	4.8
Private Consumption	2.5	2.7	5.1	6.0	6.1	6.7
Public Consumption	2.0	2.1	2.0	1.9	1.9	2.0
Total Fixed Investment	3.4	2.3	4.0	6.1	6.7	7.5
Exp. of Goods and Serv	5.8	6.1	7.7	9.3	8.1	7.1
Imp. of goods and serv.	5.2	5.4	8.8	11.0	10.7	10.3

PRICES, % CHANGE

	2001	2002	2003	2004	2005	2006
Consumer Prices	3.6	1.8	1.4	1.6	2.2	3.1
Wholesale Prices	1.8	1.0	2.5	2.5	2.5	3.2

EMPLOYMENT, % CHANGE

	2001	2002	2003	2004	2005	2006
Unemployment Rate (%)	13.0	13.0	12.5	11.9	11.3	10.5
Employment	2.0	1.6	1.6	1.6	1.6	1.8
Labour Force	0.8	1.5	1.1	0.9	0.8	0.8

EXTERNAL TRADE (BOP)

	2001	2002	2003	2004	2005	2006
Visible Trade Balance	-6404.0	-7316.9	-8270.9	-9557.4	-11255.4	-13064.0
Curr Acc and Cap Mov	-3183.8	-4436.5	-5301.0	-6487.8	-8131.3	-10250.4
As % GDP	-3.0	-4.0	-4.5	-5.2	-6.1	-7.1

GOVERNMENT ACCOUNTS

	2001	2002	2003	2004	2005	2006
Current Revenues % of GDP	38.4	37.5	36.0	34.6	33.1	31.5
Current Expend % of GDP	38.1	37.2	35.6	34.0	32.3	30.5
Net Lending As % GDP	-0.1	0.0	0.1	0.3	0.5	0.7
Gross Debt % of GDP	65.5	63.0	59.6	55.9	52.0	47.6

INTERNATIONAL INDICATORS

	2001	2002	2003	2004	2005	2006
Exch. Rate Euro vs US$	0.9	0.9	1.0	1.0	1.1	1.1
World Trade Index	1.8	2.6	8.7	9.3	7.6	7.2
World Price of Raw Materials	-13.7	-1.8	2.1	0.3	0.6	0.6
World Price of Oil	24.6	20.6	23.4	25.4	26.2	26.8
Capacity Utilization	79.4	77.6	79.4	81.3	83.1	85.2

Lower spending, lower taxes, lower interest rates

GDP AT CONSTANT PRICES

	2001	2002	2003	2004	2005	2006
Gross Domestic Product	2.7	2.7	4.0	4.0	4.1	4.3
Private Consumption	2.5	2.8	4.9	5.2	5.5	6.2
Public Consumption	2.0	2.1	2.0	1.9	1.9	2.0
Total Fixed Investment	3.4	2.4	3.9	4.9	5.1	5.5
Exp. of Goods and Serv	5.8	6.2	7.3	8.2	7.5	7.0
Imp. of goods and serv.	5.2	5.5	8.7	9.2	9.3	9.4

PRICES, % CHANGE

	2001	2002	2003	2004	2005	2006
Consumer Prices	3.6	1.8	1.5	1.6	1.7	1.8
Wholesale Prices	1.8	1.1	2.5	2.3	1.9	2.1

EMPLOYMENT, % CHANGE

	2001	2002	2003	2004	2005	2006
Unemployment Rate (%)	13.0	12.9	12.6	12.2	11.6	10.9
Employment	2.0	1.6	1.5	1.4	1.4	1.6
Labour Force	0.8	1.5	1.1	0.9	0.8	0.8

EXTERNAL TRADE (BOP)

	2001	2002	2003	2004	2005	2006
Visible Trade Balance	-6404.0	-7351.4	-8293.4	-9083.9	-10235.8	-11426.9
Curr Acc and Cap Mov	-3183.8	-4461.8	-5335.9	-6105.4	-7276.8	-8824.4
As % GDP	-3.0	-4.0	-4.5	-4.9	-5.5	-6.3

GOVERNMENT ACCOUNTS

	2001	2002	2003	2004	2005	2006
Current Revenues % of GDP	38.4	37.5	36.1	34.6	33.1	31.5
Current Expend % of GDP	38.1	37.1	35.7	34.2	32.8	31.2
Net Lending As % GDP	-0.1	0.0	0.0	0.1	0.1	0.0
Gross Debt % of GDP	65.5	62.9	59.6	56.4	53.3	50.0

INTERNATIONAL INDICATORS

	2001	2002	2003	2004	2005	2006
Exch. Rate Euro vs US$	0.9	0.9	1.0	1.0	1.1	1.1
World Trade Index	1.8	2.7	8.3	8.1	7.1	7.1
World Price of Raw Materials	-13.7	-1.9	2.6	0.5	0.8	0.6
World Price of Oil	24.6	20.6	23.4	25.4	26.2	26.8
Capacity Utilization	79.4	77.7	79.2	80.4	81.6	83.1

France

Baseline

GDP AT CONSTANT PRICES

	2001	2002	2003	2004	2005	2006
Gross Domestic Product	2.10	1.40	3.20	3.00	2.50	2.60
Private Consumption	2.70	1.60	2.90	3.10	2.50	2.70
Public Consumption	2.30	1.20	0.60	0.60	0.60	0.80
Total Fixed Investment	2.70	1.00	6.90	5.00	3.60	3.40
Exp. of Goods and Serv	2.00	0.80	7.90	8.50	6.00	5.60
Imp. of goods and serv.	1.00	2.20	7.90	8.20	5.60	5.40

PRICES, % CHANGE

	2001	2002	2003	2004	2005	2006
Consumer Prices	1.70	1.50	1.90	1.80	1.70	1.70
Wholesale Prices	1.30	0.50	4.10	2.00	1.70	1.70

EMPLOYMENT, % CHANGE

	2001	2002	2003	2004	2005	2006
Unemployment Rate (%)	8.90	9.30	8.50	7.90	7.50	7.40
Employment	1.20	0.30	0.90	0.80	0.70	0.70
Labour Force	0.40	0.60	0.00	0.20	0.30	0.60

EXTERNAL TRADE (BOP)

	2001	2002	2003	2004	2005	2006
Visible Trade Balance	33.70	37.30	40.40	42.80	45.70	48.90
Curr Acc and Cap Mov	187.80	178.30	183.70	193.50	195.90	197.10
As % GDP	2.00	1.80	1.80	1.80	1.70	1.70

GOVERNMENT ACCOUNTS

	2001	2002	2003	2004	2005	2006
Current Revenues % of GDP	54.74	54.69	54.50	54.22	54.05	53.81
Current Expend % of GDP	56.20	56.55	55.65	55.04	54.81	54.51
Net Lending As % GDP	-1.47	-1.86	-1.16	-0.82	-0.77	-0.70
Gross Debt % of GDP	63.14	62.95	61.16	59.18	57.55	55.89

INTERNATIONAL INDICATORS

	2001	2002	2003	2004	2005	2006
Exch. Rate Euro vs US$	0.89	0.94	0.98	1.04	1.09	1.10
World Trade Index	2.20	2.80	8.00	7.40	6.80	6.50
World Price of Raw Materials	-13.70	-1.80	2.60	0.60	0.70	0.40
World Price of Oil	24.58	20.61	23.43	25.36	26.17	26.84
Capacity Utilization	83.86	82.42	83.54	84.40	84.49	84.78

"Do it yourself" model

GDP AT CONSTANT PRICES

	2001	2002	2003	2004	2005	2006
Gross Domestic Product	2.10	1.30	3.60	3.90	3.70	4.00
Private Consumption	2.70	1.10	2.20	3.00	2.90	3.50
Public Consumption	2.30	1.20	0.60	0.60	0.60	0.80
Total Fixed Investment	2.70	0.80	6.90	6.40	5.00	4.70
Exp. of Goods and Serv	2.00	0.70	8.10	9.50	6.90	6.20
Imp. of goods and serv.	1.00	1.40	7.10	9.10	6.90	6.90

PRICES, % CHANGE

	2001	2002	2003	2004	2005	2006
Consumer Prices	1.70	1.50	1.80	1.10	0.80	0.80
Wholesale Prices	1.30	0.50	3.90	1.50	1.00	1.10

EMPLOYMENT, % CHANGE

	2001	2002	2003	2004	2005	2006
Unemployment Rate (%)	8.90	9.30	8.50	7.40	6.00	4.30
Employment	1.20	0.20	0.90	1.30	1.50	1.50
Labour Force	0.40	0.60	1.00	1.00	1.00	1.00

EXTERNAL TRADE (BOP)

	2001	2002	2003	2004	2005	2006
Visible Trade Balance	33.70	56.60	87.80	92.90	83.70	54.30
Curr Acc and Cap Mov	187.80	198.60	234.30	248.20	238.60	206.00
As % GDP	2.00	2.00	2.30	2.30	2.10	1.80

GOVERNMENT ACCOUNTS

	2001	2002	2003	2004	2005	2006
Current Revenues % of GD	54.74	54.61	53.89	52.19	50.96	49.71
Current Expend % of GDP	56.20	55.70	53.88	52.18	50.95	49.69
Net Lending As % GDP	-1.47	-1.08	0.00	0.01	0.01	0.02
Gross Debt % of GDP	63.14	62.64	60.01	57.30	55.25	53.26

INTERNATIONAL INDICATORS

	2001	2002	2003	2004	2005	2006
Exch. Rate Euro vs US$	0.89	0.93	0.98	1.03	1.08	1.10
World Trade Index	2.20	2.70	8.00	7.80	7.10	6.60
World Price of Raw Mater	-13.70	-1.90	2.40	0.60	0.70	0.30
World Price of Oil	24.58	20.61	23.43	25.36	26.17	26.84
Capacity Utilization	83.86	82.09	82.92	84.25	85.1	86.28

Lower Spending and Lower Taxes

GDP AT CONSTANT PRICES

	2001	2002	2003	2004	2005	2006
Gross Domestic Product	2.10	1.50	3.70	4.10	3.60	3.80
Private Consumption	2.70	1.20	2.30	2.90	2.80	3.30
Public Consumption	2.30	1.20	0.60	0.60	0.60	0.80
Total Fixed Investment	2.70	1.00	7.10	6.10	4.70	4.50
Exp. of Goods and Serv	2.00	1.10	8.60	9.30	6.70	6.30
Imp. of goods and serv.	1.00	1.90	7.60	8.90	6.60	6.90

PRICES, % CHANGE

	2001	2002	2003	2004	2005	2006
Consumer Prices	1.70	1.50	1.80	1.20	0.80	0.70
Wholesale Prices	1.30	0.50	4.00	1.60	0.90	0.90

EMPLOYMENT, % CHANGE

	2001	2002	2003	2004	2005	2006
Unemployment Rate (%)	8.90	9.30	8.50	7.40	6.10	4.70
Employment	1.20	0.20	0.90	1.30	1.40	1.50
Labour Force	0.40	0.60	0.00	0.10	0.00	0.00

EXTERNAL TRADE (BOP)

	2001	2002	2003	2004	2005	2006
Visible Trade Balance	33.70	55.40	88.40	99.80	100.30	78.50
Curr Acc and Cap Mov	187.80	197.40	234.70	255.60	257.10	234.40
As % GDP	2.00	2.00	2.30	2.40	2.30	2.00

GOVERNMENT ACCOUNTS

	2001	2002	2003	2004	2005	2006
Current Revenues % of GDP	54.74	54.58	53.83	52.17	50.95	49.67
Current Expend % of GDP	56.20	55.62	53.75	52.12	50.94	49.75
Net Lending As % GDP	-1.47	-1.04	0.08	0.06	0.00	-0.08
Gross Debt % of GDP	63.14	62.53	59.75	57.03	55.06	53.26

INTERNATIONAL INDICATORS

	2001	2002	2003	2004	2005	2006
Exch. Rate Euro vs US$	0.89	0.93	0.98	1.04	1.10	1.13
World Trade Index	2.20	3.30	8.80	8.20	7.60	7.50
World Price of Raw Materials	-13.70	-1.90	2.60	0.50	0.80	0.60
World Price of Oil	24.58	20.61	23.43	25.36	26.17	26.84
Capacity Utilization	83.86	82.25	83.21	84.32	84.95	85.96

Lower spending, lower taxes, lower interest rates

GDP AT CONSTANT PRICES

	2001	2002	2003	2004	2005	2006
Gross Domestic Product	2.10	1.20	3.50	3.90	3.00	2.80
Private Consumption	2.70	1.10	2.50	3.40	3.10	3.40
Public Consumption	2.30	1.20	0.60	0.60	0.60	0.80
Total Fixed Investment	2.70	0.60	7.00	6.70	4.60	3.60
Exp. of Goods and Serv	2.00	1.00	8.90	10.60	7.30	6.50
Imp. of goods and serv.	1.00	1.60	8.20	10.70	7.30	6.80

PRICES, % CHANGE

	2001	2002	2003	2004	2005	2006
Consumer Prices	1.70	1.50	1.80	1.30	1.20	1.40
Wholesale Prices	1.30	0.50	4.00	1.90	1.50	1.60

EMPLOYMENT, % CHANGE

	2001	2002	2003	2004	2005	2006
Unemployment Rate (%)	8.90	9.30	8.50	7.20	5.90	4.60
Employment	1.20	0.20	1.00	1.50	1.40	1.40
Labour Force	0.40	0.60	0.00	0.10	0.00	0.00

EXTERNAL TRADE (BOP)

	2001	2002	2003	2004	2005	2006
Visible Trade Balance	33.70	58.60	81.20	67.80	59.50	43.80
Curr Acc and Cap Mov	187.80	200.70	227.80	221.40	210.30	190.10
As % GDP	2.00	2.00	2.20	2.00	1.90	1.60

GOVERNMENT ACCOUNTS

	2001	2002	2003	2004	2005	2006
Current Revenues % of GDP	54.74	54.59	53.82	52.10	50.89	49.66
Current Expend % of GDP	56.20	55.67	53.69	51.76	50.43	49.15
Net Lending As % GDP	-1.47	-1.08	0.12	0.34	0.46	0.52
Gross Debt % of GDP	63.14	62.60	59.72	56.44	53.79	51.16

INTERNATIONAL INDICATORS

	2001	2002	2003	2004	2005	2006
Exch. Rate Euro vs US$	0.89	0.94	0.98	1.01	1.06	1.09
World Trade Index	2.20	3.20	9.10	9.20	8.10	7.70
World Price of Raw Materials	-13.70	-1.80	2.10	0.30	0.60	0.60
World Price of Oil	24.58	20.61	23.43	25.36	26.17	26.84
Capacity Utilization	83.86	82.15	83.36	85.22	86.16	87.14

Belgium

Baseline

GDP AT CONSTANT PRICES

	2001	2002	2003	2004	2005	2006
Gross Domestic Product	1.3	1.7	2.4	2.4	2.6	2.5
Private Consumption	1.4	1.0	1.4	2.5	3.4	3.0
Public Consumption	1.6	0.1	1.2	1.3	1.3	1.3
Total Fixed Investment	-0.1	0.5	7.8	7.8	3.6	2.6
Exp. of Goods and Serv	1.5	3.7	9.3	6.4	5.8	5.9
Imp. of goods and serv.	1.4	2.4	10.4	7.7	6.5	6.1

PRICES, % CHANGE

	2001	2002	2003	2004	2005	2006
Consumer Prices	2.5	1.2	1.9	1.9	1.9	2.0
Wholesale Prices	3.2	1.3	1.6	1.5	1.6	1.7

EMPLOYMENT, % CHANGE

	2001	2002	2003	2004	2005	2006
Unemployment Rate (%)	10.8	11.0	10.8	10.6	10.4	10.1
Employment	1.1	0.4	0.2	0.2	0.1	0.0
Labour Force	0.7	0.6	0.0	0.0	0.0	0.0

EXTERNAL TRADE (BOP)

	2001	2002	2003	2004	2005	2006
Visible Trade Balance	572.7	770.9	781.8	783.6	770.2	718.8
Curr Acc and Cap Mov	543.5	567.0	580.7	583.9	575.2	564.4
As % GDP	5.3	5.3	5.2	5.0	4.7	4.4

GOVERNMENT ACCOUNTS

	2001	2002	2003	2004	2005	2006
Current Revenues % of GDP	46.7	46.1	45.8	45.2	44.5	44.0
Current Expend % of GDP	46.5	46.0	45.4	44.7	44.0	43.5
Net Lending As % GDP	0.2	0.0	0.5	0.5	0.5	0.5
Gross Debt % of GDP	106.0	102.1	97.3	92.4	87.8	83.6

INTERNATIONAL INDICATORS

	2001	2002	2003	2004	2005	2006
Exch. Rate Euro vs US$	0.9	0.9	1.0	1.0	1.1	1.1
World Trade Index	1.8	2.3	8.1	7.7	6.7	6.4
World Price of Raw Materials	-13.7	-1.8	2.6	0.6	0.7	0.4
World Price of Oil	24.6	20.6	23.4	25.4	26.2	26.8

"Do it yourself" model

GDP AT CONSTANT PRICES

	2001	2002	2003	2004	2005	2006
Gross Domestic Product	1.3	1.9	2.5	2.5	2.6	2.7
Private Consumption	1.4	1.4	2.3	3.2	3.8	3.5
Public Consumption	1.6	0.1	1.2	1.3	1.3	1.3
Total Fixed Investment	-0.1	0.6	8.1	8.3	4.2	3.1
Exp. of Goods and Serv	1.5	3.7	9.3	6.5	5.8	5.9
Imp. of goods and serv.	1.4	2.6	11.0	8.2	6.8	6.2

PRICES, % CHANGE

	2001	2002	2003	2004	2005	2006
Consumer Prices	2.5	1.3	2.1	2.3	2.2	2.2
Wholesale Prices	3.2	1.4	1.8	1.9	1.9	1.8

EMPLOYMENT, % CHANGE

	2001	2002	2003	2004	2005	2006
Unemployment Rate (%)	10.8	10.9	10.6	10.4	10.2	9.9
Employment	1.1	0.5	0.3	0.3	0.1	0.0
Labour Force	0.7	0.6	-0.1	0.1	-0.2	-0.3

EXTERNAL TRADE (BOP)

	2001	2002	2003	2004	2005	2006
Visible Trade Balance	572.7	709.4	651.8	616.5	569.6	497.4
Curr Acc and Cap Mov	543.5	504.1	448.0	412.4	369.7	338.0
As % GDP	5.3	4.7	4.0	3.5	3.0	2.6

GOVERNMENT ACCOUNTS

	2001	2002	2003	2004	2005	2006
Current Revenues % of GDP	46.7	46.1	44.2	43.5	42.9	42.3
Current Expend % of GDP	46.5	46.0	44.2	43.4	42.8	42.3
Net Lending As % GDP	0.2	0.0	0.0	0.0	0.0	0.0
Gross Debt % of GDP	106.0	101.8	97.0	92.2	87.7	83.8

INTERNATIONAL INDICATORS

	2001	2002	2003	2004	2005	2006
Exch. Rate Euro vs US$	0.9	0.9	1.0	1.0	1.1	1.1
World Trade Index	1.8	2.3	8.1	7.7	6.6	6.4
World Price of Raw Materials	-13.7	-1.7	2.6	0.6	0.7	0.4
World Price of Oil	24.6	20.6	23.4	25.4	26.2	26.8

Lower Spending and Lower Taxes

GDP AT CONSTANT PRICES

	2001	2002	2003	2004	2005	2006
Gross Domestic Product	1.3	1.9	2.5	2.4	2.4	2.5
Private Consumption	1.4	1.5	2.3	3.1	3.7	3.3
Public Consumption	1.6	0.1	1.2	1.3	1.3	1.3
Total Fixed Investment	-0.1	0.7	8.2	8.3	3.9	2.3
Exp. of Goods and Serv	1.5	4.0	9.7	6.6	6.1	6.6
Imp. of goods and serv.	1.4	2.9	11.5	8.5	7.2	6.8

PRICES, % CHANGE

	2001	2002	2003	2004	2005	2006
Consumer Prices	2.5	1.3	1.9	2.0	1.8	1.3
Wholesale Prices	3.2	1.3	1.6	1.6	1.5	0.9

EMPLOYMENT, % CHANGE

	2001	2002	2003	2004	2005	2006
Unemployment Rate (%)	10.8	11.0	10.7	10.5	10.5	10.5
Employment	1.1	0.4	0.3	0.2	0.0	0.0
Labour Force	0.7	0.6	0.0	0.0	0.0	0.0

EXTERNAL TRADE (BOP)

	2001	2002	2003	2004	2005	2006
Visible Trade Balance	572.7	749.3	710.6	665.2	608.4	540.2
Curr Acc and Cap Mov	543.5	545.2	509.4	465.6	414.9	388.4
As % GDP	5.3	5.1	4.5	3.9	3.4	3.0

GOVERNMENT ACCOUNTS

	2001	2002	2003	2004	2005	2006
Current Revenues % of GDP	46.7	46.1	43.3	41.6	39.9	38.3
Current Expend % of GDP	46.5	46.0	43.3	41.6	40.1	38.7
Net Lending As % GDP	0.2	0.0	0.0	0.0	-0.2	-0.4
Gross Debt % of GDP	106.0	102.1	97.5	93.0	89.1	86.0

INTERNATIONAL INDICATORS

	2001	2002	2003	2004	2005	2006
Exch. Rate Euro vs US$	0.9	0.9	1.0	1.0	1.1	1.1
World Trade Index	1.8	2.7	8.7	8.5	7.6	7.7
World Price of Raw Materials	-13.7	-1.9	2.6	0.5	0.8	0.6
World Price of Oil	24.6	20.6	23.4	25.4	26.2	26.8

Lower spending, lower taxes, lower interest rates

GDP AT CONSTANT PRICES

	2001	2002	2003	2004	2005	2006
Gross Domestic Product	1.3	1.8	2.7	2.7	2.8	2.6
Private Consumption	1.4	1.4	2.5	3.6	4.1	3.5
Public Consumption	1.6	0.1	1.2	1.3	1.3	1.3
Total Fixed Investment	-0.1	0.6	8.3	9.4	5.4	3.9
Exp. of Goods and Serv	1.5	3.8	10.1	7.9	6.6	6.5
Imp. of goods and serv.	1.4	2.7	11.8	10.0	7.9	7.1

PRICES, % CHANGE

	2001	2002	2003	2004	2005	2006
Consumer Prices	2.5	1.2	1.9	2.4	2.6	2.4
Wholesale Prices	3.2	1.3	1.6	2.1	2.3	2.1

EMPLOYMENT, % CHANGE

	2001	2002	2003	2004	2005	2006
Unemployment Rate (%)	10.8	11.0	10.7	10.3	10.1	10.0
Employment	1.1	0.4	0.3	0.4	0.2	0.1
Labour Force	0.7	0.6	0.0	0.0	0.0	0.0

EXTERNAL TRADE (BOP)

	2001	2002	2003	2004	2005	2006
Visible Trade Balance	572.7	751.8	704.2	639.0	572.0	452.6
Curr Acc and Cap Mov	543.5	548.0	502.4	438.3	376.3	297.4
As % GDP	5.3	5.1	4.5	3.7	3.0	2.3

GOVERNMENT ACCOUNTS

	2001	2002	2003	2004	2005	2006
Current Revenues % of GDP	46.7	44.9	43.3	41.6	39.9	38.3
Current Expend % of GDP	46.5	45.0	43.2	41.3	39.5	37.8
Net Lending As % GDP	0.2	-0.2	0.1	0.3	0.4	0.4
Gross Debt % of GDP	106.0	102.2	97.4	92.1	86.9	82.2

INTERNATIONAL INDICATORS

	2001	2002	2003	2004	2005	2006
Exch. Rate Euro vs US$	0.9	0.9	1.0	1.0	1.1	1.1
World Trade Index	1.8	2.5	9.1	9.7	8.1	7.7
World Price of Raw Materials	-13.7	-1.8	2.1	0.3	0.6	0.6
World Price of Oil	24.6	20.6	23.4	25.4	26.2	26.8

Finland

Baseline

GDP AT CONSTANT PRICES

	2001	2002	2003	2004	2005	2006
Gross Domestic Product	0.3	1.3	3.6	3.5	3.2	3.1
Private Consumption	1.7	1.2	3.1	2.9	3.0	2.9
Public Consumption	1.7	1.4	1.5	1.4	1.3	1.5
Total Fixed Investment	2.2	0.7	4.5	4.6	4.1	3.9
Exp. of Goods and Serv	-3.6	1.3	8.1	6.4	6.3	6.2
Imp. of goods and serv.	-2.6	2.4	9.0	6.7	6.3	6.3

PRICES, % CHANGE

	2001	2002	2003	2004	2005	2006
Consumer Prices	2.6	1.7	2.0	2.0	1.9	1.8
Wholesale Prices	n.a	n.a	n.a	n.a	n.a	n.a

EMPLOYMENT, % CHANGE

	2001	2002	2003	2004	2005	2006
Unemployment Rate (%)	9.2	9.5	9.1	8.7	8.3	7.9
Employment	1.1	0.2	0.8	0.8	0.8	0.8
Labour Force	0.5	0.5	0.3	0.3	0.3	0.3

EXTERNAL TRADE (BOP)

	2001	2002	2003	2004	2005	2006
Visible Trade Balance	69077.9	66356.2	69910.6	74540.7	80788.1	86934.3
Curr Acc and Cap Mov	43829.0	47300.2	49631.8	52721.1	57005.6	57210.8
As % GDP	5.4	5.7	5.6	5.7	5.8	5.5

GOVERNMENT ACCOUNTS

	2001	2002	2003	2004	2005	2006
Current Revenues % of GDP	49.4	49.1	48.3	47.3	46.4	45.6
Current Expend % of GDP	43.8	44.0	43.0	42.1	41.3	40.5
Net Lending As % GDP	5.6	5.2	5.2	5.2	5.1	5.0
Gross Debt % of GDP	41.3	38.7	35.2	31.6	28.2	24.8

INTERNATIONAL INDICATORS

	2001	2002	2003	2004	2005	2006
Exch. Rate Euro vs US$	0.9	0.9	1.0	1.0	1.1	1.1
World Trade Index	1.9	3.1	7.7	7.6	6.8	6.5
World Price of Raw Materials	-13.7	-1.8	2.6	0.6	0.7	0.4
World Price of Oil	24.6	20.6	23.4	25.4	26.2	26.8
Capacity Utilization	n.a	n.a	n.a	n.a	n.a	n.a

"Do it yourself" model

GDP AT CONSTANT PRICES

	2001	2002	2003	2004	2005	2006
Gross Domestic Product	0.3	1.8	4.3	4.3	4.0	3.7
Private Consumption	1.7	2.7	5.4	5.4	5.6	5.6
Public Consumption	1.7	1.4	1.5	1.4	1.3	1.5
Total Fixed Investment	2.2	0.8	4.7	5.2	5.4	5.8
Exp. of Goods and Serv	-3.6	1.4	8.3	6.6	6.3	5.8
Imp. of goods and serv.	-2.6	3.2	10.5	8.7	8.5	8.7

PRICES, % CHANGE

	2001	2002	2003	2004	2005	2006
Consumer Prices	2.6	1.5	1.9	2.0	2.1	2.0
Wholesale Prices	n.a	n.a	n.a	n.a	n.a	n.a

EMPLOYMENT, % CHANGE

	2001	2002	2003	2004	2005	2006
Unemployment Rate (%)	9.2	9.4	8.8	8.2	7.6	7.0
Employment	1.1	0.3	1.0	1.0	1.0	1.0
Labour Force	0.5	0.5	0.3	0.3	0.3	0.3

EXTERNAL TRADE (BOP)

	2001	2002	2003	2004	2005	2006
Visible Trade Balance	69077.9	64341.9	63836.6	62704.4	61027.5	56164.6
Curr Acc and Cap Mov	43829.0	45186.3	43320.6	40419.3	36410.7	25023.2
As % GDP	5.4	5.4	4.9	4.3	3.6	2.3

GOVERNMENT ACCOUNTS

	2001	2002	2003	2004	2005	2006
Current Revenues % of GDP	49.4	48.2	46.5	44.8	43.1	41.6
Current Expend % of GDP	43.8	43.8	42.6	41.4	40.3	39.4
Net Lending As % GDP	5.6	4.4	4.0	3.4	2.8	2.2
Gross Debt % of GDP	41.3	39.0	36.3	34.0	32.1	30.6

INTERNATIONAL INDICATORS

	2001	2002	2003	2004	2005	2006
Exch. Rate Euro vs US$	0.9	0.9	1.0	1.0	1.1	1.1
World Trade Index	1.9	3.2	7.8	7.8	6.9	6.5
World Price of Raw Materials	-13.7	-1.8	2.5	0.5	0.6	0.3
World Price of Oil	24.6	20.6	23.4	25.4	26.2	26.8
Capacity Utilization	n.a	n.a	n.a	n.a	n.a	n.a

Lower Spending and Lower Taxes

GDP AT CONSTANT PRICES

	2001	2002	2003	2004	2005	2006
Gross Domestic Product	0.3	1.9	4.4	4.3	3.8	3.4
Private Consumption	1.7	2.7	5.5	5.5	5.6	5.5
Public Consumption	1.7	1.4	1.5	1.4	1.3	1.5
Total Fixed Investment	2.2	0.9	5.0	5.5	5.5	5.6
Exp. of Goods and Serv	-3.6	1.7	8.7	6.7	6.4	6.0
Imp. of goods and serv.	-2.6	3.6	11.2	9.1	9.0	9.2

PRICES, % CHANGE

	2001	2002	2003	2004	2005	2006
Consumer Prices	2.6	1.5	2.0	2.1	2.2	2.1
Wholesale Prices	n.a	n.a	n.a	n.a	n.a	n.a

EMPLOYMENT, % CHANGE

	2001	2002	2003	2004	2005	2006
Unemployment Rate (%)	9.2	9.4	8.8	8.2	7.6	7.0
Employment	1.1	0.3	1.0	1.0	1.0	0.9
Labour Force	0.5	0.5	0.3	0.3	0.3	0.3

EXTERNAL TRADE (BOP)

	2001	2002	2003	2004	2005	2006
Visible Trade Balance	69077.9	64435.1	63651.6	61756.0	58560.5	52057.1
Curr Acc and Cap Mov	43829.0	45251.7	43099.8	39415.9	33893.6	20893.0
As % GDP	5.4	5.4	4.8	4.2	3.4	1.9

GOVERNMENT ACCOUNTS

	2001	2002	2003	2004	2005	2006
Current Revenues % of GDP	49.4	48.2	46.5	44.8	43.1	41.6
Current Expend % of GDP	43.8	43.8	42.5	41.3	40.3	39.5
Net Lending As % GDP	5.6	4.5	4.0	3.4	2.8	2.1
Gross Debt % of GDP	41.3	39.0	36.2	33.8	31.9	30.5

INTERNATIONAL INDICATORS

	2001	2002	2003	2004	2005	2006
Exch. Rate Euro vs US$	0.9	0.9	1.0	1.0	1.1	1.1
World Trade Index	1.9	3.5	8.3	8.2	7.5	7.3
World Price of Raw Materials	-13.7	-1.9	2.6	0.5	0.8	0.6
World Price of Oil	24.6	20.6	23.4	25.4	26.2	26.8
Capacity Utilization	n.a	n.a	n.a	n.a	n.a	n.a

Lower spending, lower taxes, lower interest rates

GDP AT CONSTANT PRICES

	2001	2002	2003	2004	2005	2006
Gross Domestic Product	0.3	1.8	4.6	4.8	4.4	3.9
Private Consumption	1.7	2.7	5.6	6.0	6.2	6.0
Public Consumption	1.7	1.4	1.5	1.4	1.3	1.5
Total Fixed Investment	2.2	0.8	5.0	6.6	7.0	7.4
Exp. of Goods and Serv	-3.6	1.6	9.0	8.0	7.1	6.2
Imp. of goods and serv.	-2.6	3.4	11.2	10.6	10.1	9.9

PRICES, % CHANGE

	2001	2002	2003	2004	2005	2006
Consumer Prices	2.6	1.5	1.9	2.3	2.8	3.6
Wholesale Prices	n.a	n.a	n.a	n.a	n.a	n.a

EMPLOYMENT, % CHANGE

	2001	2002	2003	2004	2005	2006
Unemployment Rate (%)	9.2	9.4	8.7	8.0	7.3	6.6
Employment	1.1	0.3	1.0	1.1	1.1	1.1
Labour Force	0.5	0.5	0.3	0.3	0.3	0.3

EXTERNAL TRADE (BOP)

	2001	2002	2003	2004	2005	2006
Visible Trade Balance	69077.9	64365.4	63594.1	62208.7	59493.8	51635.1
Curr Acc and Cap Mov	43829.0	45221.3	42999.7	39695.3	34464.1	19694.6
As % GDP	5.4	5.4	4.8	4.2	3.4	1.8

GOVERNMENT ACCOUNTS

	2001	2002	2003	2004	2005	2006
Current Revenues % of GDP	49.4	48.2	46.5	44.8	43.2	41.6
Current Expend % of GDP	43.8	43.8	42.5	41.1	39.9	38.8
Net Lending As % GDP	5.6	4.4	4.0	3.7	3.3	2.8
Gross Debt % of GDP	41.3	39.0	36.2	33.5	30.9	28.5

INTERNATIONAL INDICATORS

	2001	2002	2003	2004	2005	2006
Exch. Rate Euro vs US$	0.9	0.9	1.0	1.0	1.1	1.1
World Trade Index	1.9	3.4	8.5	9.1	8.0	7.4
World Price of Raw Materials	-13.7	-1.8	2.1	0.3	0.6	0.6
World Price of Oil	24.6	20.6	23.4	25.4	26.2	26.8
Capacity Utilization	n.a	n.a	n.a	n.a	n.a	n.a

Greece

Baseline

GDP AT CONSTANT PRICES

	2001	2002	2003	2004	2005	2006
Gross Domestic Product	4.2	3.2	3.8	3.8	3.6	3.5
Private Consumption	3.1	2.5	2.7	2.7	2.6	2.6
Public Consumption	1.6	1.2	0.9	0.4	0.6	0.6
Total Fixed Investment	6.7	3.6	4.7	6.5	6.3	5.9
Exp. of Goods and Serv	9.3	6.4	6.2	6.4	7.0	6.4
Imp. of goods and serv.	6.0	4.1	3.3	4.3	5.2	5.0

PRICES, % CHANGE

	2001	2002	2003	2004	2005	2006
Consumer Prices	3.4	2.5	2.6	2.4	2.7	2.6
Wholesale Prices	3.6	2.1	1.7	1.6	1.6	1.9

EMPLOYMENT, % CHANGE

	2001	2002	2003	2004	2005	2006
Unemployment Rate (%)	12.0	12.3	12.3	12.3	12.3	12.2
Employment	0.6	0.3	0.6	0.6	0.6	0.6
Labour Force	0.7	0.6	0.6	0.6	0.6	0.6

EXTERNAL TRADE (BOP)

	2001	2002	2003	2004	2005	2006
Visible Trade Balance	-18669.5	-19242.9	-19726.4	-20125.9	-20592.6	-21051.6
Curr Acc and Cap Mov	-4817.9	-4558.4	-4608.1	-4556.2	-4553.1	-4523.5
As % GDP	-3.7	-3.3	-3.2	-2.9	-2.8	-2.6

GOVERNMENT ACCOUNTS

	2001	2002	2003	2004	2005	2006
Current Revenues % of GDP	30.9	30.4	30.1	29.6	29.2	28.8
Current Expend % of GDP	31.1	30.4	30.1	29.6	29.1	28.7
Net Lending As % GDP	-0.2	0.0	0.0	0.0	0.1	0.1
Gross Debt % of GDP	98.4	93.3	87.7	82.5	77.6	73.0

INTERNATIONAL INDICATORS

	2001	2002	2003	2004	2005	2006
Exch. Rate Euro vs US$	0.9	0.9	1.0	1.0	1.1	1.1
World Trade Index	2.5	3.2	7.8	7.2	6.5	6.3
World Price of Raw Materials	-13.7	-1.8	2.6	0.6	0.7	0.4
World Price of Oil	24.6	20.6	23.4	25.4	26.2	26.8
Capacity Utilization	n.a.	n.a.	n.a.	n.a.	n.a.	n.a.

"Do it yourself" model

GDP AT CONSTANT PRICES

	2001	2002	2003	2004	2005	2006
Gross Domestic Product	4.2	3.2	3.8	3.9	3.7	3.4
Private Consumption	3.1	2.5	2.7	2.9	2.8	2.7
Public Consumption	1.6	1.2	0.9	0.4	0.6	0.6
Total Fixed Investment	6.7	3.6	4.9	7.0	6.4	5.6
Exp. of Goods and Serv	9.3	6.4	6.3	6.5	7.0	6.2
Imp. of goods and serv.	6.0	4.1	3.4	4.7	5.5	5.2

PRICES, % CHANGE

	2001	2002	2003	2004	2005	2006
Consumer Prices	3.4	2.5	2.6	2.4	2.8	2.8
Wholesale Prices	3.6	2.1	1.7	1.7	1.8	2.1

EMPLOYMENT, % CHANGE

	2001	2002	2003	2004	2005	2006
Unemployment Rate (%)	12.0	12.3	12.3	12.2	12.2	12.1
Employment	0.6	0.3	0.6	0.7	0.6	0.6
Labour Force	0.7	0.6	0.6	0.6	0.6	0.6

EXTERNAL TRADE (BOP)

	2001	2002	2003	2004	2005	2006
Visible Trade Balance	-18669.5	-19242.8	-19747.1	-20258.5	-20819.6	-21352.2
Curr Acc and Cap Mov	-4817.9	-4558.3	-4623.8	-4668.2	-4767.1	-4856.3
As % GDP	-3.7	-3.3	-3.2	-3.0	-2.9	-2.8

GOVERNMENT ACCOUNTS

	2001	2002	2003	2004	2005	2006
Current Revenues % of GDP	30.9	29.4	28.1	26.5	24.9	23.5
Current Expend % of GDP	31.1	29.4	28.1	26.5	25.0	23.5
Net Lending As % GDP	-0.2	0.0	0.0	0.0	0.0	0.0
Gross Debt % of GDP	98.4	93.3	87.7	82.3	77.3	72.8

INTERNATIONAL INDICATORS

	2001	2002	2003	2004	2005	2006
Exch. Rate Euro vs US$	0.9	0.9	1.0	1.0	1.1	1.1
World Trade Index	2.5	3.2	7.9	7.4	6.7	6.3
World Price of Raw Materials	-13.7	-1.8	2.5	0.5	0.6	0.3
World Price of Oil	24.6	20.6	23.4	25.4	26.2	26.8
Capacity Utilization	n.a.	n.a.	n.a.	n.a.	n.a.	n.a.

Lower Spending and Lower Taxes

GDP AT CONSTANT PRICES	2001	2002	2003	2004	2005	2006
Gross Domestic Product	4.2	3.3	3.8	3.6	3.2	3.0
Private Consumption	3.1	2.5	2.7	2.8	2.7	2.6
Public Consumption	1.6	1.2	0.9	0.4	0.6	0.6
Total Fixed Investment	6.7	4.0	4.7	6.2	5.4	4.8
Exp. of Goods and Serv	9.3	6.8	6.6	6.6	7.1	6.7
Imp. of goods and serv.	6.0	4.5	3.8	4.9	5.9	5.8
PRICES, % CHANGE						
Consumer Prices	3.4	2.5	2.6	2.4	2.5	2.0
Wholesale Prices	3.6	2.1	1.8	1.6	1.3	1.2
EMPLOYMENT, % CHANGE						
Unemployment Rate (%)	12.0	12.3	12.3	12.3	12.4	12.6
Employment	0.6	0.3	0.6	0.5	0.4	0.4
Labour Force	0.7	0.6	0.6	0.6	0.6	0.6
EXTERNAL TRADE (BOP)						
Visible Trade Balance	-18669.5	-19349.4	-19897.7	-20379.3	-20867.0	-21276.1
Curr Acc and Cap Mov	-4817.9	-4632.8	-4699.8	-4730.4	-4806.5	-4835.7
As % GDP	-3.7	-3.4	-3.2	-3.0	-2.9	-2.8
GOVERNMENT ACCOUNTS						
Current Revenues % of GDP	30.9	29.4	28.0	26.5	25.2	24.0
Current Expend % of GDP	31.1	29.3	27.9	26.4	25.0	23.8
Net Lending As % GDP	-0.2	0.1	0.1	0.2	0.2	0.2
Gross Debt % of GDP	98.4	93.2	87.4	82.1	77.5	73.6
INTERNATIONAL INDICATORS						
Exch. Rate Euro vs US$	0.9	0.9	1.0	1.0	1.1	1.1
World Trade Index	2.5	3.6	8.5	7.9	7.3	7.4
World Price of Raw Materials	-13.7	-1.9	2.6	0.5	0.8	0.6
World Price of Oil	24.6	20.6	23.4	25.4	26.2	26.8
Capacity Utilization	n.a.	n.a.	n.a.	n.a.	n.a.	n.a.

Lower spending, lower taxes, lower interest rates

GDP AT CONSTANT PRICES	2001	2002	2003	2004	2005	2006
Gross Domestic Product	4.2	3.2	4.2	4.6	3.4	2.4
Private Consumption	3.1	2.5	2.9	3.4	2.9	2.3
Public Consumption	1.6	1.2	0.9	0.4	0.6	0.6
Total Fixed Investment	6.7	3.5	6.3	8.9	5.3	3.1
Exp. of Goods and Serv	9.3	6.6	7.0	7.6	7.3	6.3
Imp. of goods and serv.	6.0	4.3	4.3	6.2	6.0	5.4
PRICES, % CHANGE						
Consumer Prices	3.4	2.5	2.5	2.7	3.5	3.4
Wholesale Prices	3.6	2.1	1.8	2.2	2.6	2.7
EMPLOYMENT, % CHANGE						
Unemployment Rate (%)	12.0	12.3	12.2	11.9	11.8	12.0
Employment	0.6	0.3	0.7	1.0	0.7	0.3
Labour Force	0.7	0.6	0.6	0.6	0.6	0.6
EXTERNAL TRADE (BOP)						
Visible Trade Balance	-18669.5	-19256.4	-20081.8	-21151.9	-21779.6	-22237.4
Curr Acc and Cap Mov	-4817.9	-4557.0	-4869.3	-5308.4	-5301.3	-5151.0
As % GDP	-3.7	-3.3	-3.3	-3.4	-3.1	-2.9
GOVERNMENT ACCOUNTS						
Current Revenues % of GDP	30.9	29.4	28.0	26.1	24.5	23.1
Current Expend % of GDP	31.1	29.4	27.6	25.6	24.0	22.9
Net Lending As % GDP	-0.2	0.0	0.3	0.6	0.5	0.2
Gross Debt % of GDP	98.4	93.4	87.2	80.5	74.7	70.1
INTERNATIONAL INDICATORS						
Exch. Rate Euro vs US$	0.9	0.9	1.0	1.0	1.1	1.1
World Trade Index	2.5	3.5	8.7	8.8	7.8	7.4
World Price of Raw Materials	-13.7	-1.8	2.1	0.3	0.6	0.6
World Price of Oil	24.6	20.6	23.4	25.4	26.2	26.8
Capacity Utilization	n.a.	n.a.	n.a.	n.a.	n.a.	n.a.

Netherlands

Baseline

GDP AT CONSTANT PRICES

	2001	2002	2003	2004	2005	2006
Gross Domestic Product	0.80	1.10	3.90	3.30	3.20	3.10
Private Consumption	1.20	1.00	3.00	2.70	2.10	2.60
Public Consumption	2.90	1.90	1.90	1.90	1.90	1.90
Total Fixed Investment	-2.10	-1.40	4.20	4.50	4.40	4.20
Exp. of Goods and Serv	2.10	2.10	8.90	7.10	6.70	6.50
Imp. of goods and serv.	2.20	1.80	8.50	7.00	6.40	6.00

PRICES, % CHANGE

	2001	2002	2003	2004	2005	2006
Consumer Prices	4.50	2.40	2.00	1.90	1.90	1.90
Wholesale Prices	2.10	0.30	3.40	3.20	1.90	1.90

EMPLOYMENT, % CHANGE

	2001	2002	2003	2004	2005	2006
Unemployment Rate (%)	2.00	2.30	2.60	3.10	3.50	3.90
Employment	2.00	0.10	0.00	-0.20	-0.10	-0.10
Labour Force	1.50	0.40	0.30	0.30	0.30	0.30

EXTERNAL TRADE (BOP)

	2001	2002	2003	2004	2005	2006
Visible Trade Balance	54579.30	53287.30	59202.70	63046.30	71024.60	80147.30
Curr Acc and Cap Mov	37512.20	38179.70	38911.30	40061.40	41922.00	44336.50
As % GDP	4.10	4.00	3.90	3.80	3.70	3.70

GOVERNMENT ACCOUNTS

	2001	2002	2003	2004	2005	2006
Current Revenues % of GDP	42.90	42.85	42.67	42.61	42.48	42.44
Current Expend % of GDP	42.27	42.21	42.06	42.08	41.97	42.05
Net Lending As % GDP	0.63	0.64	0.61	0.53	0.51	0.39
Gross Debt % of GDP	54.03	52.21	48.41	45.28	42.38	39.74

INTERNATIONAL INDICATORS

	2001	2002	2003	2004	2005	2006
Exch. Rate Euro vs US$	0.89	0.94	0.98	1.04	1.09	1.10
World Trade Index	1.80	2.30	8.20	7.40	6.60	6.30
World Price of Raw Materials	-13.70	-1.80	2.60	0.60	0.70	0.40
World Price of Oil	24.58	20.61	23.43	25.36	26.17	26.84
Capacity Utilization	81.62	80.22	81.06	81.54	81.94	82.38

Lower Spending and Lower Taxes

GDP AT CONSTANT PRICES

	2001	2002	2003	2004	2005	2006
Gross Domestic Product	0.80	1.2	4.2	4.2	3.5	2.8
Private Consumption	1.20	1	3	2.8	2.2	2.6
Public Consumption	2.90	1.9	1.9	1.9	1.9	1.9
Total Fixed Investment	-2.10	-1.4	4.5	5.7	4.9	4.1
Exp. of Goods and Serv	2.10	2.3	9.8	8.9	7.6	6.7
Imp. of goods and serv.	2.20	2	9.2	8.3	7.1	6.6

PRICES, % CHANGE

	2001	2002	2003	2004	2005	2006
Consumer Prices	4.50	2.4	2	2.3	2.8	3.2
Wholesale Prices	2.10	0.3	3.5	3.7	2.9	3.1

EMPLOYMENT, % CHANGE

	2001	2002	2003	2004	2005	2006
Unemployment Rate (%)	2.00	2.3	2.5	2.9	3.1	3.5
Employment	2.00	0.1	0	0	0.1	-0.1
Labour Force	1.50	0.4	0.3	0.3	0.3	0.3

EXTERNAL TRADE (BOP)

	2001	2002	2003	2004	2005	2006
Visible Trade Balance	54579.30	53792.1	60208.8	68783.3	81934.5	90893.5
Curr Acc and Cap Mov	37512.20	38699.6	39896.6	45193.1	51499.6	53734
As % GDP	4.10	4.1	3.9	4.2	4.5	4.4

GOVERNMENT ACCOUNTS

	2001	2002	2003	2004	2005	2006
Current Revenues % of GDP	42.90	42.84	42.58	42.27	41.96	41.89
Current Expend % of GDP	42.27	42.16	41.76	41.02	40.4	40.62
Net Lending As % GDP	0.63	0.67	0.82	1.25	1.56	1.27
Gross Debt % of GDP	54.03	52.17	48.1	44.03	39.75	35.91

INTERNATIONAL INDICATORS

	2001	2002	2003	2004	2005	2006
Exch. Rate Euro vs US$	0.89	0.94	0.98	1.01	1.06	1.09
World Trade Index	1.80	2.7	9.3	9.5	8.1	7.7
World Price of Raw Materials	-13.70	-1.8	2.1	0.3	0.6	0.6
World Price of Oil	24.58	20.61	23.43	25.36	26.17	26.84
Capacity Utilization	81.62	80.26	81.31	82.42	83.04	83.17

Lower spending, lower taxes, lower interest rates

GDP AT CONSTANT PRICES

	2001	2002	2003	2004	2005	2006
Gross Domestic Product	0.80	1.30	4.10	3.30	3.00	2.80
Private Consumption	1.20	1.10	3.00	2.70	2.10	2.60
Public Consumption	2.90	1.90	1.90	1.90	1.90	1.90
Total Fixed Investment	-2.10	-1.30	4.40	4.60	4.30	3.80
Exp. of Goods and Serv	2.10	2.40	9.40	7.40	6.90	6.70
Imp. of goods and serv.	2.20	2.10	8.90	7.40	6.90	6.60

PRICES, % CHANGE

Consumer Prices	4.50	2.40	2.10	2.20	2.20	2.00
Wholesale Prices	2.10	0.30	3.50	3.40	2.10	1.80

EMPLOYMENT, % CHANGE

Unemployment Rate (%)	2.00	2.20	2.50	3.00	3.40	3.90
Employment	2.00	0.10	0.00	-0.20	-0.10	-0.20
Labour Force	1.50	0.40	0.30	0.30	0.30	0.30

EXTERNAL TRADE (BOP)

Visible Trade Balance	54579.30	53774.00	61525.10	65873.30	73634.50	80912.90
Curr Acc and Cap Mov	37512.20	38649.30	41119.50	42876.10	44856.10	46128.30
As % GDP	4.10	4.10	4.10	4.00	4.00	3.90

GOVERNMENT ACCOUNTS

Current Revenues % of GDP	42.90	42.82	42.57	42.48	42.37	42.39
Current Expend % of GDP	42.27	42.10	41.73	41.70	41.71	42.07
Net Lending As % GDP	0.63	0.72	0.84	0.78	0.66	0.32
Gross Debt % of GDP	54.03	52.12	48.01	44.56	41.44	38.87

INTERNATIONAL INDICATORS

Exch. Rate Euro vs US$	0.89	0.93	0.98	1.04	1.10	1.13
World Trade Index	1.80	2.90	9.00	8.30	7.60	7.70
World Price of Raw Materials	-13.70	-1.90	2.60	0.50	0.80	0.60
World Price of Oil	24.58	20.61	23.43	25.36	26.17	26.84
Capacity Utilization	81.62	80.32	81.29	81.75	82.01	82.16

Ireland

Baseline

GDP AT CONSTANT PRICES

	2001	2002	2003	2004	2005	2006
Gross Domestic Product	5.8	3.0	5.1	5.2	4.7	4.7
Private Consumption	4.1	3.0	5.5	3.8	3.9	3.7
Public Consumption	5.4	5.1	4.6	4.0	3.1	2.9
Total Fixed Investment	1.8	-1.4	4.5	4.9	5.0	4.3
Exp. of Goods and Serv	5.2	2.4	8.1	8.8	6.9	7.0
Imp. of goods and serv.	3.4	1.8	8.8	8.5	6.8	6.7

PRICES, % CHANGE

Consumer Prices	4.8	3.1	2.6	2.5	2.6	2.5
Wholesale Prices	1.8	0.7	1.2	1.6	1.5	2.0

EMPLOYMENT, % CHANGE

Unemployment Rate (%)	4.0	4.2	4.3	4.4	4.5	4.6
Employment	3.2	1.6	4.2	3.3	2.6	2.3
Labour Force	2.9	1.8	4.3	3.4	2.8	2.4

EXTERNAL TRADE (BOP)

Visible Trade Balance	26735.3	24783.2	26387.4	28327.5	30823.6	33433.8
Curr Acc and Cap Mov	-1051.0	-425.0	-207.0	-81.5	-3.8	-0.9
As % GDP	-1.2	-0.4	-0.2	-0.1	0.0	0.0

GOVERNMENT ACCOUNTS

Current Revenues % of GDP	25.1	25.2	24.4	23.5	22.9	22.2
Current Expend % of GDP	23.4	24.2	23.9	23.4	23.1	22.5
Net Lending As % GDP	1.7	0.9	0.5	0.1	-0.2	-0.3
Gross Debt % of GDP	34.1	31.5	28.4	25.9	24.1	22.6

INTERNATIONAL INDICATORS

Exch. Rate Euro vs US$	0.9	0.9	1.0	1.0	1.1	1.1
World Trade Index	1.5	2.6	8.0	7.3	6.5	6.3
World Price of Raw Materials	-13.7	-1.8	2.6	0.6	0.7	0.4
World Price of Oil	24.6	20.6	23.4	25.4	26.2	26.8
Capacity Utilization	n.a	n.a	n.a	n.a	n.a	n.a

Lower Spending and Lower Taxes

GDP AT CONSTANT PRICES

	2001	2002	2003	2004	2005	2006
Gross Domestic Product	5.8	3.2	5.4	5.5	4.9	4.8
Private Consumption	4.1	3.1	5.7	4.0	4.2	3.9
Public Consumption	5.4	5.1	4.6	4.0	3.1	2.9
Total Fixed Investment	1.8	-1.2	5.1	5.4	5.2	4.2
Exp. of Goods and Serv	5.2	2.8	8.6	9.2	7.2	7.5
Imp. of goods and serv.	3.4	2.1	9.4	9.0	7.2	7.2

PRICES, % CHANGE

Consumer Prices	4.8	3.1	2.6	2.5	2.7	2.7
Wholesale Prices	1.8	0.7	1.3	1.7	1.7	2.2

EMPLOYMENT, % CHANGE

Unemployment Rate (%)	4.0	4.1	4.1	4.1	4.2	4.3
Employment	3.2	1.6	4.3	3.4	2.7	2.3
Labour Force	2.9	1.8	4.3	3.4	2.8	2.4

EXTERNAL TRADE (BOP)

Visible Trade Balance	26735.3	24882.2	26564.6	28547.4	31003.7	33507.9
Curr Acc and Cap Mov	-1051.0	-380.5	-133.7	20.2	110.2	127.8
As % GDP	-1.2	-0.4	-0.1	0.0	0.1	0.1

GOVERNMENT ACCOUNTS

Current Revenues % of GDP	25.1	25.1	24.3	23.4	22.8	22.1
Current Expend % of GDP	23.4	24.1	23.7	23.1	22.8	22.2
Net Lending As % GDP	1.7	1.0	0.6	0.3	0.1	-0.1
Gross Debt % of GDP	34.1	31.4	28.1	25.4	23.4	21.6

INTERNATIONAL INDICATORS

Exch. Rate Euro vs US$	0.9	0.9	1.0	1.0	1.1	1.1
World Trade Index	1.5	2.9	8.6	7.9	7.2	7.2
World Price of Raw Materials	-13.7	-1.9	2.6	0.5	0.8	0.6
World Price of Oil	24.6	20.6	23.4	25.4	26.2	26.8
Capacity Utilization	n.a	n.a	n.a	n.a	n.a	n.a

Lower spending, lower taxes, lower interest rates

GDP AT CONSTANT PRICES	2001	2002	2003	2004	2005	2006
Gross Domestic Product	5.8	3.1	5.6	6.4	5.7	5.3
Private Consumption	4.1	3.0	5.8	4.6	4.9	4.4
Public Consumption	5.4	5.1	4.6	4.0	3.1	2.9
Total Fixed Investment	1.8	-1.4	5.6	7.5	6.9	4.9
Exp. of Goods and Serv	5.2	2.6	9.0	10.6	7.9	7.6
Imp. of goods and serv.	3.4	1.9	9.8	10.4	7.8	7.2
PRICES, % CHANGE						
Consumer Prices	4.8	3.1	2.6	2.7	3.0	3.2
Wholesale Prices	1.8	0.7	1.3	1.9	2.1	3.0
EMPLOYMENT, % CHANGE						
Unemployment Rate (%)	4.0	4.2	4.1	3.8	3.6	3.5
Employment	3.2	1.6	4.3	3.8	3.0	2.4
Labour Force	2.9	1.8	4.3	3.4	2.8	2.4
EXTERNAL TRADE (BOP)						
Visible Trade Balance	26735.3	24821.3	26634.3	29078.3	31946.9	34873.6
Curr Acc and Cap Mov	-1051.0	-394.6	-138.8	116.3	400.3	653.6
As % GDP	-1.2	-0.4	-0.1	0.1	0.3	0.5
GOVERNMENT ACCOUNTS						
Current Revenues % of GDP	25.1	25.1	24.3	23.3	22.7	21.9
Current Expend % of GDP	23.4	24.2	23.6	22.7	22.1	21.4
Net Lending As % GDP	1.7	1.0	0.7	0.6	0.6	0.4
Gross Debt % of GDP	34.1	31.4	28.1	25.0	22.3	19.9
INTERNATIONAL INDICATORS						
Exch. Rate Euro vs US$	0.9	0.9	1.0	1.0	1.1	1.1
World Trade Index	1.5	2.8	8.8	9.0	7.7	7.2
World Price of Raw Materials	-13.7	-1.8	2.1	0.3	0.6	0.6
World Price of Oil	24.6	20.6	23.4	25.4	26.2	26.8
Capacity Utilization	n.a	n.a	n.a	n.a	n.a	n.a

Austria

Baseline

GDP AT CONSTANT PRICES

	2001	2002	2003	2004	2005	2006
Gross Domestic Product	1.0	0.9	3.5	3.2	2.7	2.5
Private Consumption	1.1	1.1	3.3	2.4	2.3	2.3
Public Consumption	-0.3	1.5	1.4	1.4	1.5	1.5
Total Fixed Investment	0.5	0.9	6.1	3.5	3.3	3.0
Exp. of Goods and Serv	7.5	1.2	6.8	7.4	6.2	5.9
Imp. of goods and serv.	6.1	1.9	8.4	5.8	5.6	5.6

PRICES, % CHANGE

	2001	2002	2003	2004	2005	2006
Consumer Prices	2.7	1.1	1.2	1.4	1.4	1.4
Wholesale Prices	1.8	1.0	2.4	2.6	2.3	2.1

EMPLOYMENT, % CHANGE

	2001	2002	2003	2004	2005	2006
Unemployment Rate (%)	4.7	4.9	4.9	5.0	5.0	5.1
Employment	0.3	0.2	0.4	0.7	1.0	0.9
Labour Force	0.4	0.8	0.7	0.6	0.6	0.6

EXTERNAL TRADE (BOP)

	2001	2002	2003	2004	2005	2006
Visible Trade Balance	-47.9	-44.1	-45.6	-54.4	-57.2	-62.4
Curr Acc and Cap Mov	-87.3	-92.0	-95.6	-99.4	-101.0	-102.3
As % GDP	-3.0	-3.1	-3.0	-3.0	-2.9	-2.8

GOVERNMENT ACCOUNTS

	2001	2002	2003	2004	2005	2006
Current Revenues % of GDP	47.3	47.8	47.4	47.2	47.0	47.1
Current Expend % of GDP	48.2	48.7	47.8	47.1	46.7	46.6
Net Lending As % GDP	-0.9	-1.0	-0.4	0.1	0.4	0.4
Gross Debt % of GDP	61.6	61.0	58.4	55.7	53.0	50.4

INTERNATIONAL INDICATORS

	2001	2002	2003	2004	2005	2006
Exch. Rate Euro vs US$	0.9	0.9	1.0	1.0	1.1	1.1
World Trade Index	2.9	2.7	7.8	7.3	6.4	6.2
World Price of Raw Materials	-13.7	-1.8	2.6	0.6	0.7	0.4
World Price of Oil	24.6	20.6	23.4	25.4	26.2	26.8

Lower Spending and Lower Taxes

GDP AT CONSTANT PRICES

	2001	2002	2003	2004	2005	2006
Gross Domestic Product	1.0	1.0	3.5	3.2	2.5	2.1
Private Consumption	1.1	1.2	3.4	2.4	2.3	2.1
Public Consumption	-0.3	1.5	1.4	1.4	1.5	1.5
Total Fixed Investment	0.5	1.0	6.3	3.8	3.4	2.7
Exp. of Goods and Serv	7.5	1.5	7.2	7.8	6.4	6.2
Imp. of goods and serv.	6.1	2.3	9.0	6.4	6.1	6.2

PRICES, % CHANGE

	2001	2002	2003	2004	2005	2006
Consumer Prices	2.7	1.1	1.3	1.5	1.5	1.3
Wholesale Prices	1.8	1.0	2.4	2.6	2.2	1.8

EMPLOYMENT, % CHANGE

	2001	2002	2003	2004	2005	2006
Unemployment Rate (%)	4.7	4.8	4.9	5.0	5.1	5.2
Employment	0.3	0.2	0.4	0.7	0.9	0.8
Labour Force	0.4	0.8	0.7	0.6	0.6	0.6

EXTERNAL TRADE (BOP)

	2001	2002	2003	2004	2005	2006
Visible Trade Balance	-47.9	-45.0	-48.0	-60.2	-67.3	-75.2
Curr Acc and Cap Mov	-87.3	-92.8	-97.6	-104.2	-109.1	-111.6
As % GDP	-3.0	-3.1	-3.1	-3.1	-3.1	-3.1

GOVERNMENT ACCOUNTS

	2001	2002	2003	2004	2005	2006
Current Revenues % of GDP	47.3	47.8	47.4	47.2	47.1	47.1
Current Expend % of GDP	48.2	48.7	47.7	47.1	46.7	46.9
Net Lending As % GDP	-0.9	-0.9	-0.3	0.2	0.4	0.3
Gross Debt % of GDP	61.6	60.9	58.3	55.4	52.8	50.5

INTERNATIONAL INDICATORS

	2001	2002	2003	2004	2005	2006
Exch. Rate Euro vs US$	0.9	0.9	1.0	1.0	1.1	1.1
World Trade Index	2.9	3.3	8.6	8.2	7.4	7.6
World Price of Raw Materials	-13.7	-1.9	2.6	0.5	0.8	0.6
World Price of Oil	24.6	20.6	23.4	25.4	26.2	26.8

Lower spending, lower taxes, lower interest rates

GDP AT CONSTANT PRICES						
	2001	2002	2003	2004	2005	2006
Gross Domestic Product	1.0	0.9	3.8	3.7	2.9	2.5
Private Consumption	1.1	1.1	3.6	2.9	2.7	2.4
Public Consumption	-0.3	1.5	1.4	1.4	1.5	1.5
Total Fixed Investment	0.5	0.9	6.4	4.8	4.7	4.2
Exp. of Goods and Serv	7.5	1.4	7.6	8.8	6.9	6.3
Imp. of goods and serv.	6.1	2.2	9.1	7.6	6.9	6.7
PRICES, % CHANGE						
Consumer Prices	2.7	1.1	1.2	1.6	1.9	2.2
Wholesale Prices	1.8	1.0	2.4	2.9	2.8	2.8
EMPLOYMENT, % CHANGE						
Unemployment Rate (%)	4.7	4.9	4.9	4.8	4.8	4.8
Employment	0.3	0.2	0.4	0.9	1.0	0.9
Labour Force	0.4	0.8	0.7	0.6	0.6	0.6
EXTERNAL TRADE (BOP)						
Visible Trade Balance	-47.9	-44.3	-48.5	-68.4	-82.7	-102.5
Curr Acc and Cap Mov	-87.3	-92.0	-98.4	-112.8	-125.1	-140.2
As % GDP	-3.0	-3.1	-3.1	-3.4	-3.5	-3.8
GOVERNMENT ACCOUNTS						
Current Revenues % of GDP	47.3	47.8	47.4	47.2	47.1	47.1
Current Expend % of GDP	48.2	48.8	47.6	46.7	46.1	45.9
Net Lending As % GDP	-0.9	-1.0	-0.2	0.5	1.0	1.2
Gross Debt % of GDP	61.6	61.0	58.3	54.9	51.4	47.8
INTERNATIONAL INDICATORS						
Exch. Rate Euro vs US$	0.9	0.9	1.0	1.0	1.1	1.1
World Trade Index	2.9	3.2	8.9	9.2	7.9	7.6
World Price of Raw Materials	-13.7	-1.8	2.1	0.3	0.6	0.6
World Price of Oil	24.6	20.6	23.4	25.4	26.2	26.8

Portugal

Baseline

GDP AT CONSTANT PRICES

	2001	2002	2003	2004	2005	2006
Gross Domestic Product	1.9	2.0	3.2	2.9	2.7	2.7
Private Consumption	1.4	1.9	2.2	2.2	2.3	2.3
Public Consumption	2.3	2.4	2.0	1.9	1.9	1.9
Total Fixed Investment	0.0	2.2	3.8	3.8	3.5	3.1
Exp. of Goods and Serv	6.4	2.5	5.0	4.4	4.3	4.3
Imp. of goods and serv.	2.9	2.7	4.0	3.6	3.6	3.5

PRICES, % CHANGE

	2001	2002	2003	2004	2005	2006
Consumer Prices	4.3	2.5	2.1	2.1	2.0	2.0
Wholesale Prices	1.3	-0.4	2.6	2.4	2.3	2.4

EMPLOYMENT, % CHANGE

	2001	2002	2003	2004	2005	2006
Unemployment Rate (%)	4.1	4.2	3.9	3.8	3.8	3.8
Employment	1.2	-0.8	0.5	0.3	0.3	0.2
Labour Force	0.5	0.3	0.2	0.2	0.2	0.2

EXTERNAL TRADE (BOP)

	2001	2002	2003	2004	2005	2006
Visible Trade Balance	-3101.8	-3247.5	-3017.1	-2682.9	-2373.6	-2089.4
Curr Acc and Cap Mov	-2308.1	-1864.8	-1949.3	-1889.0	-1862.4	-1766.8
As % GDP	-9.5	-7.9	-8.0	-7.5	-7.1	-6.4

GOVERNMENT ACCOUNTS

	2001	2002	2003	2004	2005	2006
Current Revenues % of GDP	41.9	45.5	46.9	47.7	48.3	48.8
Current Expend % of GDP	43.8	47.5	48.5	49.1	49.5	49.8
Net Lending As % GDP	-1.9	-2.0	-1.6	-1.4	-1.2	-1.1
Gross Debt % of GDP	52.4	55.7	55.8	55.0	54.1	53.0

INTERNATIONAL INDICATORS

	2001	2002	2003	2004	2005	2006
Exch. Rate Euro vs US$	0.9	0.9	1.0	1.0	1.1	1.1
World Trade Index	2.2	2.7	7.7	7.4	6.7	6.4
World Price of Raw Materials	-13.7	-1.8	2.6	0.6	0.7	0.4
World Price of Oil	24.6	20.6	23.4	25.4	26.2	26.8
Capacity Utilization	n.a.	n.a.	n.a.	n.a.	n.a.	n.a.

Lower Spending and Lower Taxes

GDP AT CONSTANT PRICES

	2001	2002	2003	2004	2005	2006
Gross Domestic Product	1.9	2.1	3.2	2.7	2.3	2.2
Private Consumption	1.4	2.0	2.3	2.4	2.4	2.2
Public Consumption	2.3	2.4	2.0	1.9	1.9	1.9
Total Fixed Investment	0.0	2.7	4.0	3.5	2.7	2.2
Exp. of Goods and Serv	6.4	3.0	5.7	4.8	4.8	5.1
Imp. of goods and serv.	2.9	3.1	4.6	4.3	4.5	4.4

PRICES, % CHANGE

	2001	2002	2003	2004	2005	2006
Consumer Prices	4.3	2.5	2.3	2.5	2.3	1.9
Wholesale Prices	1.3	-0.4	2.8	2.8	2.5	2.0

EMPLOYMENT, % CHANGE

	2001	2002	2003	2004	2005	2006
Unemployment Rate (%)	4.1	4.1	3.9	3.8	3.9	3.9
Employment	1.2	-0.7	0.5	0.3	0.2	0.2
Labour Force	0.5	0.3	0.2	0.2	0.2	0.2

EXTERNAL TRADE (BOP)

	2001	2002	2003	2004	2005	2006
Visible Trade Balance	-3101.8	-3258.8	-3033.3	-2723.3	-2439.2	-2149.1
Curr Acc and Cap Mov	-2308.1	-1872.5	-1952.5	-1909.7	-1900.4	-1785.9
As % GDP	-9.5	-7.9	-8.0	-7.5	-7.1	-6.5

GOVERNMENT ACCOUNTS

	2001	2002	2003	2004	2005	2006
Current Revenues % of GDP	41.9	45.4	46.8	47.6	48.4	49.0
Current Expend % of GDP	43.8	47.3	48.1	48.8	49.5	50.3
Net Lending As % GDP	-1.9	-1.9	-1.3	-1.2	-1.2	-1.3
Gross Debt % of GDP	52.4	55.6	55.3	54.2	53.2	52.5

INTERNATIONAL INDICATORS

	2001	2002	2003	2004	2005	2006
Exch. Rate Euro vs US$	0.9	0.9	1.0	1.0	1.1	1.1
World Trade Index	2.2	3.2	8.7	8.4	7.8	8.0
World Price of Raw Materials	-13.7	-1.9	2.6	0.5	0.8	0.6
World Price of Oil	24.6	20.6	23.4	25.4	26.2	26.8
Capacity Utilization	n.a.	n.a.	n.a.	n.a.	n.a.	n.a.

Lower spending, lower taxes, lower interest rates

GDP AT CONSTANT PRICES	2001	2002	2003	2004	2005	2006
Gross Domestic Product	1.9	2.0	3.2	2.9	2.7	2.7
Private Consumption	1.4	1.9	2.2	2.2	2.3	2.3
Public Consumption	2.3	2.4	2.0	1.9	1.9	1.9
Total Fixed Investment	0.0	2.2	3.8	3.8	3.5	3.1
Exp. of Goods and Serv	6.4	2.5	5.0	4.4	4.3	4.3
Imp. of goods and serv.	2.9	2.7	4.0	3.6	3.6	3.5
PRICES, % CHANGE						
Consumer Prices	4.3	2.5	2.1	2.1	2.0	2.0
Wholesale Prices	1.3	-0.4	2.6	2.4	2.3	2.4
EMPLOYMENT, % CHANGE						
Unemployment Rate (%)	4.1	4.2	3.9	3.8	3.8	3.8
Employment	1.2	-0.8	0.5	0.3	0.3	0.2
Labour Force	0.5	0.3	0.2	0.2	0.2	0.2
EXTERNAL TRADE (BOP)						
Visible Trade Balance	-3101.8	-3247.5	-3017.1	-2682.9	-2373.6	-2089.4
Curr Acc and Cap Mov	-2308.1	-1864.8	-1949.3	-1889.0	-1862.4	-1766.8
As % GDP	-9.5	-7.9	-8.0	-7.5	-7.1	-6.4
GOVERNMENT ACCOUNTS						
Current Revenues % of GDP	41.9	45.5	46.9	47.7	48.3	48.8
Current Expend % of GDP	43.8	47.5	48.5	49.1	49.5	49.8
Net Lending As % GDP	-1.9	-2.0	-1.6	-1.4	-1.2	-1.1
Gross Debt % of GDP	52.4	55.7	55.8	55.0	54.1	53.0
INTERNATIONAL INDICATORS						
Exch. Rate Euro vs US$	0.9	0.9	1.0	1.0	1.1	1.1
World Trade Index	2.2	2.7	7.7	7.4	6.7	6.4
World Price of Raw Materials	-13.7	-1.8	2.6	0.6	0.7	0.4
World Price of Oil	24.6	20.6	23.4	25.4	26.2	26.8
Capacity Utilization	n.a.	n.a.	n.a.	n.a.	n.a.	n.a.

10. References

1. Aghion P., Comment on "Macroeconomic Lessons from Ten Years of Transition," by Charles Wyplosz, and "Restructuring in Transition Economies: Ownership, Competition, and Regulation," by Simon Commander, Mark Dutz, and Nicholas Stern, Annual World Bank Conference on Development Economics, 1999. 2000, pp. 374-76

2. Aghion P. and Howitt P., On the Macroeconomic Effects of Major Technological Change, The economics and econometrics of innovation. 2000, pp. 31-53

3. Aghion P. and Howitt P. W., Endogenous Growth Theory, MIT Press, 1997

4. Alesina A. and Rodrik D., Distributive Politics and Economic Growth, The Quarterly Journal of Economics, Vol. 109, No. 2. (May, 1994), pp. 465-490.

5. Baldassarri M., Spesa Pubblica, Inflazione e Crescita (Public Expenditure, Inflation and Growth), Il Mulino, Bologna, 1978.

6. Baldassarri M., Modigliani F., Castiglionesi F., Il miracolo possibile: un programma per l'economia italiana (The Possible Miracle: a Program for the Italian Economy), Bari, Laterza, 1996

7. Baldassarri M., Malgarini M., Valente G., "Il secondo miracolo possibile: la sconfitta dell'inflazione, un progetto per la piena occupazione (The Second Possibile Miracle: the Defeat of Inflation, a Project toward Full Employment) ", Milano, Editrice Il Sole 24 Ore, 1999

8. Baldassarri, M., Government Deficit, Inflation and Growth in a Two-Country Model of International Trade: Who Bears the

Burden? Economia Internazionale, vol. 33, no. 1, Feb. 1980, pp. 1-25

9. Baldassarri M. and Piga G., Distributive Equity and Economic Efficiency: Trade-off and Synergy, Equity, efficiency and growth: The future of the welfare state. 1996, Rivista di Politica Economica, pp. 257-75

10. Barro R. J. and Sala-i-Martin X., Economic Growth, MIT Press, 1998

11. Benabou R., Inequality and Growth, National Bureau of Economic Research Working Paper: 5658, July 1996

12. Blanchard O. and Giavazzi F., Reforms that can be done: improving the SGP through a proper accounting of public investment, mimeo, November 2002.

13. Busato F. and Chiarini B., 2003, Market and Underground Activities in a Two Sector Dynamic Equilibrium Model, forthcoming Economic Theory.

14. Cova P. Risorse Primarie, Squilibri Reali Nord-Sud, ed il Ruolo Del WTO nel 21 Secolo (Primary Resources, North-South Real Disequilibria, and the Role of WTO in the 21st Century), 1996, doctoral thesis.

15. Collier P. and Gunning, J. W., Explaining African Economic Performance, Journal of Economic Literature, vol. 37, no. 1, March 1999, pp. 64-111

16. Correia I., Neves J. C and Rebelo S., Business Cycles in a Small Open Economy European Economic Review, vol. 39, no. 6, June 1995, pp. 1089-1113

17. Cournot, Augustin. Recherches sur les Principes Mathematiques de la Theorie des Richesses, Paris: Hachette, 1838. (Italian translation in Biblioteca Dell'Econ., 1875. English translation by N. T. Bacon published in Economic Classics [Macmillan, 1897] and reprinted in 1960 by Augustus M. Kelly.)

18. Easterly, W. and Levine R., Africa's Growth Tragedy: Policies and Ethnic Divisions, Quarterly Journal of Economics, vol. 112, no. 4, November 1997, pp. 1203-50

19. Fama E., Efficient Capital Markets: a Review of Theory and Empirical Work, Jounal of Finance, 1970.

20. Fiorito R., Piu' incompleto che stupido: osservazioni e proposte sul Patto di stabilita' e crescita, nota presentata al Convegno ISCONA ("Finanza pubblica e contabilita' nazionale"), novembre 2002.

21. Fitoussi J. P and Creel J. , "How to Reform the European Central Bank", Center for European Reforms.

22. Galor O. and Zeira, J., Income Distribution and Macroeconomics, Review of Economic Studies, vol. 60, no. 1, January 1993, pp. 35-52

23. Haavelmo T., Multiplier Effects of a Balanced Budget, Econometrica, Vol. 13, No. 4. (Oct., 1945), pp. 311-318.

24. Masson, P., Fiscal Policy and Growth in the Context of European Integration, International Monetary Fund Working Paper: WP/00/133, July 2000.

25. Mendoza, E. G, Terms-of-Trade Uncertainty and Economic Growth, Journal of Development Economics, vol. 54, no. 2, December 1997, pp. 323-56

26. Murphy K. M., A. Shleifer and R. W. Vishny, Why Is Rent-Seeking So Costly to Growth?, The American Economic Review, Vol. 83, No. 2, Papers and Proceedings of the Hundred and Fifth Annual Meeting of the American Economic Association. (May, 1993), pp. 409-414.

27. Persson T. and Tabellini G, Is Inequality Harmful for Growth?, The American Economic Review, Vol. 84, No. 3. (Jun., 1994), pp. 600-621.

28. Perotti R., Political Equilibrium, Income Distribution, and Growth, The Review of Economic Studies, Vol. 60, No. 4. (Oct., 1993), pp. 755-776.

29. Sala-i-Martin, X. and Subramanian, A., "The Nigerian Disaster", Mimeo Columbia University, September 2002.

30. Solow, R. M. A Contribution to the Theory of Economic Growth, The Quarterly Journal of Economics, Vol. 70, No. 1. (Feb., 1956), pp. 65-94.

31. Schumpeter J. A., Business Cycles: A theoretical, historical and statistical analysis of the Capitalist process, 1939

32. Stokey N., Lucas R.E., with E.C. Prescott, Recursive Methods in Economics Dynamics, (Harvard University Press, Cambridge MA, 1989)

33. Tanzi, V. and Zee, H. H., Fiscal Policy and Long-Run Growth, International Monetary Fund Working Paper: WP/96/119, October 1996,

34. Wyplotz C., The Stability Pact Meets is Fate, paper prepared for the "Euro 50 group", Paris, November 2002.

11. Index